Analytic Ph

Continuum Studies in Philosophy
Series Editor: James Fieser, University of Tennessee at Martin, USA

Continuum Studies in Philosophy is a major monograph series from Continuum. The series features first-class scholarly research monographs across the whole field of philosophy. Each work makes a major contribution to the field of philosophical research.

Aesthetic in Kant, James Kirwan
Analytic Philosophy: The History of an Illusion, Aaron Preston
Aquinas and the Ship of Theseus, Christopher Brown
Augustine and Roman Virtue, Brian Harding
The Challenge of Relativism, Patrick Phillips
Demands of Taste in Kant's Aesthetics, Brent Kalar
Descartes and the Metaphysics of Human Nature, Justin Skirry
Descartes' Theory of Ideas, David Clemenson
Dialectic of Romanticism, Peter Murphy and David Roberts
Duns Scotus and the Problem of Universals, Todd Bates
Hegel's Philosophy of Language, Jim Vernon
Hegel's Philosophy of Right, David James
Hegel's Theory of Recognition, Sybol S.C. Anderson
The History of Intentionality, Ryan Hickerson
Kantian Deeds, Henrik Jøker Bjerre
Kierkegaard, Metaphysics and Political Theory, Alison Assiter
Kierkegaard's Analysis of Radical Evil, David A. Roberts
Leibniz Re-interpreted, Lloyd Strickland
Metaphysics and the End of Philosophy, HO Mounce
Nietzsche and the Greeks, Dale Wilkerson
Origins of Analytic Philosophy, Delbert Reed
Philosophy of Miracles, David Corner
Platonism, Music and the Listener's Share, Christopher Norris
Popper's Theory of Science, Carlos Garcia
Postanalytic and Metacontinental, edited by James Williams, Jack Reynolds, James Chase and Ed Mares
Rationality and Feminist Philosophy, Deborah K. Heikes
Re-thinking the Cogito, Christopher Norris
Role of God in Spinoza's Metaphysics, Sherry Deveaux
Rousseau and Radical Democracy, Kevin Inston
Rousseau and the Ethics of Virtue, James Delaney
Rousseau's Theory of Freedom, Matthew Simpson
Spinoza and the Stoics, Firmin DeBrabander
Spinoza's Radical Cartesian Mind, Tammy Nyden-Bullock
St. Augustine and the Theory of Just War, John Mark Mattox
St. Augustine of Hippo, R.W. Dyson
Thomas Aquinas & John Duns Scotus, Alex Hall
Tolerance and the Ethical Life, Andrew Fiala

Analytic Philosophy

The History of an Illusion

Aaron Preston

continuum

Continuum International Publishing Group
The Tower Building   80 Maiden Lane
11 York Road   Suite 704
London SE1 7NX   New York NY 10038

www.continuumbooks.com

First published 2007
Paperback edition 2010

British Library Cataloguing-in-Publication Data
A catalogue record for this book is available from the British Library.

ISBN: PB: 978-1-4411-3196-6

Library of Congress Cataloguing-in-Publication Data
A catalog record for this book is available from the Library of Congress.

Typeset by Fakenham Photosetting Limited, Fakenham, Norfolk

To Dallas Willard and Kevin Robb –
For teaching me what philosophy was in the beginning,
what it always has been, and what it can and should be today.

This transformation [in British philosophy] ... has become by now a sufficiently conspicuous fact. It has been often remarked upon, sometimes with satisfaction, sometimes with lamentation and dismay. It has almost as often been misunderstood. It has been said to have generated a kind of 'revolutionary illusion', through which neither its friends nor its enemies can see the case clearly. It stands, in fact, in need of explanation.

G.J. Warnock (1958: 1f)

... the historian endeavors, not only to bring the unknown to light, but also to bring the known closer to us, to bring it to adequate intuition in its very nature.

Adolph Reinach (1914: 200)

... the historical approach, when wisely cultivated, can frequently produce the same kind of intellectual catharsis and *dis*solution of pseudo-problems as does the analytic method.

Ernest Nagel (1936a: 7)

Very general remarks may be helpful, and are not always untrue.

G.J. Warnock (1958: 52)

Contents

Preface

This is a book on the history and nature of analytic philosophy (AP). It is not a book on some topic *in* the history of AP. Rather, it is concerned with AP holistically, as a philosophical school or movement. For good or for ill, this holistic approach sets the book apart from much recent work in the emerging 'history of AP' genre. With some notable exceptions, works in this genre tend to focus on isolated figures and factions *in* the history of AP, rather than *on* AP as a whole, and its history. Remarkable as many of these are as examples of scholarship, and helpful as they are in generating a better understanding of their respective subjects, they have done little to illuminate the history and nature of AP *as such*. This is not to say that they have no bearing on our holistic understanding of AP. To the contrary, many of these studies reveal facts of tremendous import. However, this is not always noticed, and their implications are not drawn out. I will attempt to draw them out.

To a large extent, this focus on the more fine-grained is borne of a desire for careful and accurate scholarship. The ground-level details certainly have the larger part of the say in determining historical truth, and a book like this could not easily have been written without having many excellent fine-grained studies to draw upon. Once the details are sufficiently clear, however, nothing prevents us from ascending to a higher, more coarse-grained level to try to achieve what Warnock (1958) was fond of calling an 'Olympian view' of the historical situation. As Scott Soames has recently said:

> analytic philosophers – including historians – need to do more than investigate highly specialized topics in finer and finer detail. In addition, we should try to construct larger, synthetic pictures which, while informed by precise and detailed understandings of particular issues, transcend that. In the history of philosophy, this means … attempting to develop a broad and useable picture of where we are now and how we got there. (Soames 2006: 655)

Although the present study may go beyond what Soames has in mind in terms of constructing a larger synthetic picture, his words aptly capture what I have tried to accomplish.

The respect in which it may go beyond what Soames has in mind, and beyond what most others seem comfortable with, is that it is not merely summative but holistic. However, this is justified by the fact that there are, in the history of AP, not only facts about particular analysts and their relations, but also about the movement as a whole – or at least about how it, as a whole, was perceived by those who saw it born and then grow. Should our suspicion of the coarse-grained, the general, and the holistic lead us to refuse these facts a place in our scholarly understanding of AP, we would be cutting ourselves off from some of the plain data of history, and hence from some of the truth. This bespeaks not a concern for careful scholarship but an 'atomistic' orientation that is the natural manifestation of what I shall argue is AP's fundamental commitment, captured equally well (or badly) by terms like 'positivism', 'naturalism', and 'scientism'.[1] Thanks to this orientation, it is quickly becoming a matter of accepted wisdom that to think of AP in holistic terms, as a school capable of adequate, general characterization, is an error of naïve oversimplification. Thus, even those works that do attempt to treat AP in a more holistic fashion frequently end up characterizing it as merely a loose network of partially overlapping but ultimately discrete figures and factions which seem to form a unit only to those who neglect the philosophical details.

In an important sense, this is the truth of the matter. However, it presents us with a serious problem. One expects that a group meriting the designation 'philosophical school' should be identifiable in terms of some set of philosophical views unique (within a limited context, at least) to its members – its *defining doctrines*, as I call them. To deny that AP can be characterized in this way is tantamount to claiming that it is not, after all, a philosophical school. This shocking possibility is too often ignored in works controlled by the positivistic predilection for correlating otherwise isolated bits of minutia and the attendant aversion to substantive generalization. It will not be ignored here. Instead, the issue will be raised explicitly, and the current trend resisted on the grounds that it is not in keeping with the norms for group-formation derived from a traditional understanding of philosophy itself.

To characterize AP without reference to defining doctrines not only ignores the centrality of views, ideas, or theories to the concept *philosophical school*, but also involves an implicit dismissal – or possibly ignorance – of the fact that a view-centered conception was part of the reference-fixing content of 'analytic philosophy' as the term was originally used by analysts and non-analysts alike. As we shall see, the belief that AP had at least one defining doctrine – a metaphilosophical view that I call the *linguistic thesis* – was the norm from the early 1930s, when the name 'analytic philosophy' was first introduced, through at least the mid-1960s, when AP lost its linguistic character. It is no coincidence that this was also the period when AP achieved dominance in the British and American universities, for – as I shall argue – the illusion that AP was defined by a specific approach to philosophy endorsed by many of the greatest philosophical minds of the era was of crucial importance to this social achievement.

The notion that AP was ideationally unified by defining doctrines persisted even after its linguistic veneer wore away. In the 1970s and after, characterizations of AP frequently point to views other than the linguistic thesis as its defining doctrine(s), but the belief that there is *some* ideational unity is still clearly present. Only in the last decade or so has this begun to change, with the effect that the sense of 'analytic philosophy' has begun to undergo a radical shift. Resisting this unwarranted revision of language, this study insists not only that AP can be treated as an ideationally unified school, but that it must be so treated; for only thus do we do justice to both the facts of history and the nature of philosophy.

This book is intended to be accessible to anyone capable of reading college-level English – no facility with symbolic logic is required, nor does one need to be up on the secondary literature on logical positivism, for example. Still, it will be the most interesting, and most intelligible, to those who already have some knowledge of AP, its major figures, factions and phases. Since our efforts will be directed toward AP as a whole, little effort will be given to providing a systematic introduction to its parts. Thus, if one has never heard of Moore, Russell, Wittgenstein, the Vienna Circle, logical atomism, logical positivism, and so on, it would be wise to acquaint oneself with them before reading this book. Several fine book-length introductions exist, and are listed in the bibliography. Though not nearly so detailed as these monographs, my entry on 'Analytic Philosophy' in the *Internet Encyclopedia of Philosophy* (Preston 2006b) gives enough background to make the project of this book intelligible, and has the virtues of being both widely accessible and free.

This book is the culmination of a research project that began with my doctoral dissertation at the University of Southern California. Thanks are due to the philosophy faculty there, and especially to Dallas Willard, Kevin Robb, John Dreher, Ed McCann and Walter Fisher, all of whom served on various committees that helped to see the project along its way. I also wish to thank David Kasmir, Walter Hopp and John Williston, my fellow graduate students around the turn of the millennium, for their interest, insight and support. After leaving USC, I had the good fortune to connect with a network of scholars associated with the History of Early Analytic Philosophy Society, the Bertrand Russell Society, and the email discussion group Russell-l. I am grateful for the role these scholars and organizations have played in occasionally serving as sounding boards for some of the ideas advanced in the book, and in expanding my own understanding of the history of AP. From this group I wish to single out for special thanks John Ongley and Rosalind Carey, who initially got me involved with the discussion group and the societies, Chris Pincock for good discussions at various APA (American Philosophical Association) meetings, and Michael Beaney, whose support for the book at the proposal stage meant more than he could know. Material from several chapters first appeared in *The Monist, Metaphilosophy* and the *Bertrand Russell Society Quarterly*, and appears here with the kind permission of their editors and of the Hegeler Institute. Malone College, now my home institution, awarded me several research grants that helped to take the project from dissertation to book. The encouragement and camaraderie of my colleagues there has been a continual source of refreshment. Thanks are also due to the staff at Thoemmes Continuum, for their support and expertise.

The life of scholarship requires substantial sacrifices of time and energy. These are made not by the scholar alone, but by his family as well. Apologies to my young son, Ethan, for the hours I should have been playing ball, but had to work instead. My greatest debt of gratitude is to my wife, Nicole, for her unflagging support through the entire process. She has seen the project grow from seed to plant and has made sure that I had a life beyond cultivating it. She also performed the laborious work of a copy-editor (at which she is excellent); whatever surface errors remain would have been multiplied many times over without her keen eye.

Errors of substance are, of course, another matter. As I hinted earlier, huge literatures have grown up around a number of narrower topics on the history of AP. The interpretation of Wittgenstein has become a cottage industry; one could almost say the same for Russell, and, to a lesser extent, Carnap and Quine. I have attempted to deal competently with these bodies of research in formulating my own coarse-grained views about AP, but approaching one's subject at a very low level of granularity has the unavoidable consequence that many of the details apparent in more fine-grained accounts are overlooked. Leaving matters of detail to the side does not *ipso facto* indicate error, but it does leave the door open. Should someone with a narrower specialization find fault with my treatment of his or her preferred figure or faction, I hope the fact will be communicated to me directly.

Aaron Preston
North Canton, Ohio
June 2006

Introduction: The Peculiar Career of Analytic Philosophy

For the better part of the last hundred years, Western academic philosophy has been dominated by two entities, respectively called the *analytic* and the *Continental* traditions. Both originated around the turn of the twentieth century, and, though they are opposed in many respects, both involve significant departures from the norms of *traditional philosophy* (to be elaborated further on). Their simultaneous origin in a common movement away from traditional philosophy is a phenomenon requiring explanation, but it is too large a matter for this book. Here, the focus will be upon the analytic tradition alone.

Philosophy in the analytic tradition – simply called *analytic philosophy*[1] – has long been associated with academic philosophy in the English-speaking world, principally in Britain and the United States. In fact, AP is frequently referred to as 'Anglo-American philosophy'. Some have criticized this traditional designation as misleading, noting not only that German-speaking philosophers – notably Frege, Wittgenstein and the members of the Vienna Circle – made crucial contributions to the analytic tradition, but also that the issues and ideas which originally gave rise to AP were native to the nineteenth-century Austro-German philosophical scene (cf. Dummett 1993; Bell 1999).

True as these points may be, this critique ignores the paramount significance of the fact that the name 'analytic philosophy' entered the philosophical lexicon to meet a need first felt in the British and American contexts. D.S. Clarke has observed that 'the term "analytic philosophy" seems to have been introduced in the late 1940s as a label standing for the radically new approach to philosophy then dominating discussion in Great Britain and the United States' (1997: 1). As we shall see, Clarke is right about the designation of the term, but wrong about the date of its introduction (it was in use nearly two decades earlier than he suggests). At present, the point to note is this: the very fact that AP exists as something to be discussed under a single name is historically and hence unalterably – I am tempted to say necessarily[2] – connected to its career in the British and American universities. Specifically, it is historically and hence unalterably connected to the early success of a particular philosophical outlook in

securing both (1) the attention and (2) the loyalty of academic philosophers both (3) in places that mattered (and so at *prestigious* intuitions)
and (4) in numbers large enough to generate the kind of regular and
widespread discussion that would both (5) require the coining of a new
term and (6) explain that term's subsequent entrenchment as one of the
most familiar in the philosophical lexicon – for 'analytic philosophy' is no
specialist's term; rather, it is known to everyone in the professional world
of academic philosophy today. It is used by all to discuss that world on the
large scale, and by many to identify their place in it.

It is for good reason, then, that tradition associates AP principally with
Britain and the US. There are also several other features traditionally
associated with AP. Foremost among these are the related notions that
AP originated in the 'linguistic turn', that AP is therefore linguistic
philosophy, and that this turn to language constituted an epoch-making
philosophical revolution matched only by the 'epistemological turn'
supposedly inaugurated by Descartes. The linguistic turn itself is usually
understood as the widespread adoption of linguistic analysis as the
only or at least the *preferred* philosophical method, and of a language-
centered methodology and metaphilosophy. In short, AP is traditionally
understood to be a philosophical school that took the proper work of
philosophy to be the analysis of language. For ease of reference, I shall
call this fundamentally metaphilosophical outlook the *linguistic thesis*. As
we shall see, it is this philosophical outlook to which the above-mentioned
phenomena (1)–(6) are connected. In virtue of this connection, there is
good reason for these features to be associated with AP.

In another respect, however, there is no good reason for this. On the
one hand, AP no longer embraces the linguistic thesis. Its history since
the 1960s has been characterized by a slow retreat from the outlook
that earned AP its name and its place in the academy. On the other
hand, recent historical studies on key figures in the history of AP (to be
discussed at length further on) have revealed that unanimity about the
linguistic thesis was never achieved among key, canonical analysts even
prior to 1960 – that is, among those most responsible for generating
phenomena (1)–(6).

These facts make it impossible to give an accurate general characterization of AP in terms of defining doctrines, and this creates a puzzle
about the true nature of AP. One of the fundamental theses advanced
in this book is that to lack defining doctrines is a devastating problem
for something that purports to be a philosophical school, movement or
tradition. Disagreement on this point, however, will not prevent one from
agreeing that AP has had a rather peculiar career. Specifically, it presents

us with a double peculiarity. The first is a philosophical peculiarity: AP's original philosophical outlook initially was thought to be so promising that it generated a revolution in Anglo-American philosophy, but it came to be seen as so badly flawed that it was completely abandoned, all in the span of roughly half a century. The rapidity with which AP as originally conceived rose to supremacy and then fell is unprecedented in the history of philosophy. This anomaly requires explanation.

Second, the regional dominance of AP in the world of academic philosophy presents us with a sociological peculiarity. One of the few indisputable claims that can be made about AP today is that it has dominated academic philosophy in at least the United States and Britain since at least the second quarter of the twentieth century. Ostensibly, its dominance was originally due to the overwhelmingly positive reception of its original philosophical outlook. However, given the first, philosophical peculiarity, it is clear that this reception was relatively short-lived. Thus, the sociological peculiarity consists in the fact that AP has maintained its dominant position even though the original *reason* for its dominance has long since been undermined.

In these respects, then, AP has had a peculiar career, and one which stands in need of explanation. Specifically, the following questions must be answered. First, given that its problems were both obvious enough and serious enough to bring about its total abandonment in the short span of approximately fifty years, why did AP's original program initially seem so promising to philosophers in numbers sufficient to cause its social dominance? Second, given that the original reason for its social dominance was undermined long ago, why has AP been able to maintain its position? Third, given that AP's identity as a philosophical school was conferred upon it by its original outlook, exactly what is this thing that has dominated academic philosophy ever since that outlook was abandoned? Indeed, since there never was any ideational unanimity in AP even when it appeared that there was, we may ask exactly what that entity was that dominated academic philosophy under the name 'analytic philosophy' even before its 'apparently shared' outlook was abandoned. My principal aim in this book is to answer these questions, as well as others that will emerge from the attempt.

PART I

The Crises in Analytic Philosophy

He who introduces a new conception into philosophy is under an obligation to invent acceptable terms to express it, and when he has done so, the duty of his fellow students is to accept those terms, and to resent any wresting of them from their original meanings, as not only a gross discourtesy to him to whom philosophy was indebted for each conception, but also as an injury to philosophy itself.

C.S. Peirce (1905: 104)

Chapter 1

The Identity Crisis in Analytic Philosophy

The Enigma of Analytic Philosophy

It would be both natural and desirable to begin with a general characterization of AP. To do so would orient us toward our subject and introduce
it to those who may be reading with the aim of learning just what AP is.
Unfortunately, a general characterization cannot be given, at least not
in terms that are philosophically illuminating. As Richard Rorty has
observed:

> most of those who call themselves "analytic philosophers" would now
> reject the epithet "linguistic philosophers" and would not describe
> themselves as "applying linguistic methods." Analytic philosophy is
> now the name not of the application of such methods to philosophical
> problems, but simply of the particular set of problems being discussed
> by philosophy professors in certain parts of the world. (1992: 374n)

Contemporary AP lacks even the *appearance* of a common theoretical or
methodological core. Consequently, there is not now – as there once was
– any widespread consensus about AP's nature.

Though it prevents the book from beginning the way it ought, the
lack of clear, conceptual unity in and about current AP is one half of the
situation that makes it necessary. The other half has to do with AP's social
standing. If AP was a socially insignificant school, there would be no reason
for a puzzle about its nature to evoke widespread concern. However, one
of the few indisputable facts about AP is that it has dominated academic
philosophy in the United States, Britain and elsewhere for the better part
of a century. Concerning the current situation in the States, Brian Leiter
has observed emphatically that:

> *All* the Ivy League universities, *all* the leading state research univer-
> sities, *all* the University of California campuses, most of the top liberal
> arts colleges, most of the flagship campuses of the second-tier state

research universities boast philosophy departments that *overwhelmingly* self-identify as 'analytic': it is hard to imagine a 'movement' that is more academically and professionally entrenched than analytic philosophy. (2004a [2001])[1]

The total situation represented by these two observations – Rorty's and Leiter's – calls for an inquiry into the nature of AP; for, if 'analytic philosophy' currently names little more than a loose set of problems determined by the interests of some subset of philosophy professors, it would seem that there is no principled unity to AP. In that case, it is not clear what this entity is that has ensconced itself in the philosophy departments of so many high-ranking institutions, or why it should enjoy its position of professional entrenchment.

Why We Should Care

This situation is worrisome for several reasons. First, from the perspective of traditional philosophy, which values systematic completeness, it can only be a mark of shame that a given brand of philosophy is unable to provide an adequate account of itself. Indeed, given the value analysts have traditionally placed upon clarity and rigor, one might expect that they themselves would be alarmed by the fact that what it means to be an analytic philosopher is presently unclear. That they tend not to be is a puzzle whose explanation will become clear further on. For now it should simply be noted that the failure of analytic philosophers to provide a metaphilosophical and methodological account of their manner of philosophizing counts as a tremendous oversight that makes their philos-ophizing un-philosophical in an important sense.

This is a traditional-philosopher's worry, and there is little reason to suppose it will be shared by many contemporary philosophers or by non-philosophers. However, there are other aspects of AP's present situation – practical, existential, social and ethical – that people in these categories are more likely to find worrisome. From its position of dominance, AP has managed, over the course of the twentieth century, to establish a *de facto* orthodoxy in academic philosophy, complete with 'professional standards' for judging 'good' and 'bad' philosophy. By imposing these standards on the profession, AP has shaped the Anglo-American experience with academic philosophy for the better part of a century; and, as we shall see, that experience has not been a uniformly happy one. To the extent that the dominance of AP has prevented academic philosophy from being what it could and ought to be (or have been) for those populations served by the academy, the nature of AP is a matter worthy of widespread concern.

The Normative Function of 'Analytic Philosophy'

Let us begin by noting just how close the connection is between AP and current professional standards. Brian Leiter has been remarkably transparent on this score:

> With the demise of analytic philosophy as a substantive research program since the 1960s ..., "analytic" simply demarcates a style of scholarship, writing and thinking: clarity, precision and argumentative rigor are paramount. Thus, "analytic" philosophy is now largely coextensional with good philosophy and scholarship, regardless of topic or figure. (2004a [2001])[2]

The general point could not be plainer: for practical purposes, AP is the same as good philosophy. There are two ways of reading this claim, however: as reducing good philosophy to AP, or the reverse. As we shall see, the first reading more accurately represents the current situation in academic philosophy, even though it is probably contrary to Leiter's meaning.

Leiter is best known as the editor of *The Philosophical Gourmet Report* (*PGR*), a ranking of graduate programs in philosophy. Leiter's recent work outside the *PGR* suggests that he accepts the second reading; within it, however, there are statements that pull in both directions. Since 2000, the *PGR* has heralded the collapse of a philosophically significant distinction between 'analytic' and 'Continental' philosophy. Since at least 2001, it has explicitly claimed that AP is not a 'substantive research program', and that it is characterized by *style* rather than substantive philosophical views. This suggests that there is nothing about AP sufficient to distinguish it as a unique *kind* of philosophy such as might be called a school, movement or tradition.[3] Despite this, the *PGR* seems simultaneously to insist on AP's status as a distinctive kind of philosophy. For instance, Leiter's vigorous affirmation of AP's professional entrenchment is presented as a rebuttal to 'a widespread view in the humanities that "analytic" philosophy is "dead" or "dying"'(Leiter 2004a [2001]).[4] But professional entrenchment is a sociological fact, not a philosophical one. As such, AP's professional entrenchment is consistent with its being moribund as a philosophical school (and this, as will become clear, is very likely the issue behind claims about AP's 'death'). Thus, in order for Leiter's rebuttal to count as more than a red herring, it must be read as implying that AP's social vitality is grounded in something philosophically substantive, capable of distinguishing it as a *kind* of philosophy the likes of which might be called a school.

A survey of sequential editions of the *PGR* since the late 1990s shows that Leiter's views have undergone an evolution with a very definite trajectory away from treating AP as a philosophical school. This process would seem to be the source of the tensions visible in even the most recent edition of the *PGR*. Outside the *PGR*, however, the process seems to have terminated in the *avant-garde* view that AP, understood as a distinctive *kind* of philosophy, is not merely moribund but defunct:

> ... it is time to pronounce the "bogeyman" of analytic philosophy laid to rest: so-called "analytic" philosophers now include quietists *and* naturalists; old fashioned metaphysical philosophers *and* twentieth-century linguistic philosophers, historians of philosophy *and* philosophers who show little interest in the history of the field. Given the methodological and substantive pluralism of Anglophone philosophy, "analytic" philosophy survives, if at all, as a certain style that emphasizes "logic", "rigor", and "argument" ... (Leiter 2004b: 11)

In light of this it is safe to say that Leiter no longer accepts – if indeed he ever did – the view that good philosophy can be reduced to AP; for this would require that AP be something with definite and philosophically substantive norms of its own. Leiter acknowledges that it once was that sort of thing, of course, but his current view is that *that* edifice has crumbled, and that in its place – and under its name – have emerged a variety of methods and views bound only by a common style loosely characterized in terms of clarity, precision and rigor. If anything, then, Leiter reduces AP to good philosophy, where the latter is understood as something nonsectarian and, indeed, perennial in the Western tradition.[5]

There is much to be said for Leiter's current view. However, his claim that the bogeyman of AP has been laid to rest is too optimistic. While AP *has* achieved considerable rapprochement with traditional philosophy, there are also important respects in which the two remain estranged. Traditionally, the overarching goal of philosophy is the rational construction of a general – and in that sense all-embracing – worldview that provides reasonable answers not only to metaphysical but also moral questions, thereby serving as a rough-and-ready roadmap orienting the human being toward its *summum bonum*, a life of *eudai-monia*, or 'flourishing'.[6] One way to put this is to say that the traditional *telos* of philosophy is ethical and practical, not theoretical. This will be misleading to the contemporary mind, however, as the traditional view makes philosophical theorizing partially constitutive of *eudaimonia*, and also insists that the possession of at least some theoretical understanding is necessary for guiding oneself and others into the life of *eudaimonia*. As Alexander Nehamas explains:

> During the period that began with classical Greece and ended in late pagan antiquity, philosophy was more than a merely theoretical discipline. Even when Aristotle identified philosophy with "theory," his purpose was to argue, as he does in the tenth and last book of the *Nicomachean Ethics*, that a *life* of theoretical activity, the life of philosophy, was the best life that human beings could lead. One could not lead such a life unless one acquired not only a number of philosophical views but also, over time and through serious effort, the very particular sort of character whose elements and presuppositions Aristotle described and justified in the previous nine books of the *Ethics*. The theoretical life, in turn, affects the character of those who lead it. Theory and practice, discourse and life, affect one another; people become philosophers because they are able and willing to be the best human type and to live as well as a human being possibly can. What one believes and how one lives have a direct bearing on one another. (1998: 2)

This is a far cry from the norms of AP. Whereas traditional philosophy unites the theoretical and the practical as two essential components of a complex whole, AP not only separates them but casts one of them aside as falling beyond the proper scope of philosophy. As Soames observes, 'in general, philosophy done in the analytic tradition aims at truth and knowledge, as opposed to moral or spiritual improvement ... the goal of analytic philosophy is to discover what is true, not to provide a useful recipe for living one's life' (2003: I, xiv).

Soames identifies this as one of several persistent 'underlying themes or tendencies that characterize' AP (2003: I, xiii). Another is 'a widespread presumption ... that it is often possible to make philosophical progress by intensively investigating a small, circumscribed range of philosophical issues while holding broader, systematic issues in abeyance' (xv). This is no doubt true. In fact, it is hard to see how one could make progress on specific philosophical problems without focusing principally upon the phenomena immediately involved. It is far from clear, however, that broader, systematic issues are always or ever irrelevant to narrower questions. Thus, to canonize this piecemeal approach to philosophical inquiry is to run the risk of cutting oneself off from the fruitful cross-pollination that can result from drawing upon the resources of one's total stock of views, including one's general view of 'the world'. It is true, as Soames says that, 'analytic philosophy is no stranger to grand, encompassing systems' (xv), but it is true only because some analysts have constructed systems privately which then get expressed in bits and pieces through their 'professional' work. System-building as such is neither encouraged nor rewarded by AP either in the profession or in the classroom.

This, too, is detrimental to the traditional philosophical project; for, as indicated above, philosophizing for/as *eudaimonia* requires a kind of coarse-grained systematicity that allows one to construct 'a map of the structure of all that there is' (Loux 1998: 4). Only with such a 'map' in mind can one hope to rightly order one's life by properly prioritizing the various goods present in the world – the larger part of *eudaimonia*. Traditionally, this is the mark and function of wisdom, and the goal of philosophy.[7] But these longstanding and nearly universal tendencies within AP militate against making this project the express goal of 'official' philosophical work in the forms of thought, research or teaching. AP's partial rapprochement with traditional philosophy has done little to change this; thus, their partial rapprochement notwithstanding, the remaining discrepancies between analytic and traditional philosophy reveal the former to be at best a dim reflection of what historically has counted as 'good philosophy' in the Western tradition. Consequently, we must conclude that the form of 'good philosophy' to which AP has been reduced is not nearly as perennial as Leiter suggests.

Neither is it as pluralistic as he suggests. There can be no doubt that philosophy in the analytic *context* has been moving in the direction of increasing diversity for some time. However, it is misleading to classify this diversity as either a property or an achievement of AP *itself* without significant qualification. In the American academy at least, the impetus for diversification came largely from outside the analytic mainstream. The most visible demonstration of this is the so-called 'pluralist revolt' of 1978, in which non-analysts protested at what John Lachs describes as the analysts' 'stranglehold' on the Eastern Division of the American Philosophical Association:

In the Association's dominant Eastern Division, disciplinary exclusivity was wedded to institutional nepotism in such a way that it became

nearly impossible for philosophers who were not analytic in orientation
and who did not serve in Eastern seaboard graduate schools to break
into the power circle or even into the program [of the annual meeting].
... The system of exclusion worked perfectly with regard to the presi-
dency and the other offices of the Division, as well.... (2004: 8)[8]

The hegemony of analytic philosophy transcended the governance and
activities of the APA, of course; but its manifestation there proved to be
the only front upon which its opponents could force the analysts to take
their concerns seriously. Sadly, its dismissive attitude toward alternative
philosophical approaches and those who practice them has proven to be
one of the most enduring features of AP. Lachs notes that 'the anger of
those wanting reform ... was directed not so much at the analytic style
of doing philosophy as at the arrogance of declaring analysis the only
proper method of thought', and that 'the revolt aimed not at defeating or
eliminating analytic philosophy but at establishing the legitimacy of alternative methods' (2004: 10). But this was a naïve hope. Considered in itself,
the analytic method is separable from the exclusivity that, according to
Lachs, was the real source of agitation. However, taking AP in its fullness
as not only a philosophical but also a social and historical phenomenon,
its exclusivity cannot be separated from its method: AP became the
social force that it did in the academy, and hence occupies the place in
history it does, only because a sufficient number of philosophers adopted
the analytic method *with the understanding that it was the best or only proper
philosophical method.* Indeed, as we shall demonstrate further on, at the
heart of AP is not a methodology so much as a metaphilosophy that limits
philosophy to a single method. Hence, at the time of the pluralist revolt,
it would have been just as damaging to the analytic self-image to give up
exclusivity as to give up the method of analysis itself. This is why, as Lachs
goes on to observe, although 'the organization [i.e., the Eastern APA]
is more open now than it was twenty-five years ago, ... each liberalizing
concession had to be wrung out of it' (11).

The analytic resistance to pluralism has not always taken the sinister
shape described above. Diversity comes in degrees, and which degree
seems right and reasonable will depend partly on what one recognizes as
a possible upper limit. Too narrow a view of the possibilities can enable
one, in all sincerity and with no ill-will, to suppose that an adequate
degree has been achieved when it has not. For instance, Lachs reports
that:

during the early stage of the pluralist revolt, Professor Burt Dreben spoke to an audience concerned about the openness of the profession and allowed that he was puzzled why the Harvard Department was considered narrow. "We have both Quine and Rawls," he said. "Isn't that pluralistic enough?" (2004: 11f)

Lachs rightly describes this response as 'mind-numbingly naïve' – indeed, one is reminded of a scene from the film *The Blues Brothers* in which, upon being asked what kind of music is normally played at Bob's Country Bunker, some bumpkin of a waitress answers: 'we have both kinds – Country and Western'. Still, intentional or not, exclusivity has been part of the analytic package from the beginning; and even its unintentional manifestations result from the inculcation of its core metaphilosophical commitment, which is inherently and intentionally exclusive.

In any case, since the impetus for diversification came largely from non-analysts, it hardly seems right to present this as an achievement of AP. Moreover, since an attitude of exclusivity still pervades AP, it seems no more correct to describe AP itself as pluralistic. Genuine pluralism is a view that involves a standing commitment to openness and inclusivity; but such a commitment has never been characteristic of AP at any point in its history. Thus, although AP has become more diverse, even to the point of being eclectic, it is not pluralistic in outlook. Indeed, Lachs raises the historical points he does only in the service of addressing the problem of exclusivity in the contemporary scene, a problem he illustrates with the following anecdote:

> In serving on National Endowment for the Humanities committees, I noted that members of the panel from English and history and anthropology tended to support applicants from their fields. Philosophers, by contrast, couldn't wait to light into their colleagues; they tore research proposals apart, presenting their authors as fools or as championing out-of-date, inferior ideas and methods. As a result, scholars from other fields garnered much of the money that would, under normal circumstances, have gone to philosophy. These gatekeepers to our profession thought their actions were justified by the imperative to maintain high standards; in fact, they often undertook to judge work they did not understand, and condemned styles of thought and topics of investigation simply because they had no sympathy with them.

'The contempt philosophers feel for colleagues who do not share their values and techniques', Lachs concludes, 'is nothing short of bizarre and has served to undermine the honor and integrity of the discipline' (2004: 8).

Lachs is not alone in noting the contemptuous exclusivity all too often characteristic of contemporary AP. Hans-Johann Glock observed as recently as 2004 that there is a 'prevailing scholasticism' in AP which

> shows itself in, among other things, the focus on a very narrow range of issues and authors ..., a general disinclination to explain why these issues and authors are important, the tendency to treat many fundamental issues as settled once and for all, and ... [a] predilection for technicalities irrespective of their usefulness. Finally, there is a general attitude that those who do not conform to these various standards and preconceptions, who dissent or demand explanations, for example, are simply unprofessional (except for the nonanalytic – Continental, feminist, or non-Western – colleagues in one's own department, who tend to be exempted from such damning judgments). (Glock 2004: 434)

In light of AP's persistent exclusivity, Leiter's view about the relationship of 'analytic' and 'good' philosophy lacks credibility. AP has not fully recovered from its initial rejection of traditional philosophy. It has not come full circle to embrace a standard for good philosophy that is both traditional and pluralistic. Consequently, the equation of AP and good philosophy must be read in the first way, as reducing good philosophy to AP, where the latter is construed as having unique norms of its own. And, of course, this is how it has been understood for most of the analytic era. It has only become possible to see analytic and traditional philosophy as achieving a significant level of rapprochement in the last decade or so, but the equation between analytic and good philosophy has been operative in academic philosophy for well over half a century.

As a prelude to exploring the impact of this fact, we observe that the normative role of AP has shaped academic philosophy principally by guiding decisions about the hiring and retention (i.e., tenure, promotion) of faculty, about the closely related matter of publication (acceptance or rejection), and about pedagogy (the content and manner of philosophical instruction). It is significant, for instance, that Leiter's equation of 'analytic' and 'good' philosophy is made in the *PGR*, which is, as previously mentioned, a ranking of graduate programs in philosophy at major universities in the English-speaking world. Its purpose is to meet the legitimate need of potential graduate students to know which philosophy departments are regarded as good or bad, better or worse – facts directly related to their chances of getting both a good education and a desirable job. The equation of 'analytic' with 'good' philosophy in this context reveals the strong connection between the norms of analytic philosophizing and the criteria for good pedagogy and professional success in academic philosophy today.

Until quite recently, this would also have been apparent from a look at nearly any volume of the American Philosophical Association's *Jobs for Philosophers*. Even today it is not uncommon to see departments representing themselves as analytic, soliciting applications from candidates trained in the analytic tradition, who have specializations in 'core analytic' areas, or in areas understood to be sub-disciplines within AP, and so on. Using the term in this context links it quite obviously to decisions governing the proper investment of an academic institution's resources by designating a certain kind of philosopher but not others as *prima facie* worthy of consideration for such investment.[9] While there are many reasons a department might want to invest in an analytic philosopher, including a desire for diversity among its faculty, the extent to which analysts have been sought over against philosophers from other traditions suggests that something more like a narrow parochialism is driving most of the demand.

A 1996 observation from Bernard Williams bears this out. Commenting on the distinction between analytic and Continental philosophy, he says:

> The distinctions involved are obscure, and the titles serve to conceal this fact. The term 'Continental' serves to discourage thought about the possible contrasts to analytical philosophy, and so about the identity of analytical philosophy itself. At the same time, the vague, geographical resonance of the term does carry a message, that analytical philosophy is familiar as opposed to exotic, and perhaps – if some older stereotypes are in play – that it is responsible as opposed to frivolous. This is indeed what many analytical philosophers believe about it, and they believe it not so much in contrast to activities going on in some remote continent, but, in many cases, as opposed to work done in their local departments of literature. It is not true that work in other styles does not exist in the heartlands of analytical philosophy; it merely does not exist in departments of philosophy. The distinctions involved are not geographical but professional, and what is at issue is the identity of philosophy as a discipline. (Williams 1996: 25f)

This brief statement contains a wealth of insightful observations worthy of comment. At present, we will note only that Williams acknowledges both the exclusive attitude and the attendant professional monopoly of AP.

    We must conclude, then, that the rumor of AP's death has been greatly exaggerated. The bogeyman still lives insofar as many in the profession still associate 'analytic philosophy' with something definite enough to serve as a standard for quality in philosophy.

What Makes for Good (Analytic) Philosophy?

Judgments – about good and bad, professional and unprofessional, worthy and unworthy – must be made, of course, whether by analytic standards or others. But it is surely desirable that these judgments be made in accordance with evaluative criteria clear enough to be examined and, if need be, defended. Otherwise, there is too great a danger that they will be guided by prejudice and fashion rather than principle. However, since AP itself is the model of good philosophy, the fact that its nature currently cannot be specified prevents the *de facto* standards by which these judgments are made from being articulated, scrutinized, or defended.

It is therefore no surprise that, even in the rare case that an attempt is made to articulate the analytic standards, very little of a definite nature can be said about them. For instance, in the sections of the *PGR* that fall under the title 'Methods and Criteria', we find no sustained discussion of the qualities that make for good philosophy. Though Leiter claims that 'the standards of success and accomplishment [in philosophy] are relatively clear' (2004a [2001]),[10] when it comes to instructing his staff of volunteer evaluators[11] he specifies only that they are to look to 'the quality of philosophical work and talent on the faculty [i.e., in the department], the range of areas the faculty covers, and the availability of the faculty over the next few years' (2004a).[12] Only the first two have to do with judgments about good philosophy; but, rather than specifying criteria, they assume a prior grasp of the analytic standards for philosophical talent, quality work, and relative significance among philosophical sub-disciplines (for only by making judgments of significance can one establish an ideal range against which the actual range of a given department can be judged).

Neither Leiter nor the *PGR* are to be blamed for failing to specify the analytic criteria for good philosophy. Its purpose, as Leiter says elsewhere, is '*to capture existing professional sentiment about quality* at different programs and in different fields in the English-speaking world' (2004a, my emphasis).[13] If the issue remains vague in the *PGR*, this only reflects the situation in the profession at large. As a group, analytic philosophers do not expend much effort reflecting upon their manner of philosophizing or the norms it implicitly contains – not nearly so much effort as they do employing both. At least this is the impression one gets from surveying the trends in analytic scholarship, where comparatively little of a broad, metaphilosophical nature is to be found.

And when an analyst does make the attempt, the result is usually inadequate. Consider as representative Leiter's suggestion that AP is to be understood as 'a style of scholarship, writing and thinking' in which 'clarity, precision and argumentative rigor are paramount'. *Prima facie*, this may seem to contradict the claim that AP's nature and the evaluative criteria supposedly derived from it are ill-defined. However, as Leiter himself admits, reference to these qualities does not characterize AP adequately. It indicates only 'a stylistic commitment that does little to demarcate [AP]' (2004b: 11) from alternatives, historical or contemporary.[14]

Though the *PGR* does not state or explain the standards for good/ analytic philosophy, a study of the raw-data upon which its rankings are based makes some of them plain. The sociologist Kieran Healy recently conducted such a study, and what he found will not surprise anyone familiar with the analytic ethos. First, he found that there was a high degree of consensus among the *PGR*'s staff of evaluators about the factors meriting high overall rankings for a department – so much so that he could declare philosophy 'a *very* high-consensus discipline'.[15] Second, he found that: (1) strengths in metaphysics and the philosophy of language make the greatest contribution to a department's overall ranking; (2) strengths in the philosophy of mind, of science, epistemology, ethics, as well as certain historical areas (ancient, seventeenth century, eighteenth century and Kant/German Idealism) make significant contributions, but not so much as metaphysics and language; and (3) strengths in Continental philosophy, Medieval philosophy, or the philosophy of religion contribute little.

It seems, then, that there are some objective facts about the analytic conception of 'good philosophy', at least as concerns the relative value of certain philosophical sub-disciplines. What we lack, however, is an explanation for why the analytic consensus *is* as it is, and an argument for why it *should be* as it is. We also lack a clear and defensible account of the qualities that make for good philosophy regardless of sub-discipline – the criteria for philosophical talent and quality *per se* – not to mention an account of how they relate to the high-consensus preferences for some sub-disciplines over others (for instance, do metaphysics and the philosophy of language lend themselves more easily to higher levels of clarity, precision or argumentative rigor?). It is not the sociologist's job to find these answers; rather, it is the philosopher's job to provide them. But the analysts have not provided them. Consequently, it remains unclear just what the criteria are for good philosophy on the analytic model.

Is Analytic Philosophy Good Philosophy?

Doing 'good philosophy' on the analytic model has played a significant role in making academic philosophy what it is today – indeed, what it has been for the last century. Doubtless, many analytic philosophers will regard the result as generally good. Still, only the most partisan will refuse to admit that much has gone wrong with academic philosophy over the last hundred years.

First, the fact that the analytic standards of good philosophy remain obscure suggests that they may not be legitimate standards at all, but merely practical norms grounded in the predilections and prejudices of Rorty's professors at Leiter's institutions (see pp.7f, above). The designation 'analytic' would then be little more than a label of arbitrary approval to be worn and bestowed by those with academic power and prestige. In that case, the professional entrenchment of AP would have to be seen as a case of hegemony in the worst sense, generating and sustaining an unjust professional situation in which people are hired or not, tenured or not, promoted or not, on the basis of prejudice rather than principle. And this possibility is something about which everyone involved in the profession should be concerned.

Though it is impossible to tell just how widespread it may be or have been, there is good evidence that this has been a problem in AP. In fact, the prejudicial treatment of a non-analytic philosopher provided the occasion for one of the earliest inquiries into AP's nature: Ved Mehta's *Fly and the Fly Bottle* (1963). In the opening chapter, Mehta chronicles a heated 1959 exchange in the correspondence columns of *The London Times*. The exchange was initially between Russell and Ryle, but others quickly joined the fray. The point of contention was Ryle's refusal to publish, in *Mind*, a review of Ernest Gellner's *Words and Things* (2005 [1959]). The exchange began with a searing letter in which Russell accused Ryle of abusing his position as editor by making consonance with his own philosophical predilections the standard by which other philosophical works were to be judged. *Words and Things* was itself an inquiry into the nature of AP in its ordinary-language form, and one that presented it in a very negative light. Later in that chapter, Mehta recounts an interview with Gellner in which the latter is quoted as saying:

As far as professional philosophy is concerned, 'Words and Things' ruined my future rather than secured it. I attacked the philosophical Establishment, and as long as the present philosophers remain in power, I will never have a position at an Oxford college. Whether I will be accepted again in philosophical circles remains to be seen. (Mehta 1963: 38)

He never was. Though Gellner went on to have a brilliant career working at the intersection of philosophy, anthropology and sociology, he never re-entered the philosophical mainstream.

Gellner's case is just one very public manifestation of the prejudicial environment created by the unreflective application of the analytic axiology. Cumulatively, this has resulted not only in the prejudicial treatment of individuals, but also of whole philosophical schools. Viewed broadly, one of the most conspicuous features of twentieth-century academic philosophy is the radical polarization of the analytic and Continental schools. Though analytic philosophers are becoming increasingly cognizant of the philosophical richness of Continental work, their tendency throughout most of the twentieth century was to reject it completely, frequently sight unseen. Consequently, much that was worth knowing was lost to several generations of philosophers and their students. The peculiarity and regretability of the analytic/Continental rift has been noted by a number of authors. Dummett, for example, has famously expressed his puzzlement over the divergence of the two traditions which, like the Rhine and the Danube, rise and, for a time, run together (1993: 26). Likewise, Peter Simons (2001) has argued that the rift as we know it was not, in the main, ideological, but largely the product of historical accident functioning mainly through the two world wars and the political circumstances that occasioned them. Insofar as there is blame to be assigned to philosophers and their machinations, he identifies Heidegger as having played a decisive role by derailing the phenomenological movement from the tracks upon which Husserl had originally set it. Doubtless, Simons is correct in his observations. There is more to be said about the rift, however, especially concerning the contribution from the analytic side; and it seems unlikely that the analytic axiology did not play a role.

Even more worrisome, perhaps, is the fact that by pursuing 'good work' over the course of the twentieth century, analytic philosophers managed to alienate academic philosophy both from other academic disciplines and from the general public. Tyler Burge discusses this with admirable frankness in his 1999 presidential address to the Western division of the American Philosophical Association. The bulk of twentieth-century philosophizing in the analytic line, he explains, busied itself with deflating humanity, and, along with it, philosophy. To illustrate his point, Burge presents a fictional dialogue between a certain Professor Carwittup – clearly the embodiment of twentieth-century AP – and a prospective philosophy student. As they talk, Professor Carwittup manages to dismiss as antiquated or unscientific (and thus as failing to meet the standards for 'good work' in philosophy) every topic in which the prospective student suggests he might be interested. The search for the meaning of life, the quest for truth, the attempt to discover a rational basis for moral evaluation, or to come to an understanding of free will, consciousness, or personal identity in terms that go beyond the naturalism that so often characterized analytic thought in the twentieth century – all are written off as the pipe-dreams of a now defunct discipline, namely, traditional philosophy, the kind of philosophy that existed before the analytic revolution.

The inability of Burge's student to find anything of value or interest in Professor Carwittup's version of philosophy symbolizes the experience of too many real students, not to mention large segments of both the academic and non-academic worlds. As Robert Solomon reports:

> In my travels around the country, I often meet people – successful businesspeople, artists, and others – who without any prompting regale me with a familiar confession. It begins "I had a philosophy class once, but…." I know what is coming. I cringe from the opening syllables. … Too often it is "but I hated it," typically followed by a most unflattering portrait of an uncaring, pompous teacher who was obviously too clever by half and intent on displaying this. (1999: 4)

Solomon goes on to criticize AP for endorsing a 'thin' and 'joyless' version of philosophy incommensurate with the 'thickness' and 'richness' of human experience. Constrained by worries about maintaining analytic professional standards, he explains, philosophers have tended to discount the philosophical problems that emerge naturally in ordinary human life, preferring instead more rarified problems that can be dealt with by technical methods and formal systems. In this way, he says, philosophy

> has narrowed itself to a set of conceptual skills, declared war on richness and variety in favor of a "thin" and all but exclusive preference for argument and logical analysis, and dismissed Hegel's "speculation" and his all-embracing conception of experience…. Philosophy now

requires "specialization," ... technique, narrow focus, and rigor rather than vision, curiosity, and openness. (1999: 3)

As a result, like Burge's Professor Carwittup, 'philosophers today are too often killjoys, too quick with objections, too obstinate to understand (or to listen to) imperfectly stated alternatives, too anxious to belittle both insight and enthusiasm' (1999: 4).

It is important to stress that this criticism is more than a complaint that philosophizing in the analytic mode is too difficult for the *hoi polloi*. This is true of all philosophy at some level – as anyone who teaches undergraduates knows, even reading Plato's dialogues requires a level of attention and precision to which many are unaccustomed. Though much analytic philosophizing tends to be even more difficult, the worry that is voiced here is different. Burge identifies the *deflationary* tendencies of AP, which were built into its defining methodology, as the root of the problem. Solomon also sees the problem in methodological terms: as their name suggests, analytic philosophers have tended to exalt analysis over synthesis, destruction over construction. As a result, 'the joy of philosophy becomes largely destructive, the fun of "tearing apart" and destroying ... arguments' (1999: 8) – an assessment that brings to mind Lachs' experiences with the National Endowment for the Humanities committees.

The issue is not difficulty. Rather, it is that the traditional strictures of analytic philosophizing render it methodologically ill-suited for grappling with many significant phenomena of human life in a way that is constructive and existentially meaningful.[16] Take, for instance, one of the most characteristic methodological features of AP: the use of formal logic. For over a century, an unprecedented level of philosophical effort has been given to the development and application of formal logical systems with the intention that they should make our thinking more precise in all content-areas. But this has failed to yield sure and significant results, at least in the areas of philosophy that touch 'ordinary' human life most directly, such as ethics, political philosophy and the philosophy of religion.[17]

In other areas, such as metaphysics and the philosophies of language and logic, there indeed may have been advances, but not of the kind that can easily be mapped onto ordinary human concerns. For instance, Scott Soames and Timothy Williamson both point to post-Kripkean understandings of modal and epistemic concepts as among the choicest fruit of AP. They also include aspects of our advancing understanding of the nature, limits and proper construction of formal systems themselves:

Soames refers to the formal notion of logical consequence (2003: I, xi), Williamson to our current grasp of 'the costs and benefits of analysing possibility and necessity in terms of possible worlds' and 'how close a predicate in a language can come to satisfying a full disquotational schema for that very language without incurring semantic paradoxes' (forthcoming).

Concerning these sorts of advances, three points should be noted. First, it is not certain that these actually count as advances, for there is little in the philosophies of language and logic that is not open to debate. Second, even if they do count as genuine advances, the applicability of these insights to real-world concerns has yet to be demonstrated. And third, again assuming they are sure insights, achieving them has taken so much time and effort that other very significant areas of philosophical inquiry went neglected by the philosophical mainstream for much of the twentieth century. Hans Sluga captures some of these concerns when he observes that:

> At least since Tarski's essay 'On the Concept of Truth in Formalized Languages' of 1931 it has become the common belief of linguistic philosophers that a purely formal, structural theory of meaning could be constructed. ... As long as one remains with a few simple, formalizable sentences the idea seems to hold promise. ... But there is little evidence in the actual progress of the discussion to encourage such hopes. After eighty years of debate linguistic philosophers are still not agreed on the semantics of simple proper names. How long would it take to construct a semantics of philosophical discourse? (1980: 3–4)

Though dated, Sluga's general point is still applicable: in the philosophy of language and logic, as elsewhere in philosophy, disagreements on basic issues is the norm; thus, inductively, there is little reason to think that continuing to mine this narrow vein will prove so profitable that it should rank as the most important thing philosophers might do with their time and talents. For all these reasons, then, and in light of our species' pressing need for a philosophy capable of illuminating all the areas of human life, it is not unreasonable to judge the last century's investment in formal systems as yielding too small a return to justify continued investment at the same level.

This brief digression about formal logic/semantics is intended to illustrate the general point that dissatisfaction with AP need not be a sign of intellectual weakness or vice. For instance, Williamson's claim that 'impatience with the long haul of technical reflection is a form of shallowness, often thinly disguised by histrionic advocacy of depth' (2004: 126f) simply won't do. Doubtless there are cases in which shallowness or some other intellectual vice motivates the rejection of technical philosophizing. It is just as indubitable, however, that the same rejection is frequently motivated by a virtuous concern for one's fellow human beings, a missionary sense that philosophy can do much to improve human life both individually and corporately considered, and the reasonable judgment that a philosophy not only non-technical but free of all the various strictures characteristic of AP is much better suited to this task than AP in its characteristic forms.

Moreover, neither skepticism about formal techniques nor impatience with technical reflection is required for finding fault with AP's technical preoccupations. Kevin Mulligan, Peter Simons and Barry Smith – none of them strangers to highly technical philosophizing – have recently characterized AP as driven to a highly technical form of escapism by a *horror mundi*:

> Like the braintwisters holidaymakers take onto the beach, philosophical puzzles divert from life's hardships. ... elegantly structured possible worlds are so much more pleasant places to explore than the flesh and blood reality which surrounds us here on Earth. (Mulligan *et al.*, 2006: 65)

As a consequence, AP 'is at its core a culture driven by puzzles, rather than by large-scale, systematic theoretical goals' (ibid.). And this, they observe, has implications for the profession:

> The AP system of professional philosophy encourages introspection and relative isolation because philosophy is not seen as directly relevant to the scientific concerns which prevail in the wider world. ... The quickest way to a career in the competitive world of modern AP is to pick a puzzle in a trendy area – be it vagueness, modal counterparts, rigid designation, "the hard problem" or the elimination of truth – and come up with a hitherto unsuspected twist in the dialectic, earning a few more citations in one or another of the on-going games of fashionable philosophical ping-pong. (64f.)

And, in turn, the state of the philosophical profession has consequences for the rest of the world. Whereas Solomon was concerned with the effects of AP on 'ordinary people' for whom philosophy ought to be a source of enrichment and joy, Mulligan, Simons and Smith are principally concerned with its effects – or rather its lack of effect – on other fields of inquiry, especially emerging fields with strong applied aspects that involve mechanical information processing (like bioinformatics, artificial intelligence, and the creation of a 'semantic web').[18] In such fields, they say,

> philosophical confusion is the order of the day, because AP-philosophers with some knowledge of ontology, manifesting their *horror mundi*, have shown little interest in grappling with the problems thrown up by these fields, leaving it instead to philosophically naïve exponents of other disciplines to wreak ontological havoc. Philosophers, for their part, occupy themselves with in-house puzzles, ignorant of the damage their neglect is wreaking in the wider world. (64)

A common theme runs through Burge, Solomon, Mulligan, Simons and Smith: the irrelevance of AP to real-world concerns. Though they address the problem relative to different contexts of real-world concern, all seem to acknowledge that human life needs more from philosophy than AP has been willing or able to give it. And while they all focus on AP's use of formal techniques, this in itself is not the problem. The insistence on formalization has never been universal within AP; nor is it the only source of AP's estrangement from the real world. It is simply the most obvious source – which is why it gets the lion's share of critical attention. However, estrangement from ordinary human concerns was just as much a problem for some in the ordinary-language camp, and it remains a problem even for the many contemporary analysts who rely more on natural language than formal technique. For instance, the tendency to reject 'folk psychology' in analytic philosophy of mind from Ryle and Wittgenstein through the Churchlands creates a similar estrangement without the use of formal techniques.

In short, the insistence on formalization is only one of several methodological and substantive strictures that, endorsed by the analysts, have led to unfortunate discontinuities between academic philosophy and ordinary human life – and *that* is the problem. Just as practitioners in the philosophy of mind have come to acknowledge that there is a 'psychophysical gap' that is at best very difficult to bridge and may be unbridgeable, it is time for analytic philosophers to acknowledge that there is an 'existential gap' between AP and human life that is also very difficult to bridge and may be unbridgeable. *Prima facie*, this is a good reason for thinking that AP is not a worthy model of 'good philosophy'.

The Crisis in Analytic Philosophy

A recent work on the history of AP begins with the following statement:

> It seems beyond argument that analytic philosophy has been, for some time now, in a state of crisis – dealing with its self-image, its relationships with philosophical alternatives, its fruitfulness and even legitimacy in the general philosophical community. (Biletzki and Matar 1998: xi)

The idea that there is a crisis in AP formed the basis for a recent conference at the University of Southampton, where, from 1997 to 2005, there existed a Centre for Post-Analytical Philosophy. For several years, the Centre's advertisement read:

> In recent years a feeling has been growing that the analytic tradition in philosophy, once proudly dominant and disdainful of other traditions, has been undergoing a crisis. Manifestations of this crisis can be seen in the debate now raging among analytic philosophers about what, exactly, the method of analysis is, and also in the growing interest among analytic philosophers in so-called 'Continental' philosophy.[19]

As with Leiter's pronouncement on the 'bogeyman of analytic philosophy', it is too early to herald the advent of a post-analytic era. Nonetheless, even such eminent analytic philosophers as Hilary Putnam and Jaakko Hintikka accept that something is so badly wrong with AP that its very survival is at stake. Putnam admits to 'a conviction that the present situation in [analytic] philosophy is one that calls for a revitalization, a renewal, of the subject' (1992: ix). Similarly, Hintikka has counseled that 'we have to make a new start in practically all branches of philosophical studies' and has warned that 'the survival of analytic philosophy' is at stake (1998: 260).

To philosophers who self-identify as analytic, whose philosophical careers have been devoted to some selection of the in-house puzzles mentioned by Mulligan and crew, the idea that their school is in a state of crisis will probably seem absurd. For them, discussion of these puzzles continues much as it always has, and there is no reason to think that the discussion is in danger of coming to an end. How, then, could there be a crisis in AP? The ground we have covered provides the answer. AP dominates the profession, but no one can say what it is. It has conferred its own standards upon the philosophical profession, but no one can say just what those standards are. Worst of all, AP has frequently failed to connect meaningfully with other fields of inquiry and with ordinary human concerns. Thus, despite its social vitality in the academic sphere, there is very good reason for thinking that there is a crisis in AP.

Now, if AP *could* give an account of itself and its standards that showed there was good reason for accepting the analytic model despite its 'existential gap', the crisis would be averted – or, rather, it would be shown that it is not AP that is in crisis, but the humanistic outlook that desires to have more from philosophy. If truth (or our best approximation to it) has unfortunate consequences, so be it. However, both AP's nature and its standards, and thus also the reasons in support of them, currently defy articulation. Thus, at its root, AP's crisis is not unlike the one Husserl ascribed to the 'European Sciences' in the 1930s. It is a crisis of fundamental, theoretical grounding and justification; a metaphilosophical crisis that calls for AP to clarify and to justify its nature and its methods once and for all.

Chapter 2

A Crisis within the Crisis: The Problem of Revisionist History

A New Task for History

The situation outlined in Chapter 1 calls for a careful investigation of AP's nature. However, this metaphilosophical task cannot be accomplished without a concomitant historical inquiry. AP has been with us for roughly a century now, during which time it has undergone significant metamorphoses. Consequently, it would be misleading to define it in terms drawn solely from its current or recent state(s) – and doubly so since the very fact that AP exists as something to be discussed under a single name will forever be connected to the context in which that name entered the philosophical lexicon. So, an adequate metaphilosophical account of AP will have to be not only clear and coherent but also consistent with the facts of history.

This point is fairly obvious; thus it is not surprising that *the history of AP* emerged as a new historical sub-discipline within academic philosophy just as the need for an adequate characterization of AP began to be felt in the academic community. Only a very few historical works on AP appeared before 1960. Numerous studies of individual analysts – especially Frege and Wittgenstein – appeared throughout the 60s, 70s and 80s, but little was done in the way of systematic reflection on the history or nature of AP as a whole. This slowly began to change in the 1990s, in books by Peter Hylton (1990), Nicholas Griffin (1991), the late Alberto Coffa (1991), Michael Dummett (1993) and Peter Hacker (1996), among others. John Ongley describes the emergence of this new field well:

The history of analytic philosophy movement exploded onto the philosophic scene in 1990 with the publication of Peter Hylton's study *Russell, Idealism, and the Emergence of Analytic Philosophy*. Though the movement had existed at least a decade before that, it was then that it reached critical mass. A flood of works in the subject quickly followed Hylton's

1990 book, and history of analytic philosophy emerged as a prominent part of contemporary philosophy. (2005: 3; cf. Beaney 1998)

The foci of these works were still individual figures or factions within the history of AP, but they also contained unprecedented levels of reflection on AP *as a whole* in light of what they unearthed regarding its parts.

The advent of this field has a double significance, being at once a sign of AP's crisis and its best hope for resolving it. It is a sign of the crisis in that it signifies the demise of AP's confidence in its original self-image. Being the revolutionary movement that it was, AP was initially received as rendering pre-analytic philosophy obsolete. In the minds of many analysts, this justified ignoring the history of philosophy. To the extent that analysts did engage history, they tended to do so in unhistorical ways; for instance, by creating 'rational reconstructions' of past philosophers' ideas and arguments with little regard for their historical context. Consequently, AP came to be associated with an ahistorical or anti-historical attitude. However, as its linguistic metaphilosophy – the basis for its revolutionary self-image – began to erode in the 1960s, so did the barrier between AP and the history of philosophy. Thus the emergence of history signals the disintegration of the original analytic program and self-image.

Without its single-minded devotion to linguistic analysis, not only history but many neglected fields and sub-disciplines re-emerged – or in some cases emerged for the first time – in the analytic context. This made AP highly eclectic in terms of subject matter (hence the 'pluralism' noted by Leiter). And, as AP became more eclectic through the 1980s, its lack of a unifying metaphilosophical vision became more conspicuous. Thus, ironically, the very thing that gave philosophical historians a place in the analytic context simultaneously made AP itself a puzzle for them.

The existence of this puzzle about AP's nature revealed a fundamental theoretical deficiency, and hence a metaphilosophical crisis for AP – one about which most analysts were either unaware or unconcerned. But awareness of and dissatisfaction with AP's 'existential gap' continued to increase throughout the 1990s, transforming this emerging historian's puzzle into a pressing issue for everyone concerned with the future of academic philosophy. As this crisis of theory acquired a social dimension, AP was increasingly compelled to address the long-ignored questions about its nature and legitimacy – which, of course, it could not answer successfully by looking at itself in its eclectic state. At least as a matter of practicality (since AP's nature was not clear from its contemporary state) if not also of principle (since AP is a historical entity) its nature had to be sought via an inquiry into its past.[1] Thus it is no coincidence that the history of AP movement exploded onto the scene in the 1990s, just as concern over AP's nature was reaching critical levels – it was a response to a newly felt need in the philosophical community stimulated by a dawning awareness of AP's crisis. This connection between history and metaphilosophy is not lost on Erich Reck, who observes:

> ... there seems to be an identity crisis in analytic philosophy today, a loss of certainty about what philosophy really is, or should be. ... In this situation a reflection back on early analytic philosophy is of special interest, not only to understand better when and how this particular tradition started, but also because the nature of "analytic" inquiry was at the center of discussion then. (2002: ix)

Neither is it a coincidence that, as the metaphilosophical nature of the crisis became clearer, work in the field came increasingly to focus on the nature of AP as a whole. Ongley again observes:

> One problem with early work in this new field was that it did not often ask what analytic philosophy itself was, but assumed that this was already well known. As a result, these works frequently ended up uncritically fleshing out old stories about the history and nature of analytic philosophy with new details, rather than revising our pictures of what analytic philosophy is and was. However, this shortcoming of much of the new history soon became apparent, and, toward the end of the 90s, historians of analytic philosophy increasingly began to ask the question: What is analytic philosophy? (2005: 3)

The Traditional Conception of Analytic Philosophy

The growth of historical interest in AP parallels the growth of crisis-consciousness about it; and this for the simple reason that historical inquiry is required to solve the puzzle and thereby resolve the crisis. In fact, historical inquiry seems to be our only hope for locating AP's fundamental philosophical commitments and thereby resolving the metaphilosophical aspect of its crisis. Before we discuss the findings of this historical inquiry, however, we must address an objection that threatens to stop it before it starts. Given the difficulty of defining AP, a contemporary Meno might question the possibility of fruitful inquiry into its history and nature: if we cannot define AP, how can we know what it is; and if we don't know what it is, how will we look for it?

Meno's paradox is generated by using 'knowledge' language equivo-cally. In one sense, we all know perfectly well what AP is; in another sense, we don't. We know what AP is at one level or to a certain degree; we want to come to know it on a deeper level or more fully. One begins an inquiry by setting down what one does know about the subject; thereby providing the inquiry with an initial orientation toward its subject, and delimiting the field of inquiry at least in broad strokes. One then seeks to fill in the details by scrutinizing the data that fall within those broad parameters. Ideally, this leads to a more fine-grained knowledge of the relevant data; and this in turn provides for a more complete under-standing of the whole that was initially mapped out in broad strokes – all that is required is to reflect on the whole in light of what one has learned about the parts.

What, then, do we know about AP? What are the broad strokes that orient and delimit inquiry into its history and nature? We have already mentioned several features traditionally associated with AP: its turn-of-the-twentieth-century origin, its revolutionary character, its ahistorical attitude, and, at the heart of all this, the linguistic thesis. Now the time has come for a more systematic presentation of these features which, together with its traditional anti-metaphysical stance, form what I will call the traditional conception (TC) of AP.

According to tradition, AP originated around the turn of the twentieth century, as G.E. Moore and Bertrand Russell broke away from what was then the dominant school in the British universities, Absolute Idealism. The alternative they advocated was widely interpreted as involving a metaphilosophical turn in the direction of the linguistic thesis: the view that philosophy is wholly or largely a matter of linguistic analysis. In addressing philosophical problems, Moore and Russell frequently presented themselves as exploring the possible *meanings* of the *terms* and *propositions* involved in articulating both the problems themselves and possible answers to them – a practice they called 'analysis'. Because the idiom in which they expressed their work had linguistic connotations, analysis itself was taken to be linguistic in nature. This is why AP is traditionally understood as having been born in a 'linguistic turn'.

Additionally, rather than constructing grand philosophical systems or 'worldviews', Moore and Russell focused on narrowly defined philo-sophical questions considered in isolation. This move away from traditional system-building metaphysics is the earliest and mildest manifestation of what would later come to be recognized as AP's characteristic, anti-metaphysical stance. While it was in the first instance due mainly to the narrowness of focus and trajectory toward the more fine-grained required by the practice of analysis, many interpreted Moore and Russell to be setting the bounds of meaning so that many of the more high-flying metaphysical propositions found in the history of philosophy were rendered either meaningless or false. From this point, it was a short step to the view that the problems of traditional philosophy are linguistic illusions generated by violating the boundaries of meaning, and that they are to be solved by clearly marking those boundaries and then staying within them. In the popular mind, no other view has been associated more closely with AP.

Both the linguistic conception of philosophy expressed in the linguistic thesis and the accompanying tendency of Russell and especially Moore to avoid metaphysical system-building were rightly seen as novel in the history of philosophy. It is primarily on account of these two features that AP gained the reputation for being revolutionary on a grand scale – not merely a revolt against British Idealism, but against traditional philosophy on the whole. But, having originated in this grand philosophical revolution, AP proceeded to undergo several internal micro-revolutions that parsed its history into five main phases. The first began around 1900 with Moore and Russell's linguistic turn. By around 1910, this generic turn to language began to channel itself into a more specific commitment to the use of mathematical logic, which was widely received as constituting an *ideal language* free from all forms of obscurity and imprecision. Though a number of late nineteenth- and early twentieth-century philosophers and mathematicians – of whom analysts tend to regard Gottlob Frege the most important – contributed to the development of mathematical logic, it was Bertrand Russell who popularized it and made its use a norm in AP. The turn to *logical* or *ideal-language analysis* characterizes the second and third phases of AP. They are distinguished respectively by the dominance of *logical atomism* (approximately 1910–1930s), as developed by Russell and Ludwig Wittgenstein, and *logical positivism* (approximately 1930s–1945), as developed by the members of the Vienna Circle and popularized by A.J. Ayer. The fourth phase, running approximately 1945–1965, is characterized by the turn to *ordinary-language analysis*, developed in various ways by Wittgenstein, John Wisdom, Gilbert Ryle, John Austin and Peter Strawson. Despite the disagreements they imply, these micro-revolutions are traditionally seen as subsumed within the macro-revolution of the linguistic turn, and are thought to be variations on a common theme: namely, the linguistic thesis.

The fifth and final phase, beginning in the mid 1960s and continuing beyond the end of the twentieth century, is characterized by the very eclecticism that eventually brought our puzzle to light. According to tradition, this phase was ushered in largely by the work of W.V. Quine, which undermined several key assumptions of previous philosophizing in the analytic tradition. Even so, the linguistic conception of philosophy did not die off immediately. Quine himself endorsed a technique called 'semantic ascent' – a matter of moving from philosophizing about things to philosophizing about the words that name them. He saw this as a fruitful method for finding common ground in philosophical disputes and thereby avoiding stalemate – and so as a very important philosophical method even if not the only one (see Willard 1983). Thus, only slowly did linguistic philosophy give way to the philosophy of language, and the philosophy of language to metaphysics, and metaphysics to everything else, so that, by the 1980s, the growing eclecticism in AP began to raise questions about the nature of the school itself.

This TC, here presented by way of historical synopsis, contains several elements that serve to guide further inquiry into AP. First, it provides temporal boundaries for inquiry: if AP originated around the turn of the twentieth century, it makes little sense to begin by looking to figures, factions, ideas or events that occur much earlier than that. Second, it provides geographical boundaries: if AP originated in Britain, it makes little sense to begin by looking elsewhere. Third, it provides rough extensional boundaries for AP insofar as it provides a list of paradigmatic analytic philosophers and their works. Fourth, it suggests intensional boundaries for AP insofar as it highlights the most significant attributes traditionally associated with the school: its endorsement of the linguistic thesis, its anti-metaphysical and ahistorical stances, and its revolutionary character.

The Ordinary Use of 'Analytic Philosophy'

It is important to emphasize that, despite the puzzle about its nature, the TC represents a genuine point of consensus in thinking about AP. This is true not only historically, but on the contemporary scene as well. Peter Hacker has recently dismissed this fact. Observing that 'the term "analytic philosophy" is a fairly new one', he says:

> There is no point in trying to follow Wittgenstein's advice...: "don't think, but look!" ... i.e. examine how the expression in question is in fact used. For the term does not have a well-established use that commands general consensus. Here we are free to mold the concept as we please; indeed, arguably not free, but required to do so. (1998: 14)

However, it does not follow from the fact that the term does not have a well-established use that *commands* general consensus that we may mold the concept as we please. It simply reveals that, as it is ordinarily used, 'analytic philosophy' is not as well-defined as it might be. In this it is like a vague term – and perhaps it is one. As such, it is in need of what is sometimes called a *precising definition*; but in giving a precising definition, far from being free to mold the vague concept as we please, we are constrained by the clear facts concerning the use of the vague term. This is really just another way of putting the response to Meno's paradox given above: we begin knowing vaguely what we mean by 'analytic philosophy', and we seek to know more precisely. What, then, are the clear facts concerning the ordinary, 'vague' use of 'analytic philosophy'?

Perhaps the first thing to note is that there are senses of 'analytic philosophy' that are not vague, and do not stand in need of precising definition. In what may be the broadest sense of the term, 'analytic philosophy' can be used as a description to pick out any brand of philosophy that analyzes wholes of some sort into constituents of some sort. It is this *adjectival* sense of the term that Shadworth Hodgson employs, in the first volume of *Mind*, to discuss analytic as opposed to synthetic and constructive philosophy (1876a–c). However, it is rare in contemporary parlance to see 'analytic philosophy' used in the adjectival sense, where 'analytic' serves as a mere descriptor. Instead, 'analytic' usually functions just like the words 'scholastic' and 'process' and 'Eleatic' when they occur before 'philosophy', and the whole term functions as a proper name – the name of a type or school of philosophy.[2] Thus William Charlton describes AP as 'the variety of philosophy favored by the majority of philosophers working in the English-speaking countries' (1991: 2). Used this way, the antithesis of AP is not synthetic or constructive philosophy but Continental philosophy; and it is not uncommon to see contemporary AP characterized by contrasting it with Continental philosophy, as Charlton indeed does, saying that the two differ mainly 'in how they conceive the subject and think it should be conducted' (2f) – that is, they differ metaphilosophically and methodologically. Thus, there is a sense in which 'analytic philosophy' refers to a school of philosophy, a distinctive way of doing philosophy, the way favored by most philosophers in English-speaking countries. It is clear that the puzzle, the crisis, and the surge of historical interest that has arisen alongside them have to do with AP in this *nominative* sense.

In the nominative sense, 'analytic philosophy' tends to be used in a way that is highly consistent with the TC. As we shall see, this has been constant from the moment the nominative sense of 'analytic philosophy' was added to the philosophical lexicon. For now, though, we will focus only on its use in the fifth phase of AP, the era of eclecticism. From the 1960s onward, excepting cases in which the TC is being called into question (as in much of the recent historical work on AP), talk of AP has tended to keep close to the historical, geographical, extensional and intensional boundaries it prescribes.

The clearest cases of this are overt attempts to describe or define[3] AP, the likes of which one would expect to find in anthologies and other introductory works. For instance, in an early anthology of classic analytic works, Robert Ammerman introduces AP by highlighting its turn-of-the-twentieth-century origin and its revolutionary character: 'around the turn of the [twentieth] century a revolution began in philosophy which is not yet over' (1965: 1). Ammerman identifies Moore and Russell as the two figures most responsible for this revolution (3). He notes the dominance of AP in English-speaking countries throughout much of the twentieth century, as well as its continuing influence, saying that 'some under-standing of the development and growth of analytic thought is essential if one is to understand the state of philosophy today' (1). The centrality of the linguistic thesis is a chord struck loudly and repeatedly, as Ammerman drives home the point that 'philosophical analysis is essentially the study of language' and 'all analytic philosophers would agree that the study of language is of the greatest importance' (2). Analysts disagree, he explains, only about whether ideal or ordinary language is best (2–3). Ammerman traces this linguistic orientation to the movement's beginning, explicitly describing Moore as 'interested in analyzing ordinary language' (10). Finally, he observes that the most pressing philosophical issue of the day was whether the analysts' linguistic conception of philosophy would endure – specifically, whether the Wittgensteinian hope of dissolving all philosophical problems via the analysis of language would come to fruition, or whether a new language-oriented metaphysics (perhaps of the sort Strawson was then promoting) would prove necessary (12).

In a similar work from 1966, Morris Wietz notes that it was already 'established practice' (1) to divide the history of AP into four phases: the realism of Moore and Russell, the logical analysis/logical atomism of Russell and Wittgenstein, logical positivism, and 'Linguistic, Ordinary Language, or Conceptual Analysis'. 'Analytic', he says, is to be contrasted with 'speculative' philosophy, thus alluding to AP's break with traditional philosophy (1). Wietz associates AP with the linguistic thesis, but has it occurring with Russell in the second phase of AP rather than during the first, realist phase (4–5). By the 1930s, he observes, this linguistic conception of analysis had come to be the *sine qua non* of AP (6).[4]

Likewise, in a 1970 anthology, Barry Gross names Moore and Russell as the founders of AP (9), but notes that some would name Frege (14); and he proceeds to divide its history into five stages (13f): realism, logical atomism, logical positivism, and two consecutive phases of ordinary-language philosophy (one initiated by Wittgenstein and Ryle, the other by J.L. Austin). He draws attention to AP's revolutionary reputation and discusses the reasons for it (10ff). Interestingly, he notes that this rests partly on the mistake of attributing to all analysts the logical positivists' rejection of metaphysics (10, 13).[5] Still, he describes AP as tending to be narrowly focused on analyses 'of particular concepts and notions' rather than trying to give 'a comprehensive description of the whole of reality' (9), and this, as noted previously, is itself a move away from traditional metaphysics and metaphilosophy. Finally, like Ammerman and Wietz, Gross makes the linguistic turn and the linguistic thesis central, saying, 'though analytic philosophers continued to try to understand the world, they turned more often to attempts to understand our talk about the world' (9). This, he explains, led to 'a preoccupation with language' (9) within which analytic philosophers came to believe that 'concern with language is not merely some preliminary to getting things straight, but is very close to the whole business' (19f) of philosophy.

Clearly, these characterizations keep very close to the TC, and are best taken as expressions of it. One might object that their presence in introductory works virtually guarantees that they are oversimple, and that, while suitable for the purpose of introductory works, this disqualifies them as serious, scholarly statements about the history and nature of AP. However, this would be going too far. Being simple or general does not by itself make a characterization false; and competent scholars know how to make such characterizations true. The authors in these cases were perfectly competent scholars, and they knew just what they were doing in offering their simplified characterizations of AP. For instance, Ammerman is not only aware of the possibility of oversimplification, but tells us plainly what would count as an oversimplification in the case of AP:

> ... it is misleading to speak of "analytic philosophy" as if it were homogenous and monolithic. There is no single philosophy of analysis. There is no analytic "party line," no "heresies," no pontifical authorities. The word "analysis" is here used as a way of grouping together a number of heterogeneous philosophers who share certain interests and procedures. (1965: 2)

Nearly every work on AP includes a disclaimer of this sort. And yet, the recognized differences among analytic philosophers do not prevent these early authors from grouping them together *as* 'analytic philosophers'; nor, in most cases, do they prevent them from attributing to the analysts some common view that justifies their being grouped together under a common name and as constituting a philosophical school. Thus, after clearly demarcating what would count as oversimplification, Ammerman goes on to give the very traditional characterization summarized above. He does this by focusing on what we have just seen him describe as the analysts' shared interests and procedures, saying that 'it is this common core of agreement which must be isolated before we proceed' (1965: 2). And what is this common core? Nothing other than the linguistic thesis. When Ammerman claims that 'there is no single philosophy of analysis', he means only that AP is not a traditional philosophical system that defines a comprehensive worldview – which is also what he means by denying that AP is 'homogenous and monolithic'. He does *not* mean that there are no views common to all and only analytic philosophers; for if he did, he could not go on as he does to claim that there is a common method of philosophical analysis, and that it is a matter of 'analyzing linguistic or conceptual units' in an attempt to 'understand the structure of language by a careful study of its elements and their interrelations' (2). In fact, Ammerman goes further, characterizing the analysts as unified not only by this common method, but also by a common conception of philosophy. This is clear from the way he ties the term 'analytic philosophy' to metaphilosophical considerations, saying: 'we will use the word "analysis" (or "analytic philosophy") ... to refer to any philosophy which places its greatest emphasis upon the study of language and its complexities' (2). From here, he segues into the remainder of the characterization as discussed above.

Clearly, then, Ammerman is aware of the possibility of oversimplification and is convinced that he has avoided it. Likewise with Wietz and Gross (and surely with all competent scholars who offer generalizations or simplified characterizations). Each sees himself as portraying AP accurately, despite the fact that differences among the analysts are not given detailed attention. Since their authors knew where the pitfalls were located, since they took pains to avoid them, and since their form alone gives no great cause for skepticism, there is no reason for a blanket rejection of introductory characterizations of AP, simplified though they may be. To the contrary, since introductory works tend not to aim at making contributions to the topics or debates they introduce, the views they express about those subjects are likely to avoid both controversy and idiosyncrasy and to represent popular or scholarly consensus. Moreover, their relatively simple nature derives from an effort to focus solely on

the subject's most central features. Far from disqualifying such characterizations, these facts make them of signal importance for the project of
discovering AP's fundamental commitments and hence its nature.

But talk of AP highly consistent with the TC is not limited to introductory works. Scholarly works also speak of AP in its terms. In a 1980
book on Frege, Hans Sluga places the linguistic thesis at the heart of AP:

> Of all the groups of philosophers who have been concerned with
> language, the largest and most coherent is that of analytic philosophy.
> It is the characteristic tenet of that school that the philosophy of
> language is the foundation of all the rest of philosophy. Analytic
> philosophy has tended to concern itself with language in a particular
> manner, holding that the structural, formal, logical investigation of
> language is philosophically fundamental. (1f)

A few pages later he puts the point metaphilosophically, identifying the
characteristic tenet of AP as 'the idea that … the examination of the
logical structure of language will be the proper task of philosophy' (4).
Clearly, this fits the intensional boundaries of the TC. Moreover, the
reason these points come out in a book on Frege is that – consistent with
the historical and extensional boundaries of the TC – Sluga takes Frege
to be a founder of AP.

Sluga intended his book to counteract Dummett's influential reading
of Frege, which Sluga justifiably saw as insufficiently sensitive to historical
issues. Despite their disagreements about the proper interpretation of
Frege's philosophy, they both agreed, at least early on, about the nature
of AP and Frege's status as founder. Dummett has expressed his views on
these matters in several highly similar ways, but never the same way twice;
for instance:

1. 'Only with Frege was the proper object of philosophy finally established: namely, first that the goal of philosophy is the analysis of
   thought; secondly that the study of thought is to be sharply distinguished from the study of the psychological process of thinking; and
   finally that the only proper method for analyzing thought consists in
   the analysis of language.' (1978: 458)
2. 'What distinguishes analytic philosophy, in its diverse manifestations,
   from other schools is the belief, first, that a philosophical account
   of thought can be obtained through a philosophical account of
   language, and, secondly, that a comprehensive account can only be
   so obtained.' (1993: 4f)

3. '[The] fundamental axiom of analytical philosophy [is] that the only route to the analysis of thought goes through the analysis of language.' (1993: 128)
4. 'We may characterize analytic philosophy as that which follows Frege in accepting that the philosophy of language is the foundation of the rest of the subject.' (1978: 441)
5. 'Analytical philosophy was born when the "linguistic turn" was taken.' (1993: 5)

All of these highlight the centrality of language as a subject matter for AP. (1) and (4) assume the metaphilosophical nature of AP's preoccupation with language, and (1) hints at AP's revolutionary nature. Naming Frege as founder places its origin in the late nineteenth century, but even Dummett recognizes that the movement did not come into its own until the early twentieth century (1993: viii).

Dummett's *Origins of Analytical Philosophy* (1993) was published just as the history of AP movement was gaining significant momentum, and just as AP's metaphilosophical crisis was becoming so apparent that few could continue to ignore it. For instance, in 1996, Bernard Williams foreshadowed Leiter's current views about the collapse of the analytic/ Continental distinction and with it the identity of AP, saying, 'philosophy in the United States, in other English-speaking parts of the world, and in many other countries as well, is now very largely the same. In these places there is now one philosophical culture ...' (25). This is an extreme example of a trend whose beginnings can be detected at least twenty years earlier. Beginning as early as the 1970s, commentators became increasingly circumspect in their characterizations of AP – a sign that the puzzle/crisis was coming to light even then. Despite this, few have taken the view that 'analytic philosophy' fails to pick out a distinctive kind of philosophy. This is shown by the fact that talk of AP has tended to stay close to the TC even in the mouths of those aware of the puzzle. In 1975, for instance, Michael Corrado acknowledged that analytic philosophers have trouble giving an intensional characterization of their school. 'Nonetheless,' he observed,

when analysis is opposed to other important contemporary traditions – phenomenology, for example – philosophers know pretty well who is to count as an analyst and who is not. The term *analyst* applies, in this very loose sense, to the majority of the important philosophers in the English-speaking countries, and in Scandinavia. They are philosophers who have been influenced by Bertrand Russell and G.E. Moore, Ludwig

Wittgenstein, the logical positivists, especially Rudolph Carnap, and American pragmatists, especially C.I. Lewis, or else they have been influenced by men who were influenced by those philosophers. (1975: xii)

This list fits the geographical, temporal and – with the exception of Lewis and the pragmatists – the extensional boundaries of the TC. But even this idiosyncratic departure from its extensional boundaries bears witness to the centrality of the TC for thought about AP. Lewis is best known for his contributions to mathematical logic, the abundant use of which was the most salient feature of early AP on the TC. Pierce, too, was closely connected to the development of modern logic. Beyond this, the early pragmatic movement as a whole emphasized the need to make ideas clear by looking to the practical consequences of linguistic expression in particular contexts – a point which *prima facie* might seem quite close to the logical positivists' verification principle of meaning. So, even though it is a mistake to include Lewis and the pragmatists, it is a mistake governed by, perhaps even inspired by, and certainly explicable in light of, the TC.

In 1997, Dagfinn Follesdal gave a similar extensional characterization. Follesdal distinguishes between 'two principal traditions' within AP: 'one inspired by logic, of which Bolzano, Frege, and Russell are the early main protagonists, and one oriented toward ordinary language, in which G.E. Moore, the later Wittgenstein, and J.L. Austin played a central part' (1). Like Corrado's mention of the pragmatists, Follesdal's mention of Bolzano is an idiosyncratic departure from the TC. Also like Corrado's departure, however, it is best explained by the TC's focus on the linguistic thesis and the early analytic conception of logic as an ideal language. Again, the rule is observed in the breach.

Also in 1997, Sluga provided a similar characterization without any idiosyncrasies:

Following *common practice*, I take analytic philosophy here as originating in the work of Frege, Russell, Moore, and Wittgenstein, as encompassing the logical empiricism of the Vienna Circle, English ordinary language philosophy of the post-war period, American mainstream philosophy of recent decades, as well as their worldwide affiliates and descendants. (17 n, my emphasis)

Unlike Corrado and Follesdal, Sluga does not deviate at all from the TC. Neither does Brian Leiter:

The foundational figures of this [i.e., the analytic] tradition are philosophers like Gottlob Frege, Bertrand Russell, the young Ludwig Wittgenstein and G.E. Moore; other canonical figures include Carnap, Quine, Davidson, Kripke, Rawls, Dummett, and Strawson. (2004a)[6]

The practice of giving exclusively extensional characterizations of AP is a fairly recent phenomenon, attributable to the difficulty of finding an adequate intensional characterization that covers both the linguistic and post-linguistic phases of AP – or even the latter alone. Still, some intrepid souls occasionally try to say something substantive about AP – albeit usually prefaced by caveats more emphatic than Ammerman's. What they say is frequently informed by the TC. For instance, in 1996 – alongside Williams' claim that 'analytic philosophy' no longer names anything philosophically distinctive – John Searle describes philosophy in the United States as so dominated by AP that dissenters feel the need to define themselves over against it (1). This dominance is not limited to America, he notes, but is a feature of academic philosophy in the English-speaking world at large, as well as in Scandinavia (1f). He describes the school as originating with Frege, Russell, Moore and Wittgenstein (and hence around the turn of the twentieth century), and as being perpetuated by the logical positivists of the Vienna Circle and the Oxford ordinary-language movement (2). He acknowledges the centrality of the linguistic thesis by saying that 'the simplest way to describe [AP] is to say that it is primarily concerned with the analysis of meaning' (2). Clearly, this characterization fits the TC perfectly.

As this last example shows, talk of AP in terms of the TC persists despite the increasing awareness of the puzzle/crisis. This is because, since at least the mid 1960s, 'analytic philosophy' has been used consistently to name something fitting the contours of the TC. Though both the use and the concept leave certain details unspecified and certain questions open, the basic meaning of 'analytic philosophy' is not up for grabs – contra Hacker, 'analytic philosophy' has a well-established use in connection with the TC. Thus, in 2001, Louis Pojman gave what he described as a 'simplistic but meaningful' characterization of AP as 'centered on language and logic, analyzing the meanings of words and sentences even as it analyzes arguments and builds comparatively modest epistemological and metaphysical theories' (1). Pojman was right. Despite its simplicity, his characterization is meaningful; and it is meaningful not only in the literal sense of conveying a thought, but also in the sense that it is consistent with and gives insight into the ordinary use of 'analytic philosophy'.

The Fall of the Traditional Conception

The *existence* of the TC enables historical research to begin by orienting it toward the correct subject. Moreover, the *content* of the TC offers hope that the puzzle about AP's nature might be solved, and its crisis averted, by looking to the school's past. Though there is currently no clear answer to the question 'what is AP?', the TC tells us that there was a time when it could have been answered with confidence. This was the era in which analytic philosophers accepted the linguistic thesis, and when, consequently, AP was understood to be linguistic philosophy. Given the analysts' apparent unanimity over the linguistic thesis prior to the 1960s, one might have supposed that historical work on AP in its first half-century would turn up common philosophical commitments of a more fundamental nature which, if visible in post-linguistic AP as well, might adequately define the nature of the whole.

Unfortunately, things have not turned out as hoped. Instead of finding a deeper ideational unanimity behind the linguistic thesis, historians have found that *that* unanimity was in fact illusory – Frege did not explicitly accept it, and both Moore and Russell explicitly rejected it. In fact, the most important discovery to come out of recent historical work is that *none* of AP's traditional defining doctrines or features has ever succeeded in defining or even describing it adequately – not at a single time, and certainly not over time – and thus that the TC is hopelessly flawed (see Hacker 1998: 4–14; Monk 1997; Hylton 1998; Beaney 2003). Moreover, even looking beyond those features prescribed by tradition, the historians of analytic philosophy have not been able to identify *any* set of features common to all and only canonical analysts. A close examination of some of these findings will be the task of a later chapter. Here, we may briefly note that recent scholarship is characterized by a newfound awareness of and appreciation for the differences among core, canonical analysts over such fundamentals as the procedure of philo-sophical analysis (what Michael Beaney [2002, 2003] calls the 'mode' of analysis), the nature of philosophical analysanda (the 'objects' of philo-sophical analysis), and the nature of philosophy itself. Without consensus in these areas, however, the TC unravels: if there was no shared method of linguistic analysis, then the idea that AP was unified by the linguistic thesis cannot be true; and without the linguistic thesis, we lose the traditional basis for its revolutionary character and its ahistorical and anti-metaphysical stances.

The Rise of Revisionism

One might expect that the fall of the TC would have given the historians of AP pause to consider whether and how proceeding with their investigations still makes sense. After all, in virtue of its orienting role, historical research is in some sense *based* on the TC; thus, in finding it to be false, historical inquiry might seem to have undermined itself. Far from taking pause, however, many historians have acted as if the fall of the TC is of little consequence for their work. Without a second thought, they have constructed revisionist pictures of AP which (though this was not anyone's explicit intention) serve to mask the fact that their object of study turned to dust just as they began to handle it.

Revisionism takes two forms, distinguished by the aspect of the TC each attempts to alter. Even if we take it as a characterization rather than a strict definition, the TC has the structure of a definition by genus and difference: AP is a member of the genus *philosophical school*, distinguished from other members by its unique intensional, extensional, temporal and geographical boundaries. In terms of this structure, we can say that one revisionist strategy is to alter the differentia of the TC. Usually this takes the form of assigning to AP intensional boundaries fundamentally different from those prescribed by the TC; but this inevitably forces changes in the other boundaries as well. The other revisionist strategy is to classify AP under a genus other than 'school' – such as 'tradition' or 'movement' – for which the lack of a rigorous ground of unity might seem to matter less. In the remainder of this chapter we will survey several examples of each form, and then note the consequences of revisionism for AP's metaphilosophical crisis. In the following chapter, I will argue that, in both forms, the move to revisionism is a mistake.

Differentia Revisionism

Some cases of revisionism involve altering the differentia of AP as prescribed by the TC. This usually involves a direct modification of some of the TC's intensional boundaries, but this inevitably results in an indirect modification of the other intensional boundaries and in the temporal, extensional and geographical boundaries as well. For instance, M.K. Munitz maintains that the essence of AP 'consists in the careful attention paid to the use of language as the medium of communication of thought, and to the various conditions and resources that language makes available for such communication' (1981: 9). This maintains some contact with the TC insofar as it is language-oriented, but it is far less specific in that it does not tie AP to any particular view about why or how philosophy should pay attention to language. Considered in itself, this appears to be a minor alteration to the intensional boundaries of the TC. However, taking a broader view, we see that it implies substantial alterations to every aspect of the TC. For instance, insofar as Munitz's characterization is applicable to all canonical analytic philosophers, it is also true of Aristotle in *Posterior Analytics, Categories, Rhetoric*, and more generally in his characteristic method of identifying as many senses as possible of a philosophically significant word, and of paying close attention to ordinary usage. It is also applicable to Plato in *Cratylus*, to Augustine in *De Magistro*, and so on. So, we now have AP originating in ancient Greece alongside philosophy *simpliciter*, and coexisting with it throughout Western history. Clearly, this demolishes the TC's temporal and geographical boundaries. It also overturns other intensional bound-aries: if AP is as perennial as philosophy itself, it is hard to see how it could count either as revolutionary or as outmoding all pre-twentieth-century thought. Consequently, this alteration requires that we part ways with AP's revolutionary character and anti-historical stance. Likewise, there is no clear basis here for an anti-metaphysical stance.

William Charlton's revisionist characterization of AP has the same consequences. According to Charlton (1991: 5), analytic philosophers are united in their views about what constitutes a satisfactory treatment of a topic, and about what topics are fit for philosophical treatment (and we should not miss the fact that these are issues central to any conception of 'good philosophy'). Concerning the former, it is noteworthy that Charlton does not discuss, nor does he so much as state, the supposed agreed-upon criteria for satisfactory philosophical treatment. The idea of consensus on this point is left as vague as the idea of AP itself. Concerning the second point, Charlton does have something to say. He suggests that analytic philosophers are united in their interest in the following four categories: (1) things basic to logic and mathematics, e.g., existence, truths and number; (2) things basic to physical science, e.g., time, change and causation; (3) good and evil, their varieties and the nature of the difference between them; and (4) 'mental processes, states and dispositions, especially the most general notions of belief, desire, skill, purpose and self-awareness or consciousness' (1991: 11). But then he goes on to say that 'history reveals a single philosophical tradition' (11) that consists in an ongoing discussion of these issues. By sacrificing the linguistic thesis, Charlton makes AP continuous with the whole history of philosophy, rather than a revolutionary philosophical movement that, beginning in early twentieth-century Britain, took the philosophical world by storm.

The same pattern emerges from revisionist characterizations from L.J. Cohen and Dagfinn Follesdal. Cohen contends that the unity of AP is to be found in the fact that the problems analytic philosophers are interested in 'are all, in one way or another, normative problems about reasons and reasoning' (1986: 10f). But interest in normative problems about reasons and reasoning is not unique to canonical analysts, thus Cohen admits that his definition makes AP 'a strand in the total history of western philosophy from Socrates onwards rather than just a modern movement' (49). Similarly, Follesdal (1997) characterizes AP in terms of its strong commitment to argument and justification, as opposed to the kind of philosophy done by, e.g., Heidegger and Derrida, which relies mainly on rhetoric rather than clear argument. But, as Follesdal himself notes, his definition makes Aristotle, Descartes, and perhaps even Thomas Aquinas count as analytic philosophers. As in the other cases we've seen, dropping the linguistic thesis in favor of a view, method or subject more likely to be common to all analysts requires that we also drop AP's twentieth-century, British origin, its revolutionary character, and its ahistorical and anti-metaphysical stances.

A particularly striking case of revisionism comes from Ray Monk. Using as his *definiens* a vague conception of analysis which is supposed to capture philosophical activity only (as opposed to the activity of the chemist or mathematician, say), Monk suggests that we carve up the philosophical world in such a way that Frege, Russell, Meinong and Husserl count as analytic philosophers while Wittgenstein does not (Monk 1996a). To count Meinong and Husserl among the analysts while excluding Wittgenstein is unquestionably contrary to tradition – in fact, it is hard to imagine a definition more at odds with the canon associated with the TC. And, since plenty of earlier philosophers would seem to have used *analysis* in Monk's vague sense, it also detaches AP from its turn-of-the-twentieth-century origin in Britain, its revolutionary character, and its ahistorical and anti-metaphysical stances.

Genus Revisionism

Because philosophy itself is associated with the activity of reasoning one's way to well-formulated views on various and sundry issues, it is natural to think of a 'philosophical school' or a 'school of philosophy' as something characterized primarily by a set of views, its 'defining doctrines'. In fact, 'school of philosophy' is sometimes used synonymously with 'school of thought'. As the examples above show (see pp. 30–42), the TC presents AP as a philosophical school in this sense, for they all emphasize the ideational or 'viewish' unity of AP in the linguistic thesis.

To escape the necessity of finding defining doctrines for AP, some historians have taken to calling it a 'movement' or 'tradition' rather than a 'school'. Like 'school', these terms are ordinarily used to denote collectivities – groupings of people. They differ from 'school' in that they connote change over time. For this reason, divergent views are not only permitted but expected to emerge *within* movements and traditions. For example, speaking of what he calls the German analytic tradition, Glock says: 'By a tradition, I do not mean a self-professed school like the Vienna Circle, or even one identified by adversaries, but a loose and diverse intellectual movement' (1999: 138). Similarly, upon noting that 'there are no necessary and sufficient conditions for being an analytic philosopher', James Baillie explains that:

> It is probably the best policy to regard analytic philosophy as a "form of life," in the Wittgensteinian sense. Thus, I will use the term "analytic philosophy" to mean philosophy in the *tradition* of such founders as Frege, Russell, and Wittgenstein, and which continues to constitute the dominant paradigm of philosophy as practiced in the English-speaking world. (1996: x, my emphasis)

In a similar spirit, Dale Jacquette says that 'the term *ANALYTIC PHILOSOPHY* refers to a family of related approaches to philosophical method' (2002: 11, orginal emphasis); Avrum Stroll claims that 'it is difficult to give a precise definition of "analytic philosophy" since it is not so much a specific doctrine as a loose concatenation of approaches to problems' (2000: 5); and Martinich and Sosa observe that AP

> probably defies definition, since it is not a set of doctrines and not restricted in its subject matter. It is more like a method ..., but in fact not one method but many that bear a family resemblance to each other. (2001b: 4)

Likewise, Soames says:

> The analytic *tradition* in philosophy has often been misunderstood by those outside the field, especially by traditional humanists and literary intellectuals. One persistent misconception has been to think of analytic

philosophy as a highly cohesive *school* or approach to philosophy, with a set of tightly knit *doctrines* that define it. ... If analytic philosophy is not a unified set of *doctrines* adhered to by a broad range of philosophers, what is it? The short answer is that it is a certain historical *tradition* in which the early work of G.E. Moore, Bertrand Russell, and Ludwig Wittgenstein set the agenda for later philosophers, whose work formed the starting point for the philosophers who followed them. The work done today in analytic philosophy grows out of the work done yesterday, which in turn can often be traced back to its roots in the analytic philosophers of the early part of the twentieth-century. Analytic philosophy is a trail of influence. (2003: I, xii f, my emphasis)

Revisionism and the Crisis in Analytic Philosophy

There are principled objections to both versions of revisionism, and I will make them in Chapter 3. Here we will focus on the consequences of revisionism for AP's metaphilosophical crisis, for these are objectionable enough in themselves. As we have seen, the history of AP movement has flourished largely because AP must justify itself in the face of its existential gap; but, far from being able to *justify* itself, it has not even been able to *define* itself by articulating its fundamental philosophical commitments. In this context, work on the history of AP emerged as no mere specialist's project, but as a form of service to the philosophical community at large. Though individual contributors may not see their work in this light, this is the only way to make sense of the emergence of the history of AP movement as a whole. Consequently, historical work on AP must be seen as existing principally to solve the puzzle and resolve the crisis.

Relative to this purpose, however, historical inquiry has backfired; for what it has *really* shown us by discrediting the TC is that neither the puzzle nor the metaphilosophical crisis it signifies are recent phenomena. It has shown us that, far from being a byproduct of the shift from AP's linguistic phase to its non-linguistic phase, the puzzle was extant *during* the linguistic phase, since the only answer AP had to questions about its fundamental philosophical commitments was a false one. From a purely theoretical perspective, the current situation and the pre-1960s situation are identical: the theory of AP – its metaphilosophy – was incomplete then, and it is incomplete now. Thus, we are confronted with the same situation in two different settings, or rather a single situation that has persisted unnoticed through several historical settings.

The most significant difference between present and past settings is sociological: formerly, few were asking metaphilosophical questions about AP from a position of dissatisfaction, so the lack of adequate answers was not so painfully obvious. Now, more philosophers are asking them, and it is more obvious. The fact that the principal difference between the two settings is sociological does not mean that the questions themselves are not genuinely philosophical. Nor does the fact that they *were* ignored for a time suggest that it was right to ignore them then, or that it is right to ignore them now. To the contrary, their status as genuine, philosophical questions suggests that they should have been asked long ago, and their long neglect simply reaffirms the importance of asking them now.

However, by failing to take this situation seriously in its historical setting, revisionism implicitly facilitates the *continued* disregard of AP's puzzle and attendant metaphilosophical crisis in the present. It does this by presenting the puzzle in all settings as either solved or dissolved. By giving purportedly adequate intensional characterizations of AP, differentia revisionism suggests that AP *can* articulate its fundamental commitments. Consequently, it can appear to have solved the puzzle and resolved the metaphilosophical crisis. Alternatively, genus revisionism purports to *dissolve* rather than *resolve* the puzzle and the crisis it signifies; for it implies that asking AP to articulate its fundamental philosophical commitments is misguided, a naïve failure to understand Nietzsche's maxim that 'only something which has no history can be defined'.[7]

Though these are presented as ways of addressing the puzzle mainly in its historical setting, they will apply to it in its present setting as well, since it is the same puzzle in both cases. The effect is aporetic. As we have seen, there is currently a significant amount of dissatisfaction directed toward AP on account of what it is perceived to have done to academic philosophy. The sense of dissatisfaction and the problems that have stimulated it are real. And yet, revisionism suggests that neither the problems nor the dissatisfaction can be pinned on AP, for either it is not the sort of thing that can bear corporate responsibility or, if it is, then it is simply not responsible in this case. On genus revisionism, it may be that certain figures in the analytic *tradition* contributed to these problems, but this is no reason to indict the tradition as a whole. To do so presumes that the problems emanate from fundamental, philosophical commitments common to the whole, but traditions have no such commitments. Alternatively, on differentia revisionism, AP does have fundamental, philosophical commitments, but they are not such as to have generated the problems in question. Like Leiter's current view, differentia revisionism can present AP as non-sectarian, pluralistic and perennial in the Western tradition. If AP is associated with these problems, that is only because it went through a bad patch in which a few individuals channeled those fundamental commitments into specific forms that turned out to be misguided. But, since this had nothing to do with the fundamental commitments themselves, dissatisfaction should not be directed at AP *itself.* In this way, both forms of revisionism leave the party of the dissatisfied boxing the air.

If revisionism is an error, however, all this will be a façade: the puzzle and the crisis will remain, but they will be obfuscated by the appearance of having been dismissed. Revisionism thus threatens to lull us into ignoring the puzzle and the crisis, just as has been done for most of AP's history. Moreover, supposing the standard view to be correct – namely, that the problems of academic philosophy in the analytic context are rooted in the analytic approach itself as presented in the TC – revisionism misleads us; for by convincing us that there is no systemic connection between AP and the problems, it leads us to see the latter as accidents of history, or at least to search for their sources elsewhere. Thus it gives us little reason to hope that their true source will be found and assiduously avoided in the future.

The growing acknowledgment of the puzzle/crisis and of the need for reform in academic philosophy are hopeful developments insofar as they suggest that a season of change is on the horizon in the analytic context. However, it remains to be seen whether this change will count as progress, regress, or – perhaps even worse than regress – an apparent change only, masking a deeper stagnation. In order to plot a clear course away from the problems of contemporary academic philosophy, we must have a clear view of the things that brought them to be. If there is a systemic connection between those problems and AP as traditionally understood, then we must investigate AP as traditionally understood – despite the fact that the TC is and was false. But, by revising the TC, revisionism diminishes the likelihood of ever discovering the true source of the problems; for, in doing so it detaches from the name 'analytic philosophy' those features of twentieth-century Anglo-American philosophy which, in virtue of their revolutionary character, caused it to become part of the philosophical lexicon. In this way it obscures the factors which brought AP as traditionally understood into existence, which governed its development, and which, arguably, offer the best clues as to what brought it to its current state of crisis.

In this case, AP's current situation would be like that of a patient suffering from a possibly fatal condition, but who has been misdiagnosed. Only by chance will the treatment prescribed cure the real ill. Possibly it will have no effect, and the disease will continue on its course. Possibly it will make the situation worse. Thus, assuming revisionism is an error, it constitutes a crisis within the crisis. We will now turn to investigate whether that assumption is sound.

Chapter 3

Against Revisionism

What is at Stake

What is at stake in the debate over revisionism is the proper application of those energies which, stimulated by dissatisfaction about certain features of contemporary academic philosophy, are seeking to reform and improve it. In order to be effective, the energies of reform must be directed at the source of our problems; but, if revisionism is legitimate, our sense that the source was intrinsic to AP is false, and we are sent back to the drawing board to develop new leads. If revisionism is illegitimate, however, and if we accept it despite this, then in sending us back to the drawing board it sends us onto a false trail leading away from the true source. Thus, as Bernard Williams saw, 'what is at issue' in properly demarcating analytic philosophy and distinguishing it from other philosophical alternatives 'is the identity of philosophy as a discipline' (1996: 26). With so much hanging in the balance, revisionism itself must be scrutinized before we accept it and allow it to redirect our energies.

The Fallacies of Revisionism

To anyone focused on foundational assumptions, one of the most obvious features of revisionism is the way it seems to undermine itself by dismissing the very conception that gave it its original orientation. In this section, I will explore this frequently overlooked feature of revisionism. We shall find that this dynamic plays out differently in each of the two species of revisionism; but that, either way, it confers upon revisionist inquiries the form of one or another familiar logical fallacy.

Common to both species of revisionism is the claim that there are no sharp boundaries between AP and Western philosophy *simpliciter*. For instance, in a 1997 essay, after noting the difficulty of finding unifying tenets among canonical analytic philosophers, Peter Hacker advocates using 'analytic philosophy' in what we earlier called the adjectival sense.

Used this way, it captures philosophers from every era, at least from Socrates onward. However, a year earlier, Hacker had noted that:

> If the term 'analytic philosophy' is to be useful as a classificatory term for the historian of philosophy, it must do more work than merely distinguish mainstream Western philosophy from the reflections of philosophical sages and prophets, such as Pascal or Nietzsche, and from the obscurities of speculative metaphysicians, such as Hegel, Bradley or Heidegger. (1996: 3)

Thus, in the 1997 essay, when he moves from defining AP to giving an exposition of its history, he limits his topic to what he calls 'twentieth-century analytic philosophy'; and this, he says, begins with Russell and Moore around the turn of the twentieth century. This arbitrarily imposed historical limit reflects not just the limit of Hacker's historical interest (which could be arbitrary), but also the limit of the term's objective usefulness as a historical category.

Because of this limitation, it is no surprise that historical works on AP tend to begin by using 'analytic philosophy' in its ordinary sense, to denote something identical in most respects to AP as traditionally conceived. Even if a work does not do this explicitly, it will do so implicitly by molding its content around the TC. Indeed, regardless of what they ultimately *say* about AP's intrinsic character, when determining the scope of the material covered, the majority of authors who write on its history and *all* the extant anthologies of central texts in the analytic tradition keep to the temporal, extensional and geographical boundaries prescribed by the TC.[1]

Even revisionist works make use of the TC in one of these two ways, explicitly or implicitly. The implicit form is characteristic of genus revisionism, cases of which frequently exhibit a striking incongruity between the author's choice of scope – which rarely extends much beyond the boundaries prescribed by the TC – and his or her dismissal of the TC. For example, we have seen Soames eschew a precise, intensional definition of AP, instead characterizing it as a 'trail of influence' beginning with Moore, Russell and Wittgenstein (2003: I, xii f). His two volumes follow this trail as it weaves its way among these three figures and on through the logical positivism of the Vienna Circle, Quine, Ryle, Strawson, Hare, Malcolm, Austin, Grice, Davidson and Kripke. As Soames tells the story, developments in twentieth-century philosophy of language constitute the thematic line that binds these figures and factions together. In both of these respects, his account is perfectly consistent with the TC – a fact naturally understood as a manifestation of its guiding presence, despite the fact that he explicitly rejects it. And, in fact, Soames *must* be thinking of AP as something more than a trail of influence, since otherwise it would be impossible to justify the principled selectivity he exhibits in picking the themes and figures most central to the story of AP. Trails of influence can easily be traced beyond AP's traditional boundaries. For instance, Frege and Peano influenced Russell in significant ways that helped him toward *Principia Mathematica*. In fact, Russell once said that his encounter with Peano at the 1900 International Congress of Philosophy was the most important event in his intellectual life (1944a: 12f). And yet, neither he nor Frege are included as key players in Soames' history – Frege is merely mentioned several times, and Peano not at all.

Because influence flows uninterrupted into an indefinite past, it cannot define a philosophical movement. This fact was noted by J.O. Urmson in what may be the earliest monograph on the history and nature of AP:

> One cannot understand Russell properly without some knowledge of Bradley, who again can only be fully understood in the light of his reaction to Mill and his followers, and so on through a regress to the beginnings of philosophical speculation. We must break in arbitrarily somewhere. (1956: 1)

Urmson is speaking here not about defining or delimiting AP, but about setting it against the explanatory backdrop of pre-analytic philosophy. He takes it for granted that the boundaries of AP are clear enough, and that the movement begins with Moore and Russell. Trails of influence, as he sees it, must be traced to some arbitrary point in pre-analytic history in order to *explain* how and why AP arose. But, precisely because the flow of influence can be interrupted only arbitrarily, influence cannot be used to *define* the movement. As he saw quite clearly, to *define* AP in terms of influence would be to dissolve what everyone already knew as a discrete entity into the uninterrupted flow of philosophical discourse.

Moreover, if we follow the trails of influence far enough, we will end up with a picture of AP that will not abide Soames' predilection to put the philosophy of language at the center of the analytic story. For instance, recent historical treatments have shown that early, canonical analysts were significantly influenced by the British Idealists (Griffin 1991; Hylton 1990), Leibniz, Kant, and several neo-Kantians (Coffa 1991; Glock 1999; Hanna 2001), Bolzano (Künne *et al.* 1997), Lotze (Gabriel 2002), Brentano and his school (Bell 1999), as well as more obscure figures such as Dimitri Michaltschew, one of the Greifswald objectivists (Milkov 2004).

To define AP in terms of influence would require adding these figures to the canon. It would also require a thematic revision, for to see AP in the broad scope of these connections makes the twentieth-century preoccupation with the philosophy of language tangent to a broader and more fundamental discussion about the metaphysics of human cognition.

But this is not how Soames – or anyone else – sees it. For him, only certain relations of influence are relevant to the story of AP: those that keep its origin around 1900, and its thematic focus on the philosophy of language. Either this is an arbitrary restriction of the 'influence criterion', or Soames' trail of influence is circumscribed by a different conception of AP according to which something other than influence unifies and bounds it. I submit that the latter is more likely the case, and that the best candidate for Soames' real criterion of relevance is the TC – for he focuses on just the figures and the issues *it* designates as being central to the rise and development of AP. In fact, Soames drops a hint that this is so. By neglecting Frege, Soames is aware that he is leaving 'an undeniable gap in the story' of AP (2003: II, 462). In defending his choice to leave this gap, Soames does not say that 'we must break in arbitrarily somewhere', as Urmson did in defending the need to limit the explanatory background of AP. Instead, he says that most of Frege's work, which was done in the last quarter of the nineteenth century, 'falls outside our official period' (461). Given the scope of his history, it is clear that Soames' official period begins around the turn of the twentieth century, with the work of G.E. Moore – exactly as the traditional view has it; and it is difficult to see what besides the TC could make this period 'official'.

The same implicit use of the TC is visible in a 1998 essay by Peter Hacker in which he recants his 1997 position on using 'analytic philosophy' adjectivally. There, after dismissing traditional ways of characterizing AP and insisting that 'there are no defining features that characterize the Analytic movement in all its phases,' he suggests that it is 'most illuminating and least misleading to employ the term "analytic philosophy" as the name of [the] intermingling strain of ideas distinctive of our century [that is, the twentieth century]' (1998: 24). With this in mind, Hacker makes the move to genus revisionism by suggesting that AP is best regarded as a dynamic historical movement, divisible into various phases, each of which partly overlaps with the one before it. Using the analogy of a tapestry to illustrate his view, he says:

Most (but not all) of the threads out of which the tapestry of analytic philosophy was woven can be traced back to the more or less remote past. What is most distinctive about the tapestry are the ways in which the various threads are interwoven and the character of the designs. These altered over time, some threads being either abandoned and replaced by new ones or differently used, and others becoming more prominent in the weave than hitherto, some patterns dominating one period, but sinking into the background or disappearing altogether in later periods. (1998: 14f)

Taken one way, this characterization fails to distinguish AP from philosophy at large. After all, the whole history of philosophy involves the dynamic interaction of ideas across generations of philosophers, and thus can be regarded as a dynamic historical movement. Likewise, the figure of the tapestry fits the whole history of philosophy, or any other period out of it, as well as it does the era of AP. How, then, are we to pick out just that section of the tapestry that corresponds to AP? Here, one might turn to Hacker's mention of 'the ways in which the various threads are interwoven and the character of the designs', taking these figures to refer to intrinsic features of AP that serve to unify its various phases and to distinguish the unified whole from other parts of the tapestry of philosophy-as-a-whole. But it is difficult to see what these figures could symbolize besides various theoretical positions adopted by analytic philosophers, the likes of which have served as part of the *definiens* of many a failed attempt at defining AP in terms of its traditional features. That there are any successful defining features for AP, Hacker flatly denies; so this cannot be how he intends his characterization to be taken.

Instead, it seems that when Hacker speaks of AP as a dynamic historical movement, he means to characterize it not merely as a dynamic movement that took place (as all movements do) in or across history but as a dynamic movement that took place over a *specific* period in history (the twentieth century), and in a small number of specific regions (principally Britain and America). Thus, when Hacker claims that 'the unity of Analytic philosophy in the 20th century is historical' (1998: 24) he means that all phases of twentieth-century AP have in common only that they occurred within the twentieth century. We are to pick out AP's section from the tapestry of the whole history of philosophy by superimposing a timeline and a map of the world on it and focusing only on that portion which falls within the space allotted to the twentieth century, and then only in Britain and America, and possibly Vienna. We are then to ask ourselves what are the most distinctive features that are common to these portions of the tapestry, as compared to any others; and then, certainly, things like the use of formal logic, the emphasis on language or linguistic analysis as having a primary place in philosophy, and so forth, will stand out. They will stand out as distinctive, but they are not definitive – they will not of themselves unify the movement.

Like Soames, the restrictions Hacker places on 'analytic philosophy' are not only consistent with, but explicable and justifiable only in light of the TC and the ordinary use of 'analytic philosophy' associated with it. Apart from these, there is no principled reason to impose what would otherwise be arbitrary temporal and geographical limits on a set of ideas, methods, and other features whose origins often are located far prior to the twentieth century. Hacker seems to acknowledge this implicitly when he observes that it is not only 'most illuminating' but also 'least misleading' to make the referent of 'analytic philosophy' a twentieth-century phenomenon. Here he rejects the adjectival use of 'analytic philosophy' not only because this would render it useless as a historical category by casting the historical net too broadly, but also because it would be *misleading*. Misleading to whom, and why? The answer, of course, is that it would be misleading to all who are familiar with the ordinary use of 'analytic philosophy', and hence to much of the academic world. And it would be misleading to them precisely because there *is* an ordinary use of 'analytic philosophy', a well-established use tied to the TC.

In this way, then, the genus revsionist makes use of the TC implicitly while denying it explicitly. This is a pattern of self-contradiction without which the genus revisionist would not be able to specify a non-arbitrary subject matter. The pattern is even easier to see in differentia revisionism, where it might just as well be described as equivocation rather than self-contradiction. Since differentia revisionists do not eschew making substantive claims about the intrinsic character of AP, they frequently identify their subject by using the term 'analytic philosophy' in its ordinary sense. As they attempt to clarify the concept of AP, however, they gradually coax themselves away from the original notion, ultimately breaking with it altogether and replacing it with something that does not at all fit within the parameters of the original, all the while using the same term to refer to what is given in the two incompatible notions. Clearly, this pattern is a model of equivocation.

Michael Corrado provides a clear example of this dynamic. At the beginning of his book on AP, Corrado names Russell as one of the *founders* of what he calls 'this type [that is, the analytic type] of philosophy' (1975: 3). Thus, clearly, Corrado conceives of AP as a definite kind of philosophy that originated around the early twentieth century. This suggests that he is using 'analytic philosophy' in its ordinary, nominative sense, and thus that he intends to investigate AP as traditionally conceived. However, without rejecting or revising the claim that Russell was a founder of AP, at the end of his book Corrado concludes that 'analytic philosophy is, at its best, just good philosophy, and not in any deep way distinguishable from any other sort of philosophy' (128f). These two claims appear to be inconsistent. If Russell is a founder of AP, then AP could not have existed before Russell; but surely philosophy, even good philosophy, existed before Russell. On the other hand, if AP is not distinguishable in any deep way from any other sort of philosophy, what exactly did Russell found? Founding something involves bringing into being something that has not been before; thus, in order to speak of something as being founded by a particular person at a particular time, it seems that what is founded must be distinguishable from other things that came before it. By speaking of Russell as founding the analytic type of philosophy and then denying that AP is distinguishable from any other kind of philosophy, Corrado seems to contradict himself; for this is tantamount to saying that AP is and is not a distinctive kind of philosophy founded by Russell in the early twentieth century. Thus, the same self-contradictory dynamic that we saw in genus revisionism is even more apparent in differentia revisionism. It is so apparent, in fact, that it is perhaps better described as the more subtle error of equivocation.

Of course, inquiry presupposes some flexibility to expand and even to revise our orienting concepts; however, there must be limits to this revisability. This issue is sometimes discussed by analysts under the heading of 'interpretive charity'. To exercise charity in interpretation is to choose to regard all occurrences of a term as univocal at some level despite minor differences in how the term's meaning or referent is conceptualized. Borrowing an example from Hilary Putnam, consider the word 'electron': in 1900 it was believed that electrons move in trajectories around the nucleus, but by 1934 it was believed that electrons have no trajectory. Here we have a choice to regard scientists in 1900 and scientists in 1934 (or even the same scientist, for example, Bohr, in 1900 and in 1934) as talking about the same thing or different things when they used 'electron'. Of course, it is generally accepted without question that the difference between 'electron' in 1900 and 'electron' in 1934 is not a difference in reference but a difference in beliefs about or conceptions of the same referent. On the other hand, Putnam has argued that there are cases where interpretive charity is not warranted. He considers, for example, the possibility that what some scientists once called 'phlogiston' is what contemporary scientists call 'valence electrons', and hence that phlogiston really does exist. However, Putnam points out, 'we are not prepared to say, "Phlogiston theorists were talking about valence electrons, but they had some of the properties wrong"' (1998: 14). To do so, he says, would require *excessive charity*.

It is a difficult thing to specify the conditions under which charity is warranted and those under which it is not. Nonetheless, we seem to be able to recognize warrant or lack thereof in particular cases. Putnam includes this ability among those seemingly intuitional powers that constitute Fodor's 'general intelligence'. Leaving this difficulty aside, and relying on 'general intelligence', I submit that accepting differentia revisionism requires something like the excessive charity required to treat references to phlogiston as references to valence electrons. Though specifying exact criteria for the proper exercise of charity is out of the question, the following analogy may help to show that charity is not warranted in cases of differentia revisionism.

It used to be believed that witches caused various sorts of mischief, including disease. When plague struck, one might have gone on a witch hunt in an attempt to extinguish the plague at its source. Witches, of course, don't exist (or if they do, they are not what they are popularly thought to be). Thus, arguably, no one has ever had the opportunity to acquire the kind of knowledge requisite to so much as identify a witch. How, then, would a witch hunter know when he or she had found a witch? How would one judge whether the hunt had been a success or a failure? The witch hunt would immediately run aground on the shoal of Meno's paradox but for the clear fact that witch hunters did have *some* concept of a witch. The concept was a loose and popular one – it was based not on careful study of witches but mainly upon imagination and tradition. As such, the concept is not epistemically respectable, but it is enough to get a witch hunt going.

Of course, it was eventually discovered that germs were the real culprits. But when germs were discovered, no one was tempted to claim that witches had been discovered, and that they were just a lot smaller than anyone had previously realized. Instead, the belief that witches caused disease was abandoned, and the belief that germs caused disease replaced it. Presumably this has something to do with the fact that germs are just too different from what the loose and popular concept of a witch required a witch to be. If it had turned out that there were people causing disease through some mystical means, but that they did not ride broomsticks, the traditional witch concept could have been revised and applied to them. But revising it to fit germs is too much. There is not enough of the original concept left over to justify characterizing the new concept as a revised version of the old. It is a new concept altogether.

Curiously, though, differentia revisionism seems to follow a different rule. Research into AP begins, much like a witch hunt, with the TC: a loose, pre-critical conception of AP, based not on careful study but on popular opinion and tradition. The TC, as we have seen, is quite general, leaving some of the details to be filled in through historical inquiry; but it is enough to get research into AP going. And, having begun, what the historians of AP have found is that there is no set of features shared by all and only those philosophers who count as analysts on the TC. This is tantamount to finding that there are no grounds for holding that these philosophers are members of the same school, and hence to finding that there is nothing to which the TC corresponds.

The historian is, at this point, much like the witch hunter who finds that there is nothing to which his concept of a witch corresponds, and that the real cause of disease is something altogether different. It is at this point that the witch hunter revises not his *concept* of witches but his *belief* in witches – he rejects the existence of witches and accepts the existence of germs. By contrast, differentia revisionists retain their belief in the existence of a substantive entity called 'analytic philosophy' and present themselves as merely revising the concept of it. However, as with witch and germ concepts, this involves too great a change to count as a mere revision. What we have here is an unheralded replacement of one concept with another. Indeed, differentia revisionism has the feel of someone going on a witch hunt that culminates in the discovery of germs, and then claiming that the witch hunt was successful. Not only is it reasonable to feel perplexed and dissatisfied in the face of such an outcome, it would be remarkable if we did not. When the villagers send out the hunting party, they believe that success involves a witch being brought back to the village and burnt at the stake. If the hunting party returns with only a vial of liquid and a syringe, moves about the village injecting all the inhabitants, and then claims to have successfully accomplished its task, it would be very strange indeed if the villagers failed to realize that something extraordinary was afoot.

Metaphilosophy, the Sociology of Philosophy, and Genus Revisionism

Its fallacious form is not the only questionable aspect of genus revisionism. It also involves the suspect notion that classifying AP as a movement or tradition rather than as a school renders its lack of defining doctrines unimportant. In 1998, Hans Sluga made the following observation about the emerging history of AP genre:

> … as analytic philosophers have begun to set out to retrieve their own history, they have come across questions for which their training has

not well prepared them. They write of 'authors' or 'philosophers' and their 'development'; they consider 'interpretations' of both individual 'texts' and the philosophers' 'work' as a whole; they trace 'influences' and distinguish philosophical 'schools', 'movements', and 'traditions'. Yet they have so far been inattentive to the puzzles and obscurities surrounding these terms. All these notions, in fact, require philosophical attention. Confronted with ... [Continental philosophers'] detailed examinations of the notions of authorship, work, influence, school, etc., one is forced to conclude that the historians of analytic philosophy are as yet at a naïve, prereflective state of historical thinking. (104)

Today, nearly ten years later, the situation is not much better. By and large, the historians of AP continue to use concepts like 'school', 'movement' and 'tradition' without subjecting them to rigorous analysis. In genus revisionism, the vague, connotative differences and similarities among these terms are exploited so as to evade the significance of the TC's demise.

What are these similarities and differences? To begin with a similarity, it is clear that all three can be and usually are used to pick out groups of human beings. In general, a group is a plurality of things, in themselves construed as singles, which are held together and construed as constituting a sort of 'corporate single' – the result of (as we say) 'grouping things together'. Thus, a group is something with an 'inside' and an 'outside', something to which entities may belong or from which they may be excluded. And it is natural to suppose that there must be something that accounts for the difference between those things that are 'in' and those that are 'out', something that makes it the case that those things that belong, belong, and that those that don't, don't. That is, it is natural to suppose that there will be some principle(s) of inclusion and exclusion that ground both the unity of the group's members and their difference, *qua* group members, from non-members – even if it's something as trivial as having been noticed and arbitrarily chosen to be held together by the one doing the grouping.

This should not be taken to imply that the principle(s) or criteria must be clearly defined or even clearly definable – the type and number of criteria, their level of determinacy, fluidity, permanence, and so on, will vary relative to the kind of group one is dealing with. It is here that the *differences* among 'school', 'movement' and 'tradition' come into play, for they frequently connote differing degrees of 'tightness' in the unity of a group, and this would seem to be a function of the kinds of membership criteria each involves. We have already seen both Soames and Glock distinguish among these terms in precisely this fashion: both associate 'school' with a tight form of cohesion, sharp boundaries, and membership criteria clear and distinct enough to render the group susceptible to straightforward characterization or even definition, while 'movement' and 'tradition' are associated with loose cohesion, vague boundaries and membership criteria, and a nebulousness that defies definition.

There are, of course, exceptions to these connotative rules. Artistic groups are sometimes called schools; for instance, we speak of the impressionist *school* of painting. In the case of impressionism, and of artistic schools generally, necessary and sufficient conditions are incredibly difficult to specify, and the best most of us can do is to explain the group-unity of impressionism in terms of 'family resemblance' with respect to the style of certain paintings. However, as applied to philosophy, the association between 'school', definiteness and definability is appropriate. Indeed, as applied to philosophy, the rule seems to be violated in the opposite direction: whereas an artistic school can be characterized by the looseness and vagueness usually associated with 'movement' or 'tradition', a philosophical movement or tradition cannot, but must be characterized by the tightness and definiteness normally associated with 'school'.

The basis for this resides in the nature of philosophy itself. Unlike art, philosophy essentially involves the production of theories or views. As the great nineteenth-century historian of philosophy Eduard Zeller described it, philosophy is 'a purely theoretic activity; that is, an activity which is solely concerned with the ascertainment of reality' (1881: 8). He also described it as a form of 'science': 'I see in it [philosophy] not merely thought, but thought that is methodical, and directed in a conscious manner to the cognition of things in their interdependence' (8). Few contemporary analysts would quibble with the claim that philosophy is a theoretical discipline, that its business is, minimally, the production and critical assessment of theories by means of reasoning. Theories, minimally, are sets of views, or claims, or propositions, or ideas (all of which are synonymous in this context) about the way things are, or what is the case, in some region or other – or possibly the whole – of reality. And, again minimally, in order for philosophers to deal with such views cooperatively, they must be verbally articulated in a relatively straightforward way, in the form of sufficiently clear, declarative sentences. I trust it will be recognized that this minimal conception of what philosophy is and what it involves has been widely held, at least implicitly, throughout the history of the discipline.

This minimal metaphilosophical view has implications for how the emergent social world of philosophers (academic or otherwise) *ought* to take shape. On this view, what is most fundamental to philosophy is reasoning, on the one hand, and the objects of reasoning – ideas, views, and so forth – on the other. The constant in this pair is reason, and the variables are the particular ideas or views to which reason is applied. The social world of philosophy itself is distinguished from the non-philosophical world beyond it simply by its devotion to reason. However, insofar as there are philosophically relevant divisions to be made *within* the social world of philosophy, they will be made along ideational lines. This creates a normative constraint on the initial formation and the retrospective demarcation of groups that purport to be *philosophical* in nature: namely, a philosophical group must rely for its cohesion, and hence also its existence, on a kind of unity that is constituted by agreement in theoretical matters.

It would be wrong to think that this view of philosophy and its social-historical landscape is tied to some particular philosophical outlook like Platonism or Idealism. While it might seem especially amenable to views that accept the reality of ideas-in-themselves, it is in fact compatible with many metaphysical, and even anti-metaphysical, outlooks. For instance, Moritz Schlick, founder of the Vienna Circle and co-founder of logical positivism, held such a view despite his low opinion of traditional metaphysics: 'Every philosophical movement is defined by the principles it regards as fundamental, and to which it constantly refers in its arguments' (1932: 259). The centrality of the theoretical or ideational is grounded in the nature of philosophy as such, quite apart from the metaphysical views one comes to through philosophizing.

It would also be wrong to think that I am making a claim about the propriety of describing a group as 'philosophical'. 'Philosophical' is a homonym in the Aristotelian sense, and thus can be used in many ways with different but systematically related meanings. A classic example of Aristotelian homonymy is the word 'healthy'. A human body, a diet, and a complexion can be described as 'healthy', but 'healthy' will mean something different in each case: the properties of a healthy diet (having a certain combination of nutrients, say) are not those of a healthy complexion (having a certain color and texture, say), and neither of these are identical to the properties of a healthy body (having all bodily systems functioning properly, say). And yet, these sets of properties are not unrelated: the diet is called 'healthy' because it helps to cause or maintain a state of health in the body, and the complexion is called 'healthy' because it is an effect, and hence a sign, of health in the body.

In this way, the different meanings are united by their mutual connection to a 'focal meaning' – health in the body.

Similarly, 'philosophical' can be used in a variety of ways, but all will ultimately have some connection to a focal meaning having to do with the activity of reasoning one's way to views. The diversity of its uses is such that there are cases in which it is appropriate to describe a group as 'philosophical' even though it is not characterized by theoretical agreement. For instance, a philosophy conference might be called a 'philosophical gathering', and, since its attendees constitute a group, they might be described as a 'philosophical' group despite the fact that, as conference attendees, there is no presumption of theoretical agreement among them. However, 'philosophical' in this context performs a different function than it does when combined with 'school' or 'movement' or 'tradition'. The conference and its attendees are called 'philosophical' to distinguish them from non-philosophical counterparts. To do so tells us that this is a conference having to do with the activity of reasoning one's way to views and/or with the products of that activity, and that its attendees are people who do this kind of thing or who are interested in it. Other conferences and their attendees may have nothing to do with this.

But when we call some group a philosophical school or movement or tradition, we do not mean to pick it out merely as a group devoted to the activity of reasoning one's way to views, over against groups that aren't. As Glock has observed:

> Ever since Socrates, the attempt to tackle fundamental questions by way of reasoned argument has been regarded as one of the distinguishing features of philosophy as such, e.g., vis-à-vis religion or political rhetoric, not as the hallmark of a particular philosophical movement. (1999: 138)

We use these terms not to make distinctions between the philosophical and the non-philosophical as such, but to make distinctions *within* the philosophical realm. Distinctions properly *within* that realm must be made in terms of the phenomena characteristic of it; thus, since the philosophical realm is focally characterized by the activity of reasoning one's way to views, internal distinctions can be made only along lines of method (the way the activity is employed) and view (its products). Moreover, to the extent that the activity of reasoning is not an end in itself, to the extent that finished views are its consummation, the way one employs the activity must ultimately be grounded in reasoned views about how to do so – a metho*logy*. Consequently, philosophically relevant distinctions within the realm of the philosophical must ultimately be drawn along ideational lines.

The claim that ideational factors are essential to the unity and identity of philosophical groups whether we call them schools, movements or traditions is strengthened by noting that, though all three kinds of philosophical groups *may* also be social groups (in the social-scientific sense),[2] neither schools nor traditions need be. It is not uncommon for philosophers to hold together as members of a philosophical school or tradition figures who did not have or who *could* not have had, any live contact with one another. For instance, we speak of 'the Aristotelian tradition' or the 'Aristotelian school' as including both Aristotle and Thomas Aquinas. Likewise, we may include both Plato and the Cambridge Platonists of the seventeenth century as members of the Platonist tradition or the Platonist school. In each case, the members of these philosophical groups could not have had any meaningful live interaction with each other, and thus cannot be considered social groups in the paradigmatic, social-scientific sense. Of course, we do presume a trail of influence via a chain of historical causation involving textual media as well as occasional 'live contact' among some of its members. However, this is insufficient to qualify a group as a *social* group in the eyes of most social scientists. The situation with 'school' is even more radical, for we allow ourselves to hold figures together as members of the same 'school of thought' even when both live contact *and* historical causation are absent, simply in virtue of their accepting the same views. Of our three terms, 'movement' alone seems to require the kind of live contact that most social scientists require of social groups; and yet, even a movement must have an ideational identity in order to count as philosophical in the relevant sense.

If correct, the foregoing argument from the nature of philosophy renders genus revisionism unacceptable, for the connotative differences among 'school', 'movement' and 'tradition' will be inapplicable when these terms are used to make philosophically relevant distinctions between groups within the philosophical realm. All alike should be characterizable in ideational terms. Consequently, it should be possible in principle to specify the boundaries of a philosophical group with much greater precision than is possible for an artistic group. Ideally, one would only need to look at the views that provided the original impetus for the formation of the group as they were articulated by the founders and early adherents. As soon as there is significant deviation from these views-as-originally-articulated, one would be confronted with *different* groups that may be considered as more or less closely related to the 'mainline' group depending on the degree and/or type of theoretical similarity. Schlick makes a similar observation:

... in the course of historical development, the principles [of a philosophical movement; i.e., its defining doctrines] are not apt to remain
unaltered, whether it be that they acquire new formulations, and come
to be extended or restricted, or that even their meaning gradually
undergoes noticeable modifications. At some point the question then
arises, as to whether we should still speak at all of the development of a
single movement, and retain its old name, or whether a new movement
has not in fact arisen. (1932: 259)

Of course, drawing boundaries around philosophical groups along
ideational lines may never be so simple in practice as it seems in principle.
Philosophical groups are frequently also social groups. As such they
are subject to all sorts of forces and features – such as the intrigues of
personal relationships, institutional and political influences, and so on
– that threaten to overrun the very features that pick them out as philosophical. All of these aspects of the philosophical group *qua* social group
coexist and overlap with the ideational features that constitute it a philosophical group. Though distinct, they are not separate from one another
in the lives of the group members, where all these factors exercise a
reciprocal influence in making those lives what they are. It is naïve to
think that the ideas one embraces are not affected by one's institutional,
political, and broader social settings. At the same time, it is implausible to
suppose that a person's views are merely a function of those settings; for
it seems perfectly clear that, over time, ideas can change social realities.[3]
The interplay of these factors in the lives of individual human beings
affects the character of the groups that come into being, for groups and
their features seem to supervene on individuals and their features.

All of this requires careful analysis; but this is not our task here. I wish
only to avoid the impression that, given my emphasis on the ideational,
I am somehow discounting the non-ideational, and perhaps trying to
reduce the history of philosophy to the history of ideas. To the contrary,
I concede the incontestable point that, because all of these factors inter-
mingle in the concrete lives of human beings, both on the individual
and the corporate (group) level, the history of philosophy can never
adequately be done without an eye to socio-historical issues that go
beyond the analysis of the philosophical views in isolation. In fact, this is
especially important in the case of AP. In his interesting history of the rise
of natural history in Britain, David Allen writes:

There comes a point in the history of every pursuit at which its
following becomes sufficient to entitle it to be termed a social activity.

At this stage it begins to acquire some substance. It takes on a life over and above that of its individual adherents and through the pattern of its own development starts to influence, sometimes even govern, the way in which they think and act. (1976: 3)

We are interested in AP not merely as the isolated pursuit of a few philosophers, but as a 'social activity' in Allen's sense – not merely as a school of thought, but as a school with a certain social status. As we have seen, much of the current interest in AP has been stimulated by its social dominance in the academy. Without that, there would have been no call for dissatisfaction with AP to take the forms of resistance and protest that it occasionally has (as in the pluralist revolt of 1978, for instance) – if it had not been socially dominant, it simply could have been ignored and bypassed. However, since it was and is dominant, dissatisfaction had to take the form of a struggle leading to public discussion and eventually to the scholarly work of pursuing metaphilosophical and historical questions *about* AP. Thus, it is not merely the ideational aspects of AP that we are interested in, but its social and historical features as well – and ultimately the question whether its ideational features *warrant* its social and historical features. Thus, while the ideational aspects of philosophical groups are their most fundamental features, this does not imply that other aspects of such groups can always be ignored without loss.

Even so, philosophers, *qua* philosophers, are neither historians nor social scientists, and while they may often study the same objects as these others, they hope to achieve a different kind of understanding of them, namely, *philosophical* understanding. This requires rational insight into the philosophical unity of the group, a grasp of the philosophical view(s) that ground its unity. Thus, I submit, an adequate *philosophical* understanding of the social landscape of philosophy, whether current or historical, must include a grasp of how philosophical views factor into the mix. Moreover, from the genuinely philosophical perspective, those views will be the most salient ingredients in the mix, and will be granted explanatory primacy wherever possible. Under no circumstances may they be dispensed with, as genus revisionism would have us do.

Of course, the best historians of philosophy understand this. For example, even after taking pains to ward off the supposition that 'Continental rationalism' denotes a school of thought in which every representative held all and only the same views, the respected historian of philosophy John Cottingham goes on to say that 'it is nonetheless true that they [Descartes, Spinoza and Leibniz] shared a belief that it was possible, by the use of reason, to gain a superior kind of knowledge to that derived from the senses' (1988: 4). In the end, after all misgivings have been expressed and all qualifications made, philosophy is about ideas, and philosophical groups are unified by their ideational features.

If this view is controversial, it has become significantly so only in the last half-century. While objections from earlier periods exist (I have already cited Nietzsche's maxim, for instance), it has met with significant resistance only in our own day. Ironically, much of the resistance comes from philosophers who, swimming against the analytic tide, have acquired some historical sophistication. In the field of history, rejecting the requirement that groups be defined in terms of necessary and sufficient conditions facilitates the construction of richer and more accurate historical portraits than would have been possible otherwise; and I do not wish to question the possibility that this approach might be applied profitably to the history of philosophy as well. But it will be directly profitable only for historical purposes, not for philosophical purposes; for carving up history in this way misses the uniquely philosophical interest in the history of philosophy. To satisfy *that* interest, we must see ideational factors as the rallying points of philosophical groups; and to the extent that a purportedly philosophical group cannot be characterized in ideational terms, it must be judged at least to have fallen short of a central philosophical ideal, and possibly to have fallen short of a genuinely philosophical status.

The Ineliminability of the Traditional Conception

At this point, I hope to have shown that genus revisionism is not an acceptable option. Still, one might think that differentia revisionism could be rendered acceptable if it could be shown that the TC was a late development, preceded by a significantly different *original* conception. This would give differentia revisionism an alternative conception to use as its initial 'given' for orienting its research; it would also put the facts of history on its side. The same would be true if it could be shown that, even if not a latecomer, the TC was the spurious construction of those who did not really understand AP, and that the analysts themselves understood their school in quite different terms from the beginning.

A number of authors in the analytic tradition have claimed that something like this latter scenario is true. In 1949, Arthur Pap claimed that 'the unanimous practice of the analytic method as a powerful instrument of criticism tends to blur these differences [i.e., the differences between the factions within AP] for those who look on from the other side of the fence' (1949: ix). Similarly, in 1958, G.J. Warnock observed that:

there was in philosophical circles, say 20 years ago, a large measure of uniformity in practice, overlying, and to a great extent concealing from view, considerable diversity in aims and doctrines. It is not surprising that the situation was often then, and has often been since, misunderstood. It has been particularly tempting, I believe, for *commentators outside the professional ring* to identify, first, what in fact was common to all parties – pre-occupation with analysis of language; next, to take note of the novel idea that this was the sole proper business of philosophy – an idea sponsored only by Logical Positivism; and finally, confusing this singularity of doctrine with the general uniformity of practice, to decide that all philosophers of the day were Logical Positivists. This was in fact not true at any time. (60, my emphasis)

More recently, as we have already seen, Scott Soames has suggested that it is those outside AP, mainly 'traditional humanists' and 'literary intellectuals', who have wrongly understood AP to be 'a highly cohesive school or approach to philosophy, with a set of tightly knit doctrines that define it' (2003: I, xii f). But, while it probably is the case that those outside AP have frequently overestimated or misunderstood the grounds of its unity, they cannot be blamed for concocting the notion that it was possessed of ideational unity along the lines prescribed by the TC. Far from being a latecomer or the spurious construct of non-analysts, the TC as we have it today is largely an outgrowth from the analysts' own original self-conception.

Just as the content of the TC can be discerned in the ordinary use of 'analytic philosophy', so can the content of the *original conception* be discerned in the *original use* of 'analytic philosophy'. When we speak of the original use of 'analytic philosophy', we are, of course, speaking of its use as a name rather than a description. If the TC is to be trusted, AP originated in the early twentieth century; thus the nominative use of 'analytic philosophy' should be a twentieth-century innovation. And indeed it is. Though 'analytic philosophy' was frequently used in the adjectival sense in the nineteenth century, its use as a name was unknown prior to the twentieth century. In fact, a number of scholars have observed that it seems to have become firmly ensconced in the working vocabulary of philosophers rather late in the school's history, only around the middle of the twentieth century. Glock has it catching on in the 1950s (1999: 138). Consistent with this (and with Warnock's observation about outsiders conflating AP with logical positivism), G.H. von Wright recollects:

It has struck me that the *name* 'analytic philosophy', as far as I know, became current relatively late in the history of the movement. It only gradually supplanted the label 'logical positivism' which lingered on long after it had become obsolete. To the change in terminology contributed, I should think, significantly the works of Arthur Pap [and so post-1949].... The early Cambridge analysts and the members of the Vienna Circle insisted on their method being (logical and conceptual) analysis. But they did not use the term 'analytical philosophy' for their new type of thinking. The (new) name can be said to reflect a beginning syncretism within the movement. (1993: 41–42 n)

Similarly, we have already seen D.S. Clarke claim that 'the term "analytic philosophy" seems to have been introduced in the late 1940s as a label standing for the radically new approach to philosophy then dominating discussion in Great Britain and the United States' (1997: 1).

These observations are useful so long as we are careful to understand the late 1940s or early 1950s as the period in which the term *came into widespread currency*; it was *introduced*, so far as published records can tell us, well before that. The earliest hint of its introduction comes in John Wisdom's 1931 book, *Interpretation and Analysis*. Wisdom himself is a canonical analyst in the ordinary-language camp, and his book is largely an attempt to clarify the method of his school. Wisdom does not use the term 'analytic philosophy', but he does speak of 'the analytic philosophers' (whom he also calls 'the logico-analytic philosophers') as a definite group of philosophers united in, and distinguished from others by, their use of a novel philosophical method – linguistic analysis:

> The logico-analytic philosophers are constantly asking questions such as "What does 'This is a chair' mean?" Or "Is there a sense of the word 'good' such that 'x is good' in that sense means 'I like x'?" And in discussing such questions, they use premises about the usage of language. (13)

Puzzlingly, though, Wisdom goes on to claim that:

> the work of the analytic philosopher is not a work on language. All his results could be stated in many other systems of symbols. He uses language as a description of what he analyses – "the thing called 'brother of' has such and such constituents" – he says. ... any other description would do as well ... [however] It happens that a description in terms of words is usually most convenient. (15f)

According to Wisdom, the linguistic idiom of AP is just a convenience, revealing nothing important about the method itself. However, he does not provide an alternative account of philosophical analysanda that shows them to be non-linguistic entities. Instead, he attempts to illustrate the difference between language and philosophical analysanda by giving examples:

> Take the two propositions: (1) The words "*x* is the brother of *y*" mean what the words "*x* and *y* have the same parents and *x* is male" mean; (2) The meaning of "*x* is the brother of *y*" can be analysed into what is meant by "*x* and *y* have the same parents and *x* is male". The first proposition is an interpretation. The second is an analysis. (16)

But this hardly clarifies the matter, since even proposition (2) has the appearance of being about some linguistic fact. Indeed, one gathers that philosophical analysanda are, for Wisdom, *meanings*. But, though he explicitly uses 'meaning' and its paronyms ('means', 'meant', etc.) in speaking of philosophical analysanda (never in a direct, classificatory statement, unfortunately), he never explains what he takes meanings to be or how he understands them to function. Without such an account, it is all too easy to take 'meaning' as an essentially linguistic phenomenon. Indeed, it is most natural to do so. Thus, despite his insistence to the contrary, Wisdom's characterization makes the analytic method seem essentially linguistic both in its idiom and its object – just as the TC has it.

Other elements of his account also fit the TC. For instance, Wisdom associates the method with G.E. Moore, to whom he readily points as a paradigm. He also devotes significant space to the Russellian notion of an incomplete symbol – a foundational notion in the development of the ideal-language version of AP. Finally, he notes the basis for AP's revolutionary character and its anti-metaphysical and ahistorical stances, albeit without identifying it as such:

> Much philosophy is concerned, not with the nature of the universe – that is speculative philosophy and akin to theology – but with the analysis of facts we already know. Its object is not more extensive knowledge, but more precise knowledge. ... This clearness and preciseness is what the analytic philosophers seek. (14f)

Thus there is, for Wisdom, a distinction to be made between AP and traditional, speculative philosophy in the area of aims and scope. AP rejects the 'big picture' endeavors of traditional philosophy not in principle, but in practice. Still, this is a significant departure from traditional norms, according to which analysis and speculation were complementary aspects of the total philosophical project. Thus, it is not inaccurate to see this as a genuine rejection (albeit a mild one) of those norms.

Wisdom made a second attempt at clarifying the nature of philosophical analysis in his 1934 book, *Problems of Mind and Matter*. There he does use the name 'analytic philosophy', saying that 'it is to analytic philosophy that this book is intended to be an introduction' (1), and later claiming that 'there cannot be ... an introduction to analytic philosophy' that proceeds by setting forth the fundamental 'analytic truths', as one might introduce chemistry by introducing the basic chemical truths (2). The reason, he says, is that 'there is no special set of analytic truths' (2). Consistent with his 1931 view, he says that:

> Analytic philosophy has no special subject matter. You can philosophise about Tuesday, the pound sterling and lozenges and philosophy itself. This is because the analytic philosopher, unlike the scientist, is not one who learns new truths, but one who gains new insight into old truths. (Wisdom 1934: 2)

This is presented as the basis of the distinction not only between philosophy and science, but also, as in 1931, between AP and traditional, speculative philosophy. Wisdom explains that, because his book is an introduction to *analytic* philosophy, 'it is not concerned with certain questions properly called "philosophical"' (1), concerning such things as God, the soul, immortality, or the moral and metaphysical natures of the universe. 'These speculative questions', he says,

> are clearly a great deal more important than questions of the analytic kind. ... The speculative questions are the more important because, if they could be answered, we should thereby obtain new information about matters which concern us very much, while the answering of analytic questions does not provide us with knowledge of new facts but only with clearer knowledge of facts already known. ... Speculating and analysing are operations which differ in kind; the object of the one is truth, the object of the other is clarity. (1f)

Wisdom recognized that the two operations were not mutually exclusive; however, he thought that they ought to be kept separate in order to safeguard the metaphysical neutrality of analysis: 'occasionally an analytic result bears upon a speculative theory', he noted, 'but to remember this only prejudices one's analysis' (1).

In these respects, Wisdom's two accounts are quite consistent. However, in 1934 he takes a different approach to characterizing the analysanda of philosophical analysis. Here, they are not meanings, but 'facts':

> the goal of the analytic philosopher is insight into facts; ... insight is clear apprehension of the ultimate structure of facts; ... the structure of a fact is clearly apprehended when one apprehends clearly the form, the elements, and the arrangement of the elements of that fact. (3)

Clearly, Wisdom is here influenced by the logical atomism of Russell and the early Wittgenstein; and, on the face of it, he has escaped the linguistic idiom that held him captive in 1931. However, as soon as we ask what a *fact* is, we find that he is still firmly in its grip: 'I do not attempt to define "fact". I describe a fact as what a sentence expresses' (21). The reason he offers this as a description rather than a definition is that, as he candidly admits, 'I define a sentence as what is intended to express a fact' (21 n). By making one statement a description rather than a definition, he hopes to escape the charge of formal circularity. This is a nominal achievement, however; for whether we call them definitions or descriptions, the circularity of their content renders these two statements impotent to illuminate the fundamental nature of philosophical analysanda, and hence of philosophical analysis. Wisdom was perfectly aware of this, admitting in a footnote that 'I have here provided no answer to the question "what is the ultimate nature of facts?"' (20 n). In the end, then, all that Wisdom can or is willing to say about philosophical analysis and its objects is expressed in the linguistic idiom.

This same consistency with what would ultimately become the TC is apparent in the two earliest known[4] uses of 'analytic philosophy' itself, which date from 1933: one of these comes from R.G. Collingwood,[5] Waynflete Professor of Metaphysical Philosophy at Oxford prior to Gilbert Ryle. Collingwood uses 'analytic philosophy' as a name for one of two 'skeptical positions' he wishes to criticize. As he describes it, AP is characterized by what we would now call a *metaphilosophical* view – 'the analytic view *of philosophy*', he calls it at one point (1933: 143, my emphasis). The analytic view, he says, is skeptical not about knowledge in general, but about philosophical knowledge as traditionally conceived. Specifically, AP is committed to the view that there is no knowledge to be had, philosophical or otherwise, over and above what comes from common sense and the sciences. Thus, 'philosophy cannot establish positive or constructive positions', but is limited to

> taking the propositions which we are given by science and common sense, and revealing their logical structure or 'showing exactly what

we mean when we say', for example, that there is a material world. (141f)

This is exactly the limitation that Wisdom was getting at by contrasting AP with speculative philosophy. The phrase in scare quotes is highly similar to Wisdom's descriptions of the analytic method, and both are representative of the way analytic philosophers, especially of the ordinary-language variety, frequently described their undertaking. The linguistic overtones are obvious, making this a veiled reference to the analytic philosophers' acceptance of the linguistic thesis. Though Collingwood mentions only three figures in connection with AP – Moore, Russell and Stebbing, all three canonical analysts on the TC (though not, of course, of equal stature) – he observes that 'the analytic method has been much used by well-known philosophers in this country [England] for over twenty years' (145), and so from prior to 1913. Moreover, he links his own account to Stebbing's discussion of the analytic approach given before the Aristotelian Society in 1932 (but published in 1933), in which she identifies Moore, Russell, Broad, Wittgenstein and, tentatively, the logical positivists of Vienna and Berlin[6] as proponents of the analytic method. All of this is clearly in line with what would come to be the TC.

The second 1933 occurrence comes from W.P. Montague, one of the American New Realists. Like Collingwood (and Wisdom a year later) Montague uses it to name something that fits the contours of AP on the TC, *mutatis mutandis* for the year 1933. He includes Moore, Russell and Whitehead 'in his pre-cosmological period' – i.e., the period dominated by his collaboration with Russell on *Principia Mathematica* – and Susan Stebbing 'and other members of the Aristotelian Society', and also Wittgenstein in what he initially calls 'the Cambridge School' (Montague 1933: 7), but later 'the new analytic philosophy' (8). This is ambiguous between an adjectival and a nominative use of the term, but his use of the definite article and the application to a definite set of figures construed as a philosophical school suggest a strong leaning in the nominative direction. Like Collingwood and Wisdom, Montague sees the analytic philosophers as having rejected the aims, scope and methods of traditional philosophy by restricting philosophical inquiry to what he initially describes as 'a determinedly rigorous analysis of experience and its categories' (7). However, he realizes that this description fails to distinguish 'the new analytic philosophy' from what had been going on generally in the British empirical tradition (and somewhat beyond) up through the end of the nineteenth century – one thinks preeminently of Locke and Hume, but also of James and John Stuart Mill, of Alexander

Bain, of G.C. Robertson, and even of Shadworth Hodgson, all of whom accepted, in one form or another, the restriction of philosophy to 'psychological' phenomena. Thus, Montague quickly modifies his description, noting that the analysts were on a trajectory away from investigating 'forms of experience' and toward 'forms of discourse about experience – in short, forms of grammar':

> The leading member of the group of philosophers that we are discussing [Wittgenstein] declares to us that metaphysics (old style) is nothing but "bad grammar." And a propos of this famous jibe a colleague of mine has remarked that, while the new metaphysics may be good grammar, it appears to be nothing much else. (9)

In 1936 we see Ernest Nagel using 'analytic philosophy' in much the same way, but with an important difference that we will consider again further on. Rather than a philosophical group, he uses the term to designate a set of 'tendencies still in the process of development' (1936a: 5). Apart from this, however, Nagel's conception of AP is very much in line with the TC and the earlier uses of the term. Among the characteristic analytic tendencies, Nagel includes tendencies toward (1) taking 'for granted a body of authentic knowledge acquired by the special sciences', (2) impatience with 'philosophic systems built in the traditionally grand manner', (3) treating traditional philosophical problems as pseudo-problems generated by the misuse of language, (4) having a very focused interest in questions of logic and method, (5) conceiving philosophy's task to be the clarification of meanings via an analytic method, (6) being uninterested in the history of philosophy, and (7) aspiring, in their philosophizing, to 'ethical and political neutrality' (6f). Among the leading figures whose work embodied these tendencies, Nagel includes Moore, Wittgenstein, the members of the Vienna Circle, and a group of Polish philosophers the only one of which widely known in contemporary analytic circles is Tarski. Russell is present as an important background figure. All of this is consistent with the TC.

In these four earliest instances of 'analytic philosophy' in the nominative sense, we note, first, that they are consistent with one another, and with Wisdom's 1931 description of the ways of 'the analytic philosopher'. While this could be a coincidence, it seems unlikely. More likely, all four authors were drawing upon common linguistic resources already becoming established in the broader academic community.[7] Either way, the result is the same: in the early to mid 1930s we have the first records of a philosophical school with the name 'analytic philosophy', and hence the first record of AP as a unified and significant presence on the socio-academic scene.

Second, we note that the *original conception* here associated with 'analytic philosophy' has almost exactly the same boundaries – extensional, temporal, geographical *and intensional* – as the TC, *mutatis mutandis* for the year 1933. And the single deviation from the TC – Montague's inclusion of Whitehead – is made for exactly the right reason: his involvement with Russell and *Principia Mathematica*. It is fair to say that, on that account, Whitehead probably would have been remembered as an analyst had he not gone on to work in areas taboo to the analysts (speculative metaphysics). Thus, once again the rule is observed in the breach.

Of special importance is the fact that, far from having to wait until the 1950s to notice 'a beginning syncretism within the movement', we have the conception of AP as an ideationally unified philosophical group from the very first occurrences of the term in the 1930s, as used by both analysts (Wisdom) and non-analysts (Montague, Collingwood, Nagel). Though its unifying views are not *stated* with any exactness, it is sufficiently clear that these figures all saw AP as possessed of a common metaphilosophical vision tied to a single philosophical method, thereby restricting the scope of traditional philosophical inquiry. Moreover, despite Wisdom's statements to the contrary, the method they all ascribe to it gives every appearance of being *linguistic* analysis. Indeed, the inability of any early commentator to provide an alternative idiom for the employment or description of the method suggests that, far from being a matter of convenience, the linguistic idiom was closely tied to the identity of the method itself.

This original conception of AP remained quite constant through the early 1960s, especially in the minds and mouths of analysts themselves, thereby becoming the TC. For instance, Arthur Pap's 1949 *Elements of Analytic Philosophy* (one of the works to which von Wright refers; see pp. 68f) identifies AP as a 'school of thought' (ix) and affirms that, despite significant differences among its various factions, 'the unanimous practice of the analytic method as a powerful instrument of criticism tends to blur these differences' (ix). What was this unanimously practiced analytic method? Pap preferred to call it 'logical analysis', but it is clear that he had in mind the analysis of language, broadly construed:

in general, all the typically philosophical questions of the form 'what is the nature of *X*' can be interpreted as questions of logical analysis, of the form 'what is the meaning of the word "*X*" or of any synonym thereof', or 'what is the meaning of sentences containing the word "*X*"'. (vii)

Thus, for Pap, analytic philosophers were united in their practice of the analytic method understood as the analysis of language. This is also apparent from a passage in which Pap explains AP's anti-metaphysical stance by rooting it in the analytic method:

> It is not mere 'narrowness' of interests that leads analytic philosophers to keep away from metaphysics, but positive reasons against the fertility of metaphysics as a cognitive enterprise. The evaluation of these reasons, which mainly grow in the soil of semantics, is itself a concern of analytic philosophy, not metaphysics. Hence metaphysicians have to become, at least temporarily, analytic philosophers if they seriously want to discuss the question whether metaphysics, as a cognitive enterprise, a source of genuine knowledge, is possible. (12)

This makes it even clearer that Pap took the business of analytic philosophers to be linguistic in nature, while also revealing that his conception of AP included its traditional anti-metaphysical stance.

The one respect in which Pap deviated from what eventually became the TC was his insistence that AP was not a twentieth-century innovation. In a move foreshadowing differentia revisionism, but which is its mirror image, Pap claimed:

> a history of analytic philosophy, if it should ever be written, would not have to begin with the twentieth century. It could go all the way back to Socrates, since the Socratic 'dialectic' is nothing else but a method of clarifying meanings, applied primarily to moral terms. Again, much of Aristotle's writing consists of logical analysis.... It is especially the so-called British empiricists, Locke, Hume, Berkeley and their descendants, who practiced philosophy primarily as an analytic method. To be sure, much of what they wrote belongs to psychology, but if that is deducted there still remains a conscientious preoccupation with questions of meaning, full of lasting contributions to analytic philosophy. (vii f)

Whereas differentia revisionism makes its case for continuity by assimilating AP to the history of philosophy, Pap makes his by assimilating the history of philosophy to AP – that is, it is not analytic philosophers who are construed as being concerned, as were certain figures in the history of philosophy, with normative problems about reasons and reasoning, argument and justification, causation, good and evil, mental states, and so on; rather, Pap construes our philosophical ancestors as being concerned, as analytic philosophers once were, with logico-linguistic issues. This is a bizarre aberration for which there is no explanation other than Pap's wishful thinking.

In 1956, J.O. Urmson wrote the first overtly historical work on what he called 'the analytic movement', the 'analysts', and the 'analytic philosophers' (vii f). Though he does not use the term 'analytic philosophy', it is perfectly clear that he is writing about the same group that others had called by that name; for his account is in all respects consistent with theirs, and with the TC. His story begins with the rise of logical atomism and moves thorough logical positivism to the rise of ordinary-language philosophy; thus the temporal, geographical and extensional boundaries are all in line with the TC. However, Urmson is more circumspect than Wisdom, Collingwood, Montague or Pap in giving an intensional characterization of 'the analytic movement'. Like Pap, but more strongly, he warns against the temptation to see in AP '*a definite* school, with an orthodoxy of its own, consciously moving from position to position as difficulties in the "received" view were noticed and amendments sanctioned' (ix). This is reminiscent of Ammerman's warning that it is misleading to speak of AP as if it were homogenous and monolithic. But, like Ammerman, this does not prevent Urmson from ascribing to analytic philosophers a limited but genuine ideational unity, saying that they

> were united at least in the view that analysis was at least one of the most important tasks of the philosopher; and by analysis, they meant something which, whatever precise description of it they chose, at least involved the attempt to rewrite in different and in some way more appropriate terms those statements which they found philosophically puzzling. (vii)

Like the others, Urmson takes the unifying feature of the movement to be a metaphilosophical commitment to a particular method held to be either specially important or uniquely legitimate, and he takes that method to be a form of analysis whose most significant feature – at least for the unity of AP – is its linguistic aspect.

The very same pattern is apparent in G.J. Warnock's *English Philosophy Since 1900*, published two years later (in 1958). Like Urmson, Warnock avoids using 'analytic philosophy' or any other school-name for the analytic movement as a whole; still, it is clear that this is what he has in mind when he speaks of 'contemporary philosophy' or 'the successors of the Idealist empire' or the host of other descriptions he uses to pick out his subject. Warnock's story begins with Moore and Russell, and moves through logical atomism, logical positivism, Wittgenstein, and the rise of ordinary-language philosophy, thus keeping to the extensional, temporal and geographical boundaries of the TC. His intensional characterizations are especially insightful. First, he notes that the different figures and factions in the analytic movement 'had all arrived by their different routes at the view that the day-to-day labors of the philosopher consisted overwhelmingly in the *analysis of language*', and not language as such, but 'statements of fact' (57f). 'The search for philosophical analyses', he says,

> always took the form of an attempt to formulate a sort of linguistic equation. On the left of the equation was to be the expression to be analyzed, and on the right another expression, usually longer and more explicit, designed to be synonymous with or equivalent to the first.... (59)

But unlike most other commentators from within the analytic camp, Warnock explicitly notes the metaphilosophical implications lurking just below the surface of this agreement in method, speaking not only of 'the commonly accepted notion of "analysis"' but also of 'the commonly held conviction that analysis of this type was entirely adequate for philosophical purposes' (59).

A final example comes from Peter Strawson's contribution to a 1963 collection called *The Revolution in Philosophy*. Though he does not use the term, he clearly has in mind the same group that others referred to as 'analytic philosophy' when he refers to 'the linguistic nature of the enterprise' (98) engaged in by the logical atomists, the logical positivists, and G.E. Moore. 'The general conception of analysis', he says,

> was that of a kind of translation, or, perhaps better, a kind of paraphrase. For it was to be translation within a language, not from one language to another: a translation from a less explicit to a more explicit form, or from a misleading to an unmisleading form. If your problem was, say, the nature of truth, or, say, the nature of existence, you hoped to solve it by finding a formula for translating sentences in which the adjective 'true' or the verb 'exists' occurred, into sentences in which these expressions did not occur, and in which no straightforward synonyms of them occurred either. (99f)

At this point, our survey of the use of 'analytic philosophy' connects with Chapter 2's survey of more recent uses (1965 and after). Together, these surveys point to the fact that, from its earliest uses on through to its becoming an established part of the philosophical lexicon, 'analytic philosophy' in the nominative sense was employed clearly and consistently to refer to (1) a school of philosophy (2) that had developed around the turn of the twentieth century, (3) that was distinguished by its almost exclusive use of a revolutionary method – namely, linguistic analysis – and hence by its acceptance, implicit or explicit, of the linguistic thesis, (4) that was dominating philosophical discussion in various circles, and (5) whose preeminent representatives were Moore, Russell, Wittgenstein, and the members of the Vienna Circle. These facts about how 'analytic philosophy' was originally used and how its referent was originally conceptualized are historical facts on a par with all other historical facts about AP. Thus, they can neither be ignored nor dismissed nor rewritten as we conduct our historical researches into AP.

This has far-reaching consequences some of which I will mention here, others of which we will cover in the following chapter. First, contra Soames and others who have suggested that the view of AP as an ideationally unified school was the product of facile misunderstandings by outsiders, the foregoing statements from Wisdom, Pap, Urmson, Warnock and Strawson – all canonical analysts – reveal that this was the analysts' own original and longstanding self-conception.

Second, this destroys any remaining hope that either form of revisionism might turn out to be legitimate. At the beginning of this section I suggested that differentia revisionism might be legitimate if it could be characterized as a return to some original conception of AP. What we have found, however, is that the TC is in fact closest to the original conception, and is reasonably described as the original conception itself in a later stage of development. There simply is no other historically sound conception of AP that either form of revisionism can look to in order to justify itself.

Moreover, whereas we have already seen that Hacker's claim about 'analytic philosophy' not having a well-established use is false for the period 1965 to date, we now see that it is likewise false for the period 1930–1965. Additionally, far from being vague during that early period, it portrayed AP as a school with a defining doctrine – the linguistic thesis – and hence as something that could be defined in terms of necessary and sufficient conditions that were ideational in nature. Thus, we must emphasize again that we are not free to mold the concept of AP as we please – any attempt to do so will constitute a distortion of history.

Chapter 4

On the Trail of an Illusion

Illusionism

In Chapter 2, I explained that the historians of AP have effectively undermined the TC by showing it to have been false at every stage of its development. Consequently, we can no longer think of AP – even historically – in terms of the TC. A natural response would be to reject it and to attempt to construct an accurate picture of AP via historical inquiry. This is what the revisionists have tried to do; and yet, in Chapter 3, I argued that the TC cannot be dismissed or ignored as a factor in the history of AP, that to do so is to distort history or the nature of philosophy or both. At first glance, the demands of these two chapters may seem incompatible: the one indicates that we should reject the TC as historically misleading; the other that we must retain it, since only thus conceived is 'analytic philosophy' a historically useful designation. Consequently, we are on the horns of what I will call *the historian's dilemma*: either we accept the TC as it is or we reject it and construct a revisionist conception; if the former, we end up ignoring the recent findings about its inadequacy; if the latter, we end up ignoring the historical facts about its role as the governing conception of AP for most of the movement's history. Of course, neither body of evidence can legitimately be ignored.

Fortunately there is a way to escape the historian's dilemma by going between its horns. In 1998, Bruce Aune gave a talk on 'Feigl and the Development of Analytic Philosophy at the University of Minnesota'.[1] Aune was a student at Minnesota during the 1950s, when the philosophy department was establishing itself as a bastion of AP and the philosophy of science. Almost in passing, he makes the observation highlighted below:

"Philosophical analysis" seems to have been the favorite adjective of the philosophy department in the early [nineteen] fifties. Not only did Feigl and Sellars entitle their anthology "Readings in Philosophical Analysis," but Hospers entitled his textbook, the first edition of which he published in 1953, "Introduction to Philosophical Analysis"; and Wilfrid Sellars referred to his graduate seminar as "the analysis seminar" (I think its official name was "Seminar in Philosophical Analysis.") *What did they mean by "philosophical analysis"? Probably not the same thing, though they might not have realized it [in] the early fifties* … . (2, my emphasis)

Here we have first-hand testimony that several significant analysts working in the same department (and one then on the cutting-edge of AP in America), some of whom collaborated on projects explaining and promoting 'philosophical analysis', seem not to have realized that they had differing conceptions of analysis, and hence of the scope and method of philosophy. If this situation was actual at Minnesota, it was certainly possible elsewhere in the analytic world. It is even possible that it was the norm.

The proposal that this was so is the heart of what I call *the illusionist thesis*, or simply *illusionism* (as opposed to revisionism). Illusionism accepts that the TC does not correspond, and never has corresponded, to anything in reality. Consequently it posits that, insofar as it has ever seemed to anyone that it did, that 'seeming' was an illusion. And yet illusionism also insists that it *did* seem that way to many – indeed, to many self-proclaimed analysts – during the early and middle years of the analytic movement. Consequently it posits that the illusion itself must be counted part of the movement's history. In this way, illusionism goes between the horns of the historian's dilemma.

Moreover, as I will develop it, illusionism insists that the illusion of the TC was accidental neither to the movement's successes nor its failures in the British and American academies. Rather, it was quite central to both; thus, beyond offering a way out of the dilemma, illusionism offers a way forward when it comes to explaining what I earlier (in the Introduction) called AP's 'peculiar career'. In doing so, it leads to new questions whose answers complete that explanation. And, as we shall see, explaining AP's peculiar career in this way will also reveal its true nature. Thus, the illusionist thesis serves as the cornerstone of my proposed solution to the puzzle about AP. This extended use of the illusionist thesis will require some spelling out, and it is to that task that we now turn.

Two Illusions in the TC

In order to use the illusionist thesis to explain AP's peculiar career, we must distinguish between two illusions connected to the TC. So far, our critical observations about that conception have focused on the fact that it is and always has been false. It is false in the straightforward sense that there simply was no school the likes of which it portrayed. More fundamentally, though, it is false because the philosophers it picks out as being core, canonical analysts were not ideationally unified in the linguistic thesis. On the TC, these figures' purported consensus over this novel metaphilosophical view is the ground for taking them together as members of a philosophical school at all, and also for that school's anti-metaphysical and anti-historical stances, as well as for dating its origin to the turn of the twentieth century. Thus, the notion of ideational unity in the linguistic thesis is the core of the TC, and it is principally because this core component is false that the conception as a whole is. The false notion of the movement's ideational unity is the main illusion associated with the TC. We may call it *the illusion of unity*.

While this is the main illusion, it is not the only illusion associated with the TC. One feature of AP's peculiar career is the rapidity with which AP as traditionally conceived – that is, as linguistic philosophy – rose and then fell. Its fall consisted in the abandonment of two of its most central features: the linguistic thesis and its attendant anti-metaphysical stance. Generally speaking, these features were abandoned because the analysts were unable to work out the details of the linguistic thesis, at least in a way that generated widespread consensus. We will return to this issue further on. Here, we point out only that, seeing as its problems were obvious enough to be spotted in very short order and severe enough to lead to its demise in less than half a century (a meager span for a supposedly epoch-making outlook), the early success of AP as originally conceived is immensely puzzling. Put bluntly, it is astonishing that such a badly and obviously flawed outlook managed to attract a number of philosophers sufficient to generate a revolution in the social sphere of academic philosophy. Of course, we must suppose that the linguistic thesis appeared not only plausible but promising to those who joined the emerging analytic movement. However, given that this appearance was quite obviously false, it seems to have been an illusion distinct from but intimately connected with the illusion of unity. We may call this second illusion *the illusion of promise*. Unlike the illusion of unity, it is not part of the TC's content. Rather, it is a second-order illusion bearing upon part of that content: the TC presents AP as ideationally unified in the linguistic thesis; the illusion of promise presented the linguistic thesis as an immensely promising view, and hence AP as an immensely promising movement. In the following sections, I will outline the explanatory role that the TC and its illusions play *vis-à-vis* AP's peculiar career.

Baptizing an Illusion – the Illusion as an Essential Feature of Analytic Philosophy

In the Introduction, I claimed that the very fact that AP exists as something to be discussed under a single name is historically connected to its career in the British and American universities, and specifically to the early success of a particular philosophical outlook in securing both (1) the attention and (2) the loyalty of academic philosophers both (3) in places that mattered and (4) in numbers large enough to generate the kind of regular and widespread discussion that would both (5) require the coining of a new term and (6) explain that term's subsequent entrenchment as one of the most familiar in the philosophical lexicon. From the data given in Chapter 3, we know that the outlook in question was the one attributed to AP on the TC – linguistic thesis, anti-metaphysics, anti-history – for when the name came into being, that was the outlook associated with it.

This is extremely significant for our historical understanding of AP, for it shows that the TC is intrinsic – in some sense *essential* – to AP as a social entity. Its origination as a named social object would have required that a set of common conceptualizations or 'collective intentionalities'[2] be linked to a common name via a corporate act of Kripkean baptism.[3] Again, from the data given in Chapter 3, we can be confident that the intentionalities that originally defined AP as a social entity and which served as the reference-fixing content of 'analytic philosophy' in its baptism were those of the TC. Thus, like the support beams in a mineshaft, the TC served to define and preserve a social space whose rough contours had already been carved out through the efforts of those destined to be remembered as founders of AP. Within this defining structure, what in reality had been a set of figures, views and events united only by Humean contiguity and resemblance (or Wittgensteinian 'family resemblance') came to be seen as a philosophical school united ideationally in the linguistic thesis and socially in the desire to reform philosophy along the lines it prescribed.

The TC as *Explanans*

Its role in AP's baptism and pre-baptismal rise (i.e., phenomena (1)–(6)) confers upon the TC, and hence its illusion(s), a central position, and hence significant explanatory value, *vis-à-vis* the rise of AP. But (1)–(6) are only the initial, stage-setting part of that event; for AP *as such* could not begin to rise until it was brought into being as a named social entity. The TC was just as important to this post-baptismal phase of AP's rise. We know that the TC not only provided the reference-fixing content in AP's baptism, but that it governed talk and thought about AP for more than thirty years thereafter. Consequently, we must suppose that those who aligned with AP at least from around 1933 onward understood themselves to be aligning with it as traditionally conceived – that was how it was 'advertised', and that, we must suppose, is what they were 'buying into'. Of course, there would have been more to an individual's 'conversion' to AP than the TC itself; for example, in many cases it may have been that conversion to AP was, in the first instance, conversion to Moore or Russell or Wittgenstein. Still, insofar as individuals saw themselves as part of the broader school of AP, the evidence suggests that they would have done so, and perhaps that they only *could* have done so, in terms of the TC. In this way, the TC would have continued to facilitate AP's rise even and perhaps especially in its post-baptismal era.

This prospect, grounded in the facts about the ordinary use of 'analytic philosophy', is further supported by looking to the works mentioned by Aune – the one edited by Feigl and Sellars, the other written by Hospers. Not surprisingly, what they say about philosophical analysis is largely consistent with the TC, and hence with each other. In the Preface to the former, the editors explain that:

> The conception of philosophical analysis underlying our selections springs from two major traditions in recent thought, the Cambridge movement, deriving from Moore and Russell, and the Logical Positivism of the Vienna Circle (Wittgenstein, Schlick, Carnap) together with the Scientific Empiricism of the Berlin group (led by Reichenbach). These ... have increasingly merged to create an approach to philosophical problems which we frankly consider a decisive turn in the history of philosophy. (Feigl and Sellars 1949: vi)[4]

This clearly fits the geographical, temporal and extensional boundaries of the TC. It fits the intensional boundaries insofar as it acknowledges AP's revolutionary character, thereby also implying its anti-historical stance. Other intensional boundaries are neglected in the Preface, but this is quickly made up for in the Introduction, in which Feigl presents the standard logical positivist account of philosophy: properly practiced it focuses on the questions 'what do you mean?' and 'how do you know?' (Feigl 1943: 3), philosophical analysis is linguistic analysis, traditional metaphysical problems are pseudo-problems generated by the misuse of language, traditional philosophy is 'the disease of which [analysis] should be the cure' (6). Sellars' own contribution is 'Realism and the New Way of Words' (1948). As the title suggests, his view of philosophical analysis is similarly linguistic.

Hospers also presents a predominantly linguistic conception of philosophical analysis, although – like Wisdom more than two decades earlier – he attributes this to convenience rather than the nature of analysis itself: 'Where, then, shall we begin our study [of philosophy]? Different persons may prefer to start at different places; but it will be most economical of effort in the long run if we begin with a study of language' (1953: xii). The shape of language, he says, frequently distracts from the genuinely philosophical data and leads to philosophical error; thus, to get clear on the nature of meaning will help us avoid pitfalls and keep focused on genuine philosophical issues. This is not quite the view that traditional philosophy consists in pseudo-problems generated by the misuse of language, nor is it a direct statement of the linguistic thesis, but it approximates both and is certainly in keeping with the TC.

So, the TC was central to the analytic self-image in its post-baptismal phase, and this helps to explain the illusion of promise during this period. The problem associated with the illusion of promise is that the linguistic thesis, the cornerstone of AP as traditionally conceived, was in reality not nearly so promising as it was initially taken to be. Indeed, it is not even very plausible. Even less plausible is the notion that it could be a proper foundation for a revolutionary philosophical school. Reflecting on the metaphysical puzzles surrounding the nature of language in general and words in particular, especially so-called word 'types' (as opposed to 'tokens'), Dallas Willard observes that:

> … language in general, and its elements ("words") and structures in particular, are no more clear and no more subject to consensus among philosophers – nor are they more clearly positioned in reality in such a way as to provide philosophical access to all else – than are other material objects, along with minds, experiences, and the various ranges of properties and relations, of which we speak before we make the semantic [i.e., linguistic] turn. (1983: 290)

Setting this fact against the early and mid twentieth-century analysts' hope that looking to language would solve rather than create philosophical problems, Willard notes (1983: 290) that the latter '*should* have been expected, since the only philosophically unmuddled sense of "word" is that in which words are simply one subset of physical objects and events', e.g., noises and marks on paper. Similar complexities attach to propositions and meanings. Why, then, were problems and disagreements surrounding these phenomena not expected? These and related issues in the philosophy of language were well known prior to the rise of AP. Frege, Husserl and Peirce had all grappled with them by the turn of the twentieth century. Thus, it did not require a half-century of work for the analysts to *discover* them; rather, it took that long for the analysts to *acknowledge* their depth and difficulty. Why, then, did the analysts initially have such great faith and hope in the adequacy of the linguistic thesis not only as a metaphilosophical view, but as an ideational cornerstone for their school?

One possibility is that its underlying problems were either ignored or missed by a great many analysts, despite their being obvious. Illusionism explains how this could have been, for the illusion of unity could have easily masked these problems and, even if noticed, quelled worries about them. As traditionally conceived, AP would have had tremendous power to impress and attract philosophers even and perhaps *especially* in virtue of its non-ideational aspects – and so quite apart from its problem areas. The TC portrays AP as a revolutionary approach to philosophy unanimously endorsed by some of the greatest philosophical minds (not to mention some of the most forceful, persuasive, and downright interesting personalities) of the day: initially G.E. Moore, Bertrand Russell, Ludwig Wittgenstein, and the members of the Vienna Circle; later, W.V. Quine, Peter Strawson, John Austin, and so on. Moreover, on account of their intellectual greatness, these figures acquired a large amount of prestige in the world of academic philosophy. Thus, in aligning oneself with AP as traditionally conceived, one would have been aligning oneself with intellectual and social greatness. This would have been a strong incentive to align with AP even if one did not completely understand or had doubts about the principles behind it. Moreover, the fact that all these greats were presented by the TC as endorsing the analytic metaphilosophy could easily have given the false impression that it was already on solid ground, requiring no further development, or at most just a few finishing touches. Here was a strong consensus of insuperably expert testimony validating the analytic approach. How could one go wrong by following the greats?

There is also a more sinister side to this illusory 'consensus of the greats': one must consider what would have been the consequence of going against it, of blowing the whistle on AP. Even if one was not blinded by the illusion, the fact that many others *were* established a *status quo* that served as a normative standard for work in philosophy. Bryan Magee, who had first-hand experience with academic philosophy in both Britain and America during AP's heyday, recalls that:

> There were several decades during the broad middle of the twentieth century when, in a great deal of the English-speaking world, a philosopher had to be thought to share the analytic approach if his colleagues were to regard him as a serious philosopher at all – although at the same time fierce and unforgiving battles went on among the analytic philosophers. (1997: 438)

This observation brings to mind those of Lachs and Glock (see pp. 12–15), thus revealing that 'analytic philosophy' has played a normative role in academic circles for a long while. The consequences of violating this norm can be discerned by looking to the cases of those who did, like Ernest Gellner, Brand Blanshard (1962) and R.G. Collingwood. The former was marginalized in his own lifetime (see pp. 19f). The latter two were well-established by the time the analytic *status quo* was achieved, so they were not directly threatened by it. Still, they were punished indirectly: under the normative influence of 'analytic philosophy', their work suffered such neglect that, for many decades now, it has been not only possible but normal for students to earn advanced degrees in philosophy without ever hearing their names let alone reading any of their works.

We must also consider that, if up and coming academics like Gellner could suffer marginalization for disagreeing with the *status quo*, students would have been even more vulnerable, and hence much more inclined to duck the issues even if they saw them. Returning to Aune's reflections on AP at the University of Minnesota, he recalls: 'when I wrote my Ph.D. prelims in 1959, I had a strong feeling that there was no longer a departmental consensus on how philosophy should be done' (1998: 6). Wisely, Aune tried to steer clear of the issue in those prelims, with the result that they 'were gently criticized for being excessively noncommittal on philosophical method' (6). Although the issue here is *lack* of consensus among the Minnesotans rather than the (superficial) consensus he says existed among them less than a decade earlier, the crucial point remains the same: the analysts were unyieldingly devoted to their views about proper philosophical scope and method. If one's professors happened to agree in those views, one could satisfy them all by adopting the party line; if they did not, the only way to avoid a withering attack was to tiptoe around the issue as best one could. We must not forget Magee's language when he describes the analysts' internecine battles as 'fierce and unforgiving'. As a graduate student in that context, far better to suffer gentle criticism for being noncommittal than to suffer an onslaught for being committed to the 'wrong' view!

Although we must acknowledge this sinister aspect of the illusion of unity, we must also hope and indeed suppose that its more positive attractions would have lent the greater impetus to AP's propagation. Among these attractions were not only the allure of teaming up with the greats, but also AP's purported revolutionary character. By clothing the movement in the mystique of revolution, the TC would have rendered it appealing, especially to those of a younger generation. Peter Hacker has observed that being revolutionary was a vital part of the traditional analytic self-image:

> each phase of the analytic movement [until 1970] was motivated by a revolutionary fervor. The protagonists passionately believed that they were ridding philosophy of intellectual pretensions, clearing the Augean stables of accumulated refuse, and putting the subject on a fresh footing. (1998: 24f)

Revolutionary fervor and passionate belief are just the sorts of things that tend to sweep human beings up and carry them along, often without knowing just where they're headed. This is true whether the revolution in question is political, intellectual, cultural, or whatever – and, of course, there tends to be significant mutual influence among these spheres, so that a revolution in one can quickly spread to another. Consequently, the revolutionary character ascribed to AP on the TC would certainly help to explain why philosophers might have been attracted to it despite its theoretical problems. The following reflection from a 1940s Oxford undergraduate reveals just how seductive this was:

> I recall sitting at a table in a cafe with some fellow students one morning. We were talking about philosophy in general terms, and I was struck by the fact that those present not only assumed that the ordinary language mode had superseded all other ways of doing philosophy, but agreed that the task of philosophy would soon be finished. ... There was a wonderful feeling of euphoria in the air, something for which I feel a deep nostalgia. 'Bliss was it in that dawn to be alive, but to be young

was very heaven!' It was a really wonderful feeling that something new and very important was happening here and now in philosophy, and in a way in which one could share. (quoted in Forguson 2001: 331)

The line of verse quoted by this young Oxonian is from Wordsworth's 'The French Revolution as It Appeared to Enthusiasts at its Commencement' – an allusion as telling about the effects of AP's revolutionary mystique as it is foreboding about the movement's future. But, of course, its revolutionary character was part of the illusion cast by the TC. While it presented the greats as united in a revolutionary view whose promotion was a revolutionary endeavor, the fact was that that view was not shared by all, and that, even among those who accepted it, it had not been worked out well enough to be displayed in public let alone to be publicly presented as the ideational cornerstone of a school.

In sum, with the TC simultaneously presenting AP as possessed of several very attractive features that it did not have, and concealing some very serious problems that it did, the movement was virtually guaranteed enormous growth and social success – hence its meteoric rise. But the problems with the linguistic thesis were just too obvious and too severe for its prescriptions and proscriptions to long be abided – hence the TC's quick reversal of fortune, and the fall of AP in its linguistic form. Eventually, the analysts had to acknowledge the depths of philosophical difficulty (and the attendant disagreements) lurking beneath their apparent – or at best superficial – agreement in the linguistic thesis. When they did, the illusions of promise and unity as they related to the linguistic thesis were dispelled.

As Aune's reflections suggest, and as he explicitly says, this occurred among the Minnesotans around 1960: 'though they might not have realized ... [in]the early fifties', that they had underlying disagreements about philosophical analysis, philosophical method and philosophy itself, 'they certainly did so by 1960, when I finished my Ph.D.' (1998: 2). But this awakening was not limited to Minnesota. In fact, it is something we could have predicted on the basis of the historical facts concerning thought and talk about AP in the analytic world at large. These suggest that, until the 1960s, the TC enjoyed widespread and largely unquestioning acceptance. Only in and after the 1960s do characterizations of AP become more circumspect and uses of the TC more heavily qualified. Presumably, this was due to a dawning recognition of the TC's inaccuracy; and this certainly would have included a growing sense of the miscellany of metaphilosophical and methodological views nesting together under the banner of 'analytic philosophy' – the very thing Aune says was happening at Minnesota in the late 1950s and early 60s. Given the geographic scope of this shift in the analytic self-understanding, we must take Aune to be describing the local manifestation of a global phenomenon within the analytic world. The illusions of the TC, which had held sway in the analytic world for nearly thirty years, were beginning to lose their power.

The Traditional Conception as *Explanandum*

The foregoing shows how illusionism explains certain aspects of AP's peculiar career in its post-baptismal stage. The illusion of unity, of a consensus of the greats, inspired the illusion of promise and discouraged dissent, while the attendant revolutionary mystique of the illusory school was appealing in its own right. Under these illusions, AP experienced rampant growth. But the illusions could not be sustained long – at least in their original form – for the challenges to the linguistic thesis were just too great. As Joseph Margolis rightly observes:

> The grand systems of analytic philosophy ... all simply collapsed as a result of *internal weaknesses* that could not be satisfactorily patched or papered over. They were, it seems, precocious in vision, deficient in resources, and damned by *basic errors that all who cared could see.* (2003: 1, my emphasis)

Like Willard, Margolis implies that there was something so obvious about the faults of linguistic philosophy that they should have been noticed and taken seriously much earlier than they were. In fact, if Margolis is right that AP's weaknesses and errors were so glaring that all who cared to see them could have, then we must conclude that those who didn't see them simply didn't care to. Of course, there was a mitigating factor: the TC and its illusions. To the extent that they may have masked AP's weaknesses and problems, it would have been possible for a person otherwise disposed to see them, to miss them. But this mitigating factor was operative only in the post-baptismal phase of AP's rise, for it presupposes the TC's status as the established view of AP.

Here we are confronted with the fact that the TC and its illusions, while explaining some of the peculiarities of AP's career, also add to them; for the facts that the TC and its illusions came to exist and to play the role they did are themselves peculiarities that require explanation. How, we must ask, did the illusions of unity and promise come to be in the first place? How did the false conceptualizations or intentionalities that eventually came to be associated with the TC come to exist, and to be ubiquitous enough to require the simplifying technology of a proper name? What, in other words, was responsible for facilitating the pre-baptismal, stage-setting phase of AP's rise?

Indeed, the TC and its illusions cannot provide a *complete* explanation for AP's rise even in its post-baptismal phase. Though many analysts of the rank and file may have been unwitting victims of these illusions, there is clear evidence that both leading analysts and their critics were aware of the problems that eventually led to linguistic philosophy's fall from at least the early 1930s. In fact, one of our two earliest uses of 'analytic philosophy' comes from a critique in which Collingwood charges the analysts with failing to articulate a viable metaphilosophy/methodology. As noted previously, Collingwood saw AP as a form of skepticism about traditional philosophical knowledge. According to the analysts, he says,

> ... there are many questions, traditionally referred to philosophy for decision, which, because they cannot be decided by science or common sense, cannot be decided at all. Is there a God; shall we have a future life; what is the general nature of the universe as a whole? Because we do not know the answers to these questions independently of philoso-phizing [i.e., because they are not included among the propositions of science or common sense], philosophy cannot give them. (1933: 141)

Thus, on the analytic account, 'nothing is left for philosophy except the task of analyzing the knowledge that we already possess' (141).

According to Collingwood, we can begin to summarize the analytic position by distinguishing among three classes of propositions. First, there is the class just mentioned – purported answers to traditional philosophical questions – that are unfit for use by fields in the knowledge business, such as philosophy aspired to be. Second, there are the proposi-tions of science and common sense, which are the principal vehicles of knowledge. AP has a claim to being in the knowledge business because it deals with this class of propositions: not by verifying or falsifying them, but by analyzing and thereby clarifying them. Thus, propositions in this second class serve as philosophical analysanda, what Collingwood calls 'the data of analysis'. But analyses yield further propositions, their analy-santia, and these 'results of analysis' count as a third class. Like those of the second class and unlike those of the first, these propositions are counted items of knowledge since they are just clearer versions of the members of class two. Such is the analytic view in outline.

But this cannot be all, Collingwood charges, for 'the analytic view implies [another] class of propositions: neither the data of analysis ..., nor its results ..., but the principles on which it proceeds' (143). Such principles 'constitute a theory concerning the nature and method of philosophy ... a philosophical theory, and a constructive one' (144).[5] The analyst's 'first duty', he insists, 'is to expound these' principles, this theory (145); but this is exactly what the analysts had failed to do. Here, Collingwood adverts to a 1933 paper by Susan Stebbing in which she 'reminds us that the analytic method has been much used by well-known philosophers in this country [Britain] for over twenty years, but that none has "seen fit to raise" the questions upon what presuppositions it rests and whether they can be justified' (Collingwood 1933: 145). Stebbing herself tries to address these issues, but, by her own admission, cannot come up with any persuasive arguments for what she sees as the presuppositions of analysis. She even admits that they seem 'not very plausible' (Stebbing 1933: 92) thereby coming close to questioning the illusion of promise. Thus, Collingwood concludes, 'it cannot be allowed that the ... analytic philosopher ... has even begun the task of formulating a philosophical position or programme of his own' (1933: 147).[6]

This last line may seem to overstate the case, for those at the forefront of the movement were not only aware of but preoccupied with the open questions of detail lurking beneath their apparent unity in the linguistic thesis. Reporting on his 1934–35 visits to analytic outposts in Cambridge, Vienna, Prague, Warsaw and Lwów, Ernest Nagel observed (1936a: 6) that 'as a consequence of this [i.e., the analytic] conception of philosophy, concern with formulating the *method* of philosophic analysis dominates all these places':

> Since it is held that clarity as to the method of philosophy will save men from blind-alley pursuits, and that loyalty to a secure and tested method is preferable to a dogmatism with respect to doctrine, it is natural that much of the energy should be directed toward making that method explicit. (1936a: 6)

Here fit the debates between the ideal-language philosophers and the ordinary-language philosophers, between the early Wittgenstein with his picture theory of meaning and the later Wittgenstein with his theory of meaning as use, and also – perhaps the best-known and most devastating manifestation of this general problematic – the logical positivists' struggle to find the proper formulation of the verification principle. Some of these answers turned out to be abject failures, none was a hands-down success, and none succeeded in garnering unanimous support among the analysts. In light of this, Collingwood is best read as poking a hole in the illusion of unity – not as saying that no individual analytic philosopher had tried to explain the principles of analysis, but that the analytic philosophers as a group, or 'the analytic philosopher' as a type, had been unsuccessful in articulating a common account of those principles – which is in fact exactly what he says. To say that AP had not even begun the task of formulating its position is simply a rhetorically effective way of putting the point that, as a *philosophical* movement, AP was still at square one.

Ernest Nagel was also aware of the illusory aspects of AP, and he probed both the illusion of unity and the illusion of promise – albeit more gently and at a more fine-grained level than Collingwood. For instance, Nagel's sense of the *dis*unity lurking beneath the linguistic thesis led him to characterize the referent of 'analytic philosophy' as 'a set of tendencies still in the process of development' (1936a: 5) rather than as a school of philosophy. Although he knew that its leading figures were working to make the analytic method explicit, he also knew that 'those who take a leading part in determining the direction of these [the analytic] tendencies still maintain suspended judgments on central issues' (5). Although he does not list these issues explicitly, his ensuing discussion suggests that they include such things as, for Wittgenstein, the full explication of his theory of meaning as use, and, for the logical positivists, the proper formulation of the verification principle of meaning – the very things that, if successfully formulated and promulgated among the analysts, would have answered Collingwood's charge. Moreover, Nagel realized that the avenues along which core figures were trying to work out the details of the linguistic thesis were themselves too diverse to generate consensus even in the event that one or another should lead to some measure of success. Thus, like Collingwood but at a more fine-grained level, Nagel understood that the analysts did not have a clearly articulated method or metaphilosophy in common at and after the movement's baptism.

Nagel also recognized that the characteristic analytic tendencies, even with the details worked out and consensus achieved, might not by themselves constitute an adequate approach to philosophy. For instance, he specifically criticizes the analysts' characteristic anti-historical attitude in this light:

> ... a profound admiration for the conception of philosophy here indicated [i.e., the analytic] does not stand in the way of my recognizing a danger polar to the one against which this unhistorical attitude is a

protest. I am not convinced that all of traditional philosophy is a mistake, or that valuable insights relevant to problems discussed to-day may not be obtained from its study. Indeed, it seems to me that a better knowledge of the history which they contemn would have saved many of the analytical philosophers from serious error; for ... the latter frequently discuss the traditional problems however disguised they may be by a different terminology. (1936a: 7)

Thus, like Stebbing, Nagel questioned what in retrospect we recognize as the illusion of promise.

Collingwood, Stebbing and Nagel show us that the inadequacies of AP as traditionally conceived, and particularly of the emerging TC itself, were perfectly obvious from very early in the movement's history – just as Willard and Margolis suggest. It is therefore surprising not only that the illusion enthralled people in sufficient numbers to facilitate AP's post-baptismal rise, but also – and especially – that its baptism ever occurred, that the TC, and along with it AP *as such*, came to exist in the first place. One might have supposed that philosophers would be more attentive to the theoretical details beneath the linguistic thesis, and that they would insist on having the details of a view more fully worked out before announcing the advent of a movement founded upon it. Nagel certainly seems to have felt this way. Why, then, did Wisdom and others fail to exercise the same attention and cautious restraint? Why did they present AP as a completed metaphilosophical and methodological system unanimously endorsed by the greats when it clearly was not?

Moreover, we may ask, why did these illusions last so long? Perhaps Wisdom and his contemporaries had a *prima facie* reasonable hope that the details of the linguistic thesis would be quickly worked out, and perhaps this justified their lack of restraint. However, it should have quickly become clear that this hope was vain, that they should have heeded Collingwood's criticism by exercising Nagelian restraint in speaking of their movement. At the 1934 World Congress of Philosophy in Prague, the phenomenologist Roman Ingarden became one of the first to argue that the verification principle of meaning was self-undermining;[7] but it would be more than two decades before the logical positivists finally gave up trying to find a workable revision of it.[8] Some see this as a sign of the positivists' rigor and intellectual integrity. But it is just as easily taken to signify a stubborn hope that an obviously flawed and *prima facie* implausible view could be patched up and made to seem plausible. In fact, such a hope marked the analytic movement as a whole. Like the positivists with the verification principle, the analysts at large ultimately had to abandon the linguistic thesis because they were unable to articulate a common method fitting its general parameters. Also like the positivists, they held out hope for an inordinately long time – over thirty years from the time Stebbing and then Collingwood first staked out the issue in clear terms. Why, we may ask, were the analysts so committed to set sail, and then keep sailing, on what should have been easily recognized as an unsound vessel?

To answer these questions, we must take a closer look at the phenomena that had to be ignored or overlooked, on the one hand, and focused on, on the other, for the TC, and particularly the illusion of unity, to emerge. As we shall see, there is a clear pattern among analysts who embraced the linguistic thesis and the TC of emphasizing certain kinds of phenomena and de-emphasizing others in such a way that it facilitated the rise of the illusion of unity. Moreover, this pattern bespeaks a particular philosophical outlook – *scientism* – that also explains the illusion of promise, and hence the analysts' own devotion to the doomed linguistic thesis.

PART II

Scientism and the Emergence of Analytic Philosophy

And indeed there seems to be a battle like that of the gods and the giants going on among them, because of their disagreement about existence. ... Some of them drag down everything from heaven and the invisible to earth, actually grasping rocks and trees with their hands; for they lay their hands on all such things and maintain stoutly that that alone exists which can be touched and handled; for they define existence and body, or matter, as identical, and if anyone says that anything else, which has no body, exists, they despise him utterly, and will not listen to any other theory than their own.

Plato, *Sophist* (246a–b)

Probably the most decisive division among philosophical attitudes is the one between worldly and other-worldly types of thought.

Herbert Feigl (1943: 3)

... following [Hume's] critique, a fateful "fear of metaphysics" arose which has come to be a malady of contemporary empiricistic philosophizing; this malady is the counterpart to that earlier philosophizing in the clouds, which thought it could neglect and dispense with what was given by the senses.

Albert Einstein (1944: 289)

Chapter 5

The Root of the Illusion of Unity

Getting Behind the Illusion of Unity

In Chapter 2 we surveyed some of the discoveries that prompted the fall of the TC among contemporary historians. In this chapter we will take a closer look at those discoveries that concern the early analysts' differing views about philosophical analysanda, on the one hand, and the scope and nature of philosophy, on the other; for these issues bear most directly on the illusion of unity. That illusion, again, is simply the false belief that the core, canonical analysts were ideationally unified in the linguistic thesis. It is false because several such analysts did not subscribe to the linguistic thesis at all. There are two principal ways in which a philosopher might fail to subscribe to the linguistic thesis: by denying that philosophical analysis is linguistic analysis, or by denying that philosophy is to be defined in terms of the single method or activity of analysis. Of course, these two denials are not mutually exclusive, so a philosopher might depart from the linguistic thesis in both ways. It turns out that Frege, Moore and Russell each did; and these departures are what had to be overlooked in order for the illusion of unity and the TC to emerge.

Frege and the Linguistic Thesis

The last several decades have seen heated debates over the interpretation of Frege's philosophy.[1] We will not wade into the thick of those debates here. Instead, we will note three points that seem to be decisive for determining Frege's relationship to the linguistic thesis, and hence to AP as traditionally conceived.

First, as we have seen, one of the most fundamental features of the analytic self-image for most of the twentieth century was the school's status as a revolutionary movement, a status grounded in the revolutionary nature of the linguistic thesis. However, Hacker has argued that Frege was not interested in reforming philosophy the way all the other early analysts were, and, in fact, that he had no metaphilosophical interests or motives at all: 'Frege's professional life was a single-minded pursuit of a demonstration that arithmetic had its foundations in pure logic alone ... One will search Frege's works in vain for a systematic discussion of the nature of philosophy' (1986: 5, 7). Given this lacuna in Frege's own thought, it at best a great leap to conclude that he accepted the metaphilosophical restrictions of the linguistic thesis; but our two remaining points suggest that this leap should not be made.

Second, Hacker also has drawn attention to a number of respects in which Frege stands opposed to the metaphilosophical program of AP as traditionally conceived:

> ... he thought that philosophical theses (if logicism is a philosophical thesis) could be *proved* by *a priori* argument ... [and] he thought that philosophy could make ontological *discoveries*, for example that concepts are really a species of function and that truth and falsehood are special kinds of objects, namely the values of such functions for arguments. (1986: 7, original emphasis)

These beliefs are in obvious conflict with the linguistic thesis's metaphilosophical restrictions, as well as with views traditionally thought to be corollaries of the linguistic thesis itself: e.g., that metaphysical claims are meaningless, that all *a priori* truths are tautologies grounded in the meanings of words, and hence that they revealed something about the structure of language rather than the world.

Third, even on Dummett's interpretation, which makes Frege the first to have taken the linguistic turn, it is clear that Frege's philosophical analysanda were not words or sentences but rather *propositions* construed as Ideal or Platonic entities. The view that propositions or meanings have an Ideal existence – the kind of existence traditionally attributed to Platonic Forms – was standard in Austro-German philosophy from Bolzano and Lotze to Frege and Husserl, and also among certain British philosophers like Moore and Russell in their early phases, as well as the Cambridge logician W.E. Johnson (whom Griffin [1998] notes may have been a direct influence on Moore and Russell) and Susan Stebbing. Dallas Willard has identified nine features that show up repeatedly in versions of this Platonic theory of propositions (1984: 178ff): (1) they are not spatio-temporal; (2) they are not identical with sentences, but *may* serve as the meanings or senses of sentences; (3) they cannot be perceived by the senses, though they are somehow grasped; (4) the same proposition *may* be grasped by many people; (5) they are mind-independent; (6) 'when the proposition *is* related to a mind, its relation is, or principally is, that of an *object* of thought or of the so-called "propositional-attitudes"'; (7) 'description of a proposition does not essentially involve a reference to any particular mind or act of thought with which it may be involved on occasion'; (8) 'its description does essentially involve mention of its references *to*, or intendings or meanings *of*, certain things (which it is *about*), plus description of how these references are related to one another'; and (9) 'the proposition is what is underivatively true or false, while opinions or sentences or statements are true or false only because they have a certain relationship to a proposition'. Thus understood, propositions are much like Platonic Forms: they are unchanging bearers of truth and meaning/content which are capable of existing apart from both the minds that might think them and the words that might express them.

Meaning, on this view, is not essentially linguistic; rather, as Husserl puts it, propositions or meanings 'are an ideally closed set of general objects, to which being thought or being expressed are alike contingent' (1900–01: 333). Frege makes no significant departures from this general pattern.[2] For him, language – or at least the ideal language of symbolic logic – 'mirrors' visibly the invisible structure of propositions. Hence it is a tool by means of which we can analyze propositions, but it is not itself the analysandum. Even Dummett admits that, 'as his philosophy developed, Frege became more and more insistent that thoughts [i.e. propositions], and not the sentences that express them, formed his true subject matter' (1993: 5). Consequently, Fregean philosophical analysis is not linguistic analysis in the sense characteristic of AP as traditionally conceived.

Moore and the Linguistic Thesis

Similar observations hold true of Moore. Unlike Frege, Moore did reflect quite a bit on the nature of philosophy. However, these reflections reveal that he did not accept the metaphilosophical strictures of the linguistic thesis. It is true that Moore limited his own philosophical activities to analysis; but this avoidance in practice did not reflect an 'in principle' rejection of traditional, speculative system-building. Rather, it reflected the limits of his own philosophical interests. Moore was an 'occasional philosopher'. By his own admission, he possessed no innate drive to develop a systematic philosophy; rather, he was agitated into philosophizing only by the bizarre challenges some philosophers' claims posed to his commonsense beliefs:

I do not think that the world or the sciences would ever have suggested to me any philosophical problems. What has suggested philosophical problems to me is things which other philosophers have said about the world or the sciences. (1942a: 14)

In the *Library of Living Philosophers* volume on Moore, V.J. McGill criticizes Moore's piecemeal approach to philosophy. He rightly notes that Moore attempted to develop no grand system of philosophy, but worked instead in a few specific areas. McGill blames Moore's approach to philosophy on his commitment to a method which was simply not suited to deal with other sorts of philosophical issues. In his reply to McGill, however, Moore explicitly rejects this idea:

... it is, of course, true that there are ever so many interesting philosophical problems on which I have never said a word ... Mr. McGill suggests that the reason why I have not dealt with some of these other questions may have been that I was wedded to certain particular methods, and that these methods were not suitable for dealing with them. But I think I can assure him that this was not the case. I started discussing certain kinds of questions, because they happened to be what interested me most; and I only adopted certain particular methods (so far as I had adopted them) because they seemed to me suitable for those kinds of questions. I had no preference for any method .... (1942b: 676)

Although his practice may have suggested otherwise, in word and in principle Moore clearly endorsed a very traditional view of philosophy according to which analysis and synthesis (or 'construction' or 'speculation') are complementary aspects of the philosophical project. Moreover, though complementary and ultimately inseparable, Moore acknowledged that analysis was subordinate to synthesis as means to end: the ultimate aim of philosophy, he said in 1910, is 'to give a general description of the entire universe'; this he describes as 'the most important and interesting thing that philosophers have tried to do' and 'the first and most important problem of philosophy' (1953: 1f).[3]

Moore also rejected the idea that philosophical analysis was linguistic analysis. Again, the crucial issue is the nature of philosophical analysanda. On the TC, AP began when Moore and Russell broke away from what was then the dominant school in the British universities, Absolute Idealism. When Moore and Russell articulated their alternative to Idealism they used a linguistic idiom, frequently basing their arguments on the 'meanings' of 'terms' and 'propositions'. However, from 1899 through 1910, Moore's views were much closer to the Platonic view of the standard Austro-German account than to the 'linguistic' view of traditional AP. Moreover, recent scholarship has shown that it is likely that Moore's early views were shaped by reading in that tradition (cf. Bell 1999; Milkov 2004). In fact, Moore's only significant variation on this general theme was to identify meanings/propositions with ordinary objects – tables, cats, people, and the like (cf. Baldwin 1990, 1991; Preston 2006a). This is a puzzling idiosyncrasy; still, it is clear that Moorean meanings/propositions from 1899 to 1910 are not linguistic entities.

By 1910, both Moore and Russell had abandoned this 'propositional realism'. Moore never devised a satisfactory, alternative account, and later came to exhibit uncertainty about exactly what his positive views about propositions were after 1910 (cf. Moore 1953: xii). However, he was quite certain that he never accepted the view that they were linguistic entities. Even at the end of 1910, Moore affirmed that 'I do *not* mean by a proposition any of those collections of *words* which are one of the things that are commonly called propositions. What I mean by a proposition is rather the sort of thing which these collections of words *express*' (1953: 57). He goes on to explain that a proposition is 'what is apprehended' with the mind, as opposed to what is heard with the ears, in, e.g., utterances of 'twice two are four' or 'twice four are eight' (57f).

Despite these clear statements to the contrary, Moore was widely understood to endorse a linguistic conception of analysis. This misunderstanding even found its way into the *Library of Living Philosophers* volume on Moore, where Norman Malcolm tied Moore's entire philosophical legacy to his 'linguistic method' (1942: 368; cf. 349). With characteristic humility, Moore was quick to count himself partially responsible for the linguistic interpretation of his work. 'I have often', he admitted, 'in giving analyses, used this word "means" and thus given a false impression' (1942b: 664f). Be this as it may, his was the lesser fault; for the non-linguistic nature of meanings/propositions would have been perfectly obvious to anyone familiar with the Austro-German view, or even with Moore's own early work on the nature of propositions (1899; 1953: ch. 3).

But apparently such familiarity was lacking in the populations among which the TC came to be. Thus, in 1942, Moore found himself having to correct the linguistic interpretation of his own work. 'In my usage', he insisted, 'the *analysandum must* be a concept, or idea, or proposition, and *not* a verbal expression' (1942b: 663f):

I never intended to use the word ['analysis'] in such a way that the *analysandum* would be a *verbal expression*. When I have talked of analyzing anything, *what* I have talked of analyzing has always been an idea or concept or proposition, and *not* a verbal expression; that is to say, if I talked of analyzing a "proposition," I was always using "proposition" in such a sense that no verbal expression (no sentence, for instance), can be a "proposition," in that sense. (661)

According to Moore, the analysis of a verbal expression, i.e., linguistic analysis, would involve dissecting the symbols out of which it was composed and noting their manner of combination:

consider the verbal expression "*x* is a small *y*." I should say that you could quite properly be said to be analyzing this expression if you said of it: "it contains the letter '*x*', the word 'is', the word 'a', the word 'small', and the letter '*y*'; and it begins with '*x*', 'is' comes next in it, then 'a', then 'small', and then '*y*'." (661)

This is precisely what the logical positivists did in their form of linguistic analysis. In calling philosophy 'the formal structure theory of the language of science', Carnap meant that philosophy was to be concerned with questions of linguistic form, i.e. questions about 'the arrangement and kind of symbols ... out of which a proposition is constructed, *without reference to the meaning* of the symbols and propositions' (1934: 56). By calling it 'the logical syntax of the language of science', Carnap meant that it should be concerned with questions about the proper application of the formation and transformation rules for the symbols of a language. This conception of analysis was inspired by the positivists' reading of Wittgenstein's *Tractatus*. Although that reading has come under fire from more recent interpreters, it cannot be denied a strong *prima facie* plausibility. And certainly in Wittgenstein's later work analysis is a matter of determining the proper use of symbols by observing how they are actually used in various contexts.

Moore, on the other hand, explained that 'I, when I talked of "giving an analysis," have never meant anything at all like this' and 'in my usage, both *analysandum* and *analysans* must be concepts or propositions, not mere verbal expressions' (1942b: 661 and 664). But even with this 1942 clarification in print, the linguistic interpretation of Moore persisted. Not even the 1953 publication of *Some Main Problems of Philosophy*, which contained the 1910 lecture cited above, was able to overturn this pertinacious error.[4]

Russell and the Linguistic Thesis

In the case of Russell, things are not so straightforward. Russell's views changed in significant ways over the course of his long career, and this makes it risky to label anything as Russell's 'official' view on a subject. Also, in some of his phases, Russell endorsed several traditional analytic views or at least came very close to doing so. At one point or another, he endorsed the views that:

(1) 'the essence of philosophy ... is analysis, not synthesis' (1914a: 113)
(2) philosophical analysis is logical analysis; and, in fact, 'philosophy ... [is] indistinguishable from logic' (1914a: 110)
(3) logical truths are linguistic/symbolic and tautological (1944a: 19; cf. 1959: 211f), and hence
(4) his own logical analyses were linguistic analyses (1944b: 691; 1944a: 14).

Taken together, these views imply the linguistic thesis. However, the inference is invalidated by the fact that either Russell did not hold all these views simultaneously or, if he did, this was only a brief period during one of the most significant transitions in his intellectual history – in which case they are better said to have accidentally overlapped than to have been explicitly *held* simultaneously.

Despite his evolving philosophical opinions on various topics, and in apparent or sometimes real contradiction to some of the above statements, at least three features of Russell's philosophical outlook remained fairly stable over the course of his long career, and are certainly representative of his later, mature views. These are: that philosophy is about the world and not language, that philosophical method involves analysis *and* synthesis or construction, and that propositions are not linguistic. It seems only right that these relatively stable patterns of thought and belief should carry more weight in determining 'Russell's views', and hence his relation to the linguistic thesis, than views he held only in passing.

Concerning the first point, Nicholas Griffin observes that 'one main task of philosophy, in Russell's view, was to provide a comprehensive account of the world consistent with the best scientific knowledge of the day'. 'This', he says, 'remained a constant in his philosophical career' so that, to a large extent, 'the various phases of Russell's philosophy develop out of each other as different attempts to carry forward a single philosophical project ... [namely,] to produce a system of the world' (2003: 18). Griffin's statement is accurate, but it requires careful qualification. The aim of producing a 'system of the world' sounds like the project of traditional philosophy described in Chapter 1 (and, indeed, Griffin compares Russell to Leibniz and Spinoza on this point), but Russell did not embrace *that* project during the period when he exercised his greatest influence on the development of AP (roughly 1905–1920). Specifically, by 1914, Russell had come clearly to reject the holistic and ethical aspects of the traditional philosophical project. This point comes through clearly and forcefully in his 1914 Herbert Spencer lecture, 'On Scientific Method in Philosophy', in which he dismisses as anthropomorphic projections the notions that there are facts pertaining to the universe as a whole and that some of these are ethical facts. 'The apparent oneness of the world', he says there, 'is merely the oneness of what is seen by a single spectator or apprehended by a single mind', while 'ethical metaphysics is fundamentally an attempt ... to give legislative force to our own wishes' (1914a: 99 and 107f). The latter he singles out as a very serious 'hindrance to progress in philosophy' (98; cf. 107).

Despite Russell's rejection of *the universe* as a possible object of study, he nonetheless took philosophy's subject matter to be reality, 'the world', rather than language or meaning. 'The scientific philosophy', he says, '... aims only at understanding *the world* and not directly at any other improvement of human life' (109, my emphasis). The world is distinguished from the universe in that, after the fashion of empiricists and positivists at least since Hume, the former is not to be understood as a genuine whole but as a collection of particulars (items, events, experiences or whatever), among some of which certain regular correlations obtain. Quoting William James, he says that the oneness of the world is a function of 'the fact that certain *specific and verifiable connections* are found among the parts of the experiential flux' (in Russell 1914a: 100).

Our experience of this 'world' is always partial – we only experience a limited number of particulars in their 'specific and verifiable connections'; hence our empirical knowledge remains partial as well. Projecting beyond experience by forming inductive generalizations about the universe as a whole, or even scientific 'laws' purporting to govern some region or *kind* of phenomenon in it, is mere speculation. And yet, we *can* have absolutely certain knowledge applicable equally to all particular existents. This knowledge comes from logic, whose laws tell us what is possible and impossible not merely in our world but for 'any possible world' (111; cf. 105). Russell explains this by delineating necessary features of philosophical propositions: they must be 'general' and 'applicable to everything that exists or may exist', not in the sense of 'being concerned with the whole of things collectively' but 'with all things distributively' (110f). This is, in a sense, knowledge of 'the whole world' – not, again, the world *as a whole*, as a thing in itself with properties of its own, but as the mere assemblage of all particulars.

For us, the crucial point is that Russell did not, in 1914, accept the view that philosophy was mainly or solely about language. However, in the interest of driving home the point that Russell's metaphilosophical orientation toward reality rather than language was indeed a stable feature of his philosophical outlook, it is worth noting that the distance between him and the traditional analytic line became even greater by the time AP as traditionally conceived had reached its zenith. In several pieces written between 1945 and 1964 (not all of them published during that period, however), Russell readmitted into his metaphilosophy the traditional ethical and speculative dimensions that he had rejected in 1914. To the end of his career, he endorsed a piecemeal approach to philosophical problems rather than holistic thinking in the full-blown sense of traditional metaphysics, as well as the view that 'much interesting philosophy was due to errors of syntax' (1946: 77); however, in the mid 1940s we see Russell giving wider scope to the range of legitimate philosophical problems, and yoking philosophy's metaphysical orientation to an ethical goal in the indissoluble unity of a single philosophical task. The man who in 1914 had insisted that philosophy 'cannot take account of ethical notions' because this would turn it 'aside from that submission to fact which is the essence of the scientific temper' (1914a: 109) had by now given up the idea that philosophy ought to be scientific in this way, and could say that 'philosophy differs from science ... by the fact that it is occupied with knowledge as a whole, and with the bearing of our knowledge upon questions concerning values' (1945a: 221). 'The philosopher', he explains,

> ... seeks to understand the world as far as possible, not only because he values understanding, but also because he is anxious to find out ... how far desire and fact are capable of being harmonized. Is there, within the limits of possibility, a way of living which would make most men happy? Is there ground for hope that such a way of living will be realized at some future time? (220)

His earlier confidence in the adequacy of scientific knowledge, or at least scientific method, for guiding human life had been shaken by two world wars, the failure of the Russian revolution, and the growing threat of nuclear holocaust. 'When I was young', he observed in 1946,

I supposed, ignorantly, that if people were shown quite clearly the road to general happiness, including their own, they would take it. I did not allow enough for that power of hatred and envy, which turns men's thoughts rather to bringing about the misery of others than to achieving their own welfare. (73)

The superior level of intelligence, knowledge and skill that modern man had achieved through the sciences had not been matched by a corresponding moral advance, with the result that human 'wickedness [was] more effective than at any former time' (75). Far from being our salvation, science itself had become 'the cause of our fears' (1964: 461). What was needed, Russell now saw, was 'not more [scientific] intelligence, but less destructive passions', so that we might 'learn to regard mankind as a unity, not as a collection of warring nations and creeds' (1946: 75). 'The education of desire through wisdom and discipline' (1945a: 221), as Russell described it, is the common task of traditional philosophy and the world's great religious traditions – albeit pursued by somewhat different means. But Russell distrusted religion. Hence the task fell to philosophy, which he now saw as a *via media* between science and religion/theology – respectively, Russell's archetypes for definite but value-free knowledge and deluded ignorance masquerading as knowledge. Philosophy was to accomplish this task by cultivating 'the tolerant spirit which comes of realizing the difficulties and uncertainties of what may seem like well-grounded beliefs, and the evils that result from the blind strife of rival dogmatisms' (1945b: 233). Seeing the scientific and technological advances of the mid twentieth century as sufficient to ensure physical well-being for all – if only they could be properly handled – 'nothing stands in the way' of human flourishing, said Russell, 'except the human passions of pride, envy, and hatred. These remain to be overcome. It is the duty of the philosopher to do what he can to bring about this last triumph' (1964: 461).

Assigning philosophy this task requires a very different metaphilosophy than the one Russell endorsed in 1914. Instead of seeking certainty and precision in all things, philosophy was now to teach us 'to learn to live without certainty, and yet without being paralyzed by hesitation' (1945a: 221). Philosophy, he now believed, 'must take account of possibilities and hypotheses in regions where no definite knowledge is attainable by science' (221). Here he stands in vivid contrast with ideal-language philosophy, particularly in the form of logical positivism. Speaking of 'the recently developed technique of exact [i.e., logical] analysis', he says,

It is held by a certain school of philosophy ... that this technique should henceforth be considered to be the whole of philosophy; but if philosophy is essentially concerned with what is speculative, it should not even be a part of philosophy, any more than the art of making lenses is part of astronomy'. (1945b: 225f)

It may be that the school Russell had in mind here was logical positivism specifically, and not ideal-language philosophy or AP in general. This is unimportant, however, for the actual point of disagreement fits all these possibilities equally well. But a parallel statement from the following year suggests that it is not just logical positivism that he had in mind, but ideal-language philosophy *in specie*:

Out of consideration of the [logical] paradoxes a whole new kind of philosophy has developed: the philosophy that concerns itself with logical syntax, with semantics, and with the condition that a sentence must fulfill if it is to be significant. ... There are some who maintain, in their enthusiasm for this new study, that all the old stock problems of philosophy arise from attributing significance to nonsense. I cannot agree with this point of view .... (1946: 72)

This captures the Wittgenstein of the *Tractatus* as well as the logical positivists, and so the full line of ideal-language approaches. Widening the circle even further, in a 1956 review of Urmson's *Philosophical Analysis*, Russell put all forms of linguistic philosophy – hence AP *in specie* – in his crosshairs. Again, the point of contention was Russell's view that philosophy is about the world rather than language. He begins by rejecting the ordinary-language branch of AP, especially as practiced by the later Wittgenstein (whom he here calls 'WII'):

In common with all philosophers before WII, my fundamental aim has been to understand the world ... But for WII I should not have though it worth while to state this aim, which I should have supposed could be taken for granted. But we are now told that it is not the world that we are to try to understand but only sentences, and it is assumed that all sentences can count as true except those uttered by philosophers. (1956: 615)

This much is not surprising, as Russell's opposition to 'the cult of common usage' is well known. However, Russell is usually presented as objecting to it merely or mainly because of its triviality – as he once put it,

'to discuss endlessly what silly people mean when they say silly things may
be amusing but it can hardly be important' (1953: 612). His more fundamental objection, however, was that it rejected 'the desire to understand
the world' as 'an outdated folly'. 'This', he said, 'is my most fundamental
point of disagreement with' the adherents of WII (1956: 616).

This objection applies not only to ordinary-language philosophy, but
also to ideal-language philosophy; thus, in the 1956 review, he shifts his
critique seamlessly from the one to the other:

> There is a curious suggestion, already to be found among some of the
> Logical Positivists, that the world of language can be quite divorced
> from the world of fact. ... Some Logical Positivists – Neurath and
> Hempel, and Carnap at one time – maintained explicitly that sentences
> must not be confronted with fact. They maintain that assertions are
> compared with assertions, not with experiences, and that we can never
> compare reality with propositions. (615)[5]

He then compares himself with these two main strands of AP on what
he calls the 'justification' of empirical statements: for him, this was a
matter of their 'relation to facts'; for the positivists, of 'conformity to
syntactical rules'; 'but the adherents of WII do not bother with any kind
of justification, and thus secure for language an untrammeled freedom
which it has never hitherto enjoyed' (616). The point of the comparison
is to emphasize his contempt for ordinary-language philosophy. However,
it also shows that the logical positivists were with 'WII' on the side of
linguistic philosophy, while Russell stood over against them on the side of
'reality philosophy'. And, indeed, while Russell always remained friendly
toward the ideal-language side of AP, this was only on account of their
rigor and very much *despite* their purely linguistic view of philosophy.[6]

For Russell, then, the point of philosophy is to produce a 'system of
the world'. It is as a means to this end that *analysis* enters into Russell's
metaphilosophy, as an element of proper philosophical method. To make
analysis a means to an end is not, of course, to say that it is inessential
to the task of philosophy, but only that it is not identical to it. Though
essential, it is only a part; not the whole. In fact, analysis is not even
the whole of Russell's philosophical method, let alone the whole of
his metaphilosophy. Rather, his mature and stable view is that analysis
must be coupled with synthesis (construction) in serving the end of a
scientifically informed 'system of the world' (cf. Hager 2003: 312). As he
himself once put it, 'the business of philosophy ... is essentially that of
logical analysis, *followed by logical synthesis*' (1924: 162, my emphasis). Thus

Paul Hager speaks of 'the two-directional character of his [Russell's] philosophical method' (2003: 311; cf. Klement 2005): first, via analysis, we move downward, toward the more fine-grained, or in logical terms, backward toward fundamental premises; then, via synthesis, we move upward, toward the more coarse-grained, or rather forward toward new conclusions or 'results'. The synthesis step gives philosophy the ability to 'enlarge the domains of particular subjects' (Hager 2003: 313; cf. 322) like mathematics and physics by enabling us to adopt 'fresh lines of advance after our backward journey' (Russell 1919a: 2).

Hager rightly observes that 'this capacity of the synthesis stage to expand knowledge needs emphasizing, since it has usually been overlooked' (2003: 312). Russell himself probably contributed to this situation by frequently using 'analysis' as shorthand for the whole bi-directional method. But, whatever the causes, overlooking the role of synthesis in Russell's method is precisely what was required in order to see Russell as accepting the linguistic thesis and falling under the TC; for under them, as we have seen, 'the analytic philosopher ... is not one who learns new truths' but only provides us with 'clearer knowledge of facts already known'. Thus it is important to note that, balancing Russell's sometimes exaggerated claims about the significance of analysis, there are passages in his corpus that seem to elevate synthesis more highly. For instance, he once said that scientific philosophy's most important feature was its ability 'to invent hypotheses [about the world] which, even if they are not wholly true, will yet remain fruitful after the necessary corrections have been made' (1914a: 113). Clearly, this constitutes a radical departure from the linguistic thesis.

Just as radical a departure is the fact that, insofar as analysis was a significant part of philosophical method, it was not *linguistic* analysis. Though Russell did say once that 'all sound philosophy should begin with an analysis of propositions' (1900: 8), this cannot be taken too strictly since, as Peter Hylton notes,

> any given conception of propositions and analysis, is ... inextricably tangled in metaphysics. The idea of 'finding and analyzing the proposition expressed' by a given sentence is one that makes sense only within a given philosophical context, which imposes constraints on the process; the philosophical context cannot itself, therefore, be based on a neutral or uncontroversial notion of analysis. (1996: 183)

As we have already seen in Chapter 5, talk of analysis requires an account of analysanda, and simply labeling them 'propositions' is not sufficient

– one has to specify their nature. Even in 1900, when Russell made his statement about beginning with analysis, he had a definite theory about their nature in mind. Since about 1898, Russell had held a view in essence the same as Moore's quasi-Platonic 'propositional realism' (cf. Griffin 1998: 11f; 2003: 20f). Thus, in 1903, Russell explained that:

> ... a proposition ... does not itself contain words; it contains the entities indicated by words. Thus meaning, in the sense in which words have meaning, is irrelevant to logic. But such denoting concepts as *a man* have meaning in another sense: they are, so to speak, symbolic in their own logical nature, because they have the property which I call *denoting* .... (47)

As it was with Moore, Russellian propositions are not linguistic but are what we might describe as Ideal states of affairs whose constituents are ordinary objects and the relations among them. Moore called these constituents of propositions 'concepts', but Russell called them 'terms'. This makes it sound as if they're linguistic, but they are not. Griffin explains: 'terms are neither linguistic nor psychological, but objective constituents of the world. Concepts, universals, complexes, concrete and abstract particulars, physical objects, and mental states are all terms' (2003: 20).

Just as terms and propositions are not linguistic, so the sort of meaning relevant to logic (and hence philosophy) is not linguistic meaning. Rather, it is the sort had by concepts (a kind of term) in virtue of their having the property of *denoting*. Denoting has often been taken to be a relation between *linguistic* entities and the things that *they* are about. However, as we saw above, Russell insists that denoting has to do with something's being symbolic in its own logical nature, that it is 'a logical relation between some concepts and some [other] terms, in virtue of which such concepts inherently and logically *denote* such terms' (1903: 53). The fact that denoting is an inherent relationship between concept-terms and the object-terms that they are *about* shows that denoting is not the contingent relationship that a linguistic symbol bears to the thing it symbolizes. Instead, it is more like the intentionality of what some have called 'natural signs' (cf. Addis 1989). This view is carried over into Russell's seminal essay 'On Denoting' (1905). As Ray Monk has noted:

> at the very center of his argument in 'On Denoting' is a rejection of the notion that language is the subject of the philosopher's inquiry. The pivotal step in his notorious 'Gray's Elegy' argument, for example, is

his discounting of the notion that the meaning of definite descriptions might be 'linguistic through the phrase'. His assumption, here, is that, as logicians, we are simply not interested in linguistic meaning, but rather in the purely logical relation that he calls 'denotation'. (1996a: 5)

This is significant, for the theory of descriptions that Russell develops in 'On Denoting' is commonly accepted as an example of linguistic analysis at its finest, resolving philosophical problems through the analysis of sentences.

It is true that Russell thought the grammar of ordinary language could be philosophically misleading, and that close attention to the grammatical structure of language was an indispensable guide for philosophical analysis. From the *Principles of Mathematics* come the oft-quoted lines: 'The study of grammar ... is capable of throwing far more light on philosophical questions than is commonly supposed by philosophers' and 'on the whole, grammar seems to me to bring us much nearer to a correct logic than the current opinions of philosophers' (Russell 1903: 42). But this is only because:

> every word occurring in a sentence must have *some* meaning ... [and thus] the correctness of our philosophical analysis of a proposition may ... be usefully checked by the exercise of assigning the meaning of each word in the sentence expressing the proposition. (42)

Thus it is quite clear that – like Frege – Russell took himself to be dealing ultimately with the propositions expressed in language rather than the bits of language in which propositions were expressed. At most, one can say that 'language is inescapably the medium through which philosophical analysis engages with matters that are non-linguistic' (Hager 2003: 328). As Griffin observes, 'this is certainly as close as Russell got to taking the linguistic turn' (1998: 13).

Another respect in which Russell may seem to have come close to taking the linguistic turn was his reluctant conversion, around 1913, to Wittgenstein's views on the nature of mathematical and logical truth – namely, that they are linguistic/symbolic and tautologous.[7] This 'linguistic turn' is what stands behind Russell's later admissions that he was wrong in having originally taken himself to be doing ontological work via logical analysis. For example, Russell at one point acknowledged that his original definition of 'types' in the theory of types was wrong 'because I distinguished different types of *entities*, not *symbols*' (1944b: 691; cf. 1944a: 14).

Such analyses, he came to believe, did not directly reveal truths about the world, nor even about language as such, but about what could be dropped from natural language if, for technical purposes, one wanted to create an artificial 'language' using as few symbols as possible. Thus, whereas he thought he had been studying the world, Russell's Wittgensteinian conversion convinced him that he had only been studying 'minimum vocabularies', vocabularies in which no term could be defined in terms of any of the others. It is only in the context of this project of constructing minimum vocabularies that Russell speaks of the logical analysis of *language* (1944b: 687f).

So, this was a linguistic turn of sorts, but it was not *the* linguistic turn – the acceptance of the linguistic thesis. Ultimately, Russell's linguistic turn seems to have remained limited to mathematics and logic; though there may have been a period during which it was uncertain that it would remain localized in these areas. Accepting that logical truth was linguistic saddled Russell with an inconsistent triad of beliefs: if logic is the essence of philosophy and logic is about language, how could philosophy still be about the world? Something had to give, and initially it may have appeared that Russell was willing to sacrifice his traditional metaphilosophical outlook to his new views about the nature of logic. For instance, Russell titled the second of his 1914 Lowell lectures (published as *Our Knowledge of the External World*), 'Logic as the Essence of Philosophy', and in the final paragraphs of the book affirmed that 'the study of logic becomes the central study in philosophy: it gives the method of research in philosophy just as mathematics gives the method in physics' (1914b: 259). Thus, his commitment to the centrality of logic and logical analysis seemed strong as ever, and given that his Wittgensteinian conversion was at that point certain, it would seem to follow that he had rejected the view that philosophy was about the world.

And yet 1914 was also the year of 'On Scientific Method in Philosophy', in which, as we have seen, Russell maintained that philosophy is about the world rather than language. And, in fact, the very same view is clearly represented in *Our Knowledge* ... when he affirms that 'what [philosophy] can do' via its logical method 'is to help us to understand the general aspects *of the world* and the logical analysis of familiar but complex *things*' (1914b: 18f, my emphasis). Thus, he says, 'it offers, in its own domain, the kind of satisfaction which other sciences offer' and 'by the suggestion of fruitful hypotheses, it may be indirectly useful in other sciences' (ibid.). As we saw earlier, Russell's view was that philosophy was to be a matter of logical analysis and logical synthesis leading to knowledge of the world. How could this be, given his linguistic turn?

Part of the answer, it seems, is that Russell was doing his best to make good on his social commitments while he contemplated how best to move forward. There can be no doubt that 'Wittgenstein's onslaught' (Russell 1968: 57, quoted in Stevens 2005: 108) took a tremendous toll on Russell, both intellectually and emotionally. In a letter to Ottoline Morrell, he describes it as shattering his philosophical impulse 'like a wave dashed to pieces against a breakwater', and as filling him with 'utter despair' (ibid.). And yet, he had already committed to give the Lowell lectures. Thus, he explains to Morrell,

I *had* to produce lectures for America, but I took a metaphysical subject although I was and am convinced that all fundamental work in philosophy is logical. My reason was that Wittgenstein persuaded me that what wanted doing was too difficult for me. (ibid.)

Thus, Graham Stevens describes Russell's conversion as leaving him in an 'awkward situation' in response to which he simply 'steered clear of the question' of the nature of logic (2005: 108). Like Descartes adopting his provisional code of ethics before launching himself in to systematic doubt, so Russell more or less stayed the philosophical course he had already set for himself in previous years while he puzzled over how best to pull out of the intellectual tailspin caused by 'Wittgenstein's onslaught'.

Another part of the answer is that, although Wittgenstein had shown logical truth to be linguistic, he had not shown meaning itself to be a mere matter of symbols. Though the *Tractatus*, which presents Wittgenstein's thought at this time, does endorse the linguistic thesis (in 4.0031, etc.), it also endorses the so-called 'picture theory' of meaning. A significant (meaningful) proposition is a 'logical picture' of the facts that constitute (some part of) the world in the sense that the *structure* of the proposition is identical to the *structure* of the corresponding state of affairs in the world. Thus, meaning is a matter of structural isomorphism between language and reality. But the nature of the 'logical forms' upon which the isomorphism depends is highly mysterious. As Wittgenstein saw it, they were somehow involved in language and the world but transcended both. Their natures could not, like theoretical entities in science, be elucidated by description – by definition, logical forms were the foundations for the 'picturing' relations between language and the world; hence they could not also ground picturing relations between language and themselves. Thus, as Wittgenstein put it, logical forms cannot be *said*, but only *shown* in sentences or states of affairs exhibiting them. And, since sentences purporting to be about meaning are not about any empirical state of affairs, but about logical form and the 'picturing' relation themselves, such sentences are, strictly speaking, meaningless. Hence the puzzling remarks in *Tractatus* 6.54:

> My propositions are elucidatory in this way: he who understands me finally recognizes them as senseless, when he has climbed out through them, on them, over them. (He must so to speak throw away the ladder, after he has climbed up on it.) He must transcend these propositions, and then he will see the world aright.

Thus Wittgenstein saw the joint emphases on meaning as picturing and on logical form as leading philosophy toward a kind of mysticism in which the ultimate grounds of meaning were ineffable.

This aspect of the theory was not sufficiently recognized by his contemporaries, however. As a consequence, the logical positivists developed an influential misreading of the *Tractatus* that took its theory of meaning to be purely linguistic (cf. Ayer 1982: 111). Such an interpretation did not even occur to Russell, as he was committed to a world-oriented metaphilosophy. This also would have inoculated him against Wittgenstein's mysticism, if he had recognized it.[8] Guided by his unshaken belief that philosophy must give us knowledge about non-linguistic reality, Russell went in search of an alternative way of developing the picture theory of meaning. By 1918, he had found his alternative: rather than turn to linguistic symbolism or mysticism, he turned to psychology. In his 1918 lectures on 'The Philosophy of Logical Atomism', Russell averred:

> I think that the notion of meaning is always more or less psychological, and that it is not possible to get a pure logical theory of meaning, nor therefore of symbolism. I think that it is the very essence of the explanation of what you mean by a symbol to take account of such things as knowing, of cognitive relations, and probably also of association. At any rate I am pretty clear that the theory of symbolism and the use of symbolism is not a thing that can be explained in pure logic without taking account of the various cognitive relations that you may have to things. (1918a: 186)

A year later, Russell gave a more detailed account of meaning in terms of cognitive relations. Specifically, he defended a view according to which linguistic meaning is grounded in mental images. Propositions, at this stage in Russell's career, are treated as *the contents of beliefs*; and they can be expressed either in words or images, in the form of what he calls word-propositions and image-propositions. 'As a general rule', he says, 'a word-proposition "means" an image-proposition' (1919b: 308); i.e., it is a sign for an image-proposition. An image-proposition, on the other hand, is a sign for a thing: 'some images mean particulars and others mean universals' (303).

Russell defended this view again in a 1920 *Mind* symposium with Schiller and Joachim. There he says: 'meaning, in my view, is a characteristic of "signs," and "signs" are sensible (or imaginal) phenomena which cause actions appropriate, not to themselves, but to something else with which they are associated' (Russell 1920: 402). The association of imaginal (psychological, mental) sign with meant object is facilitated by resemblance: the image, in virtue of its own intrinsic properties, resembles the object it means – a non-mystical mode of 'picturing'. The association of sensible sign (word) with meant object, on the other hand, is mediated by the imaginal sign. Sensible signs in language have no intrinsic relation (resemblance) to what they mean. Through a process of habituation, Russell argues, sensible signs come to be associated with objects and the imaginal episodes which accompany our experiences of objects. Eventually the sign comes to participate in 'mnemic causation': in virtue of the psychological faculty of memory, sensible signs can come to have some of the same causal powers had by their meant objects. For example, hearing the name of a favorite pet might cause some of the same things to happen on the part of the hearer that the presence of the pet might cause.

Michael Dummett characterizes the linguistic turn as a way of grounding the anti-psychologistic stance of late nineteenth-century logic without resorting to Platonism (1993: 131). Russell had held a psychological view of meaning prior to his turn to Platonism (cf. Russell 1894, esp. 196–97). Having now been divested of his Platonism, Russell reverted to psychologism rather than accept the linguistic thesis. He retained this psychological view of meaning for the rest of his life, affirming in 1940 that 'words are not essential to propositions' (1940: 189), and confessing in 1944 that 'the more I have thought about it, the less convinced I have become of the complete independence of logic' (1944a: 14).[9]

This last line gives us some clarity as to how Russell finally dealt with the inconsistent triad of beliefs facing him after his linguistic turn. Ultimately, rather than sacrifice his view that philosophy was about the world, Russell backed away from his view that logic was the central study of, let alone the essence of, philosophy. Since logic was merely symbolic, its connection to meaning had to be explained by studies in psychology and, Russell thought, physiology. As Ray Monk puts it, 'logic had been shown to be essentially symbolic, and therefore fairly trivial: what remained was to theorize – psychologistically – about symbolism itself' (1996a: 8).

Its symbolic nature rendered logic 'trivial' in part because, as we saw earlier, this reduced logical analysis from an ontological tool to an exercise in the construction of minimum vocabularies, and, as Russell saw it, facts about minimum vocabularies had at best a limited and vague application to the genuine philosophical task of understanding the world. 'Minimum vocabularies', he observed in 1944, 'are more instructive when they show a certain kind of term to be indispensable than when they show the opposite' (1944a: 14). Russell illustrated this with the fact that 'no vocabulary can dispense wholly with words that are more or less of the sort called "universals"', though 'probably we could be content with one such word, the word "similar"' (ibid.). 'The fact that we need the word "similar"', he says, 'indicates some fact about the world, and not only about language', but 'what fact it indicates about the world, I do not know' (ibid.). Thus, as Monk observes, 'the lesson he took from this [i.e., his "linguistic turn"] is not that philosophers should now seek to analyze sentences, but rather that logic did not have, after all, the philosophical significance he had earlier attached to it' (1996b: 56).

In sum, then, Russell was at odds with the linguistic thesis, and hence with AP on the TC, in consistently maintaining (1) that philosophy was about the world rather than language, (2) that philosophy requires synthesis as well as analysis, and (3) that propositions, or at least meanings,[10] are not essentially linguistic.

The *sine qua non* of the Illusion of Unity

We have now seen that three canonical analysts, all of whom are frequently taken to be *founders* of AP itself, did not accept the linguistic thesis. And yet under the illusion of unity, they were portrayed as accepting it. In order for this illusion to take hold in someone's mind, one would have to fail to take proper stock of the ways in which Frege, Russell and Moore departed from the linguistic thesis. Such failure might be the result of ignorance, it might be the result of judging the departures to be so insignificant as to warrant ignoring them, or it might be caused by something else; but, one way or another, these departures had to be neglected for the illusion of unity to have its effect.

It is entirely possible that the explanation for this neglect might vary from case to case. For instance, while some among the rank and file may have been ignorant of these points, it seems unlikely that those near the center of the movement would have been. Likewise, it is easier to imagine ignorance of these issues in later-generation analysts, whose whole philosophical experience and education were shaped by an already dominant AP, than it is to imagine in earlier-generation analysts, whose experience and education would have been more likely to transcend the boundaries of AP as they, and it, came to be. So, some may have been ignorant of the issues. But the more interesting possibility is that some might have judged these departures to be too insignificant to matter – just the opposite of what a traditional philosophical outlook would judge. In fact, there is evidence that this actually happened on a fairly wide scale. An examination of this evidence will move us one step closer to finding the root cause of the illusions of unity and promise, and hence of the TC.

The most obvious case comes from a 1963 essay by Peter Strawson. Strawson was unquestionably aware that there was considerable divergence of opinion among core, canonical analysts over the nature of philosophical analysanda. He even notes that the way they are characterized seems to have implications for the nature of philosophical analysis, and hence (under the linguistic thesis) of philosophy itself: 'analysis of sentences … suggests the grammarian; analysis of thoughts or beliefs, the psychologist; and analysis of statements, perhaps the policeman or the advocate' (98). Astonishingly, however, after noting these differences and their *prima facie* metaphilosophical implications, Strawson dismisses them as unimportant and affirms that the unity of AP is grounded in the unanimous practice of *linguistic* analysis:

> It does not matter much … [what we say the objects of analysis are], … Maybe it is best to say, as Moore always said, that the objects of analysis were *propositions*. This answer, whatever its shortcomings, emphasizes, without over-emphasizing, *the linguistic nature of the enterprise, the preoccupation with meaning.* (98, my emphasis)

This passage is astonishing in several respects. As we have seen, there are at least three ways to characterize propositions and meanings: as Ideal, as psychological, and as linguistic. Not only do non-linguistic approaches outnumber the linguistic approach two to one, those two also have a much broader representation than the linguistic in the history of philosophy. Moreover, by 1963, both Russell and Moore had been fairly outspoken in their opposition to the linguistic interpretation. For these reasons, Strawson should not have so easily assumed an obvious connection between propositions and linguistic meaning, or between meaning *as such* and language. Why, then, did he?

Even more astonishing, perhaps, is his explicit mention of Moore in connection with the linguistic view of propositions. This statement was made a decade after Moore's 1910 lecture was published (in 1953), and more than two decades after his emphatic 1942 repudiation of the linguistic view. These explicit repudiations in conjunction with Moore's original, quasi-Platonic conception of propositions/meanings should have been adequate to prevent a statement like this one. Why were they not?

We need not speculate about the causes of Strawson's apparent oversights, or about how or why he attributes the linguistic view of 'propositions' and 'meanings' to all analysts without a second thought. He himself reveals the *how* and the *why* immediately upon the heels of the above statement. 'It does not matter much ... [what we say the objects of analysis are]', he says,

> For, however we describe the objects of analysis, particular analyses ... always *looked* much the same. A *sentence*, representative of a class of *sentences* belonging to the same topic, was supposed to be elucidated by *the framing of another sentence.* (98, my emphasis)

Deliberately ignoring what are now coming to be seen as substantive philosophical differences among the early analysts (for these are the very things that have caused the fall of the TC), Strawson focuses completely upon the empirical – in this case *visual* – features of the expression of particular analyses, which happened to consist in superficially similar patterns of (mostly linguistic) behavior and their symbolic components and products. Only by emphasizing these features of the *practice* of analysis and the *expression* of analyses while simultaneously de-emphasizing the theoretical disagreements lurking just beneath them could Strawson hope to justify his claim that linguistic analysis was the common analytic method.

Strawson was not alone in this. Nearly all the statements surveyed in Chapter 2 and Chapter 3 exhibit the very same pattern of glossing over Frege's, Moore's and Russell's departures from the linguistic thesis and hence from the TC; and several of them combine this with an emphasis on the empirical over the ideational or theoretical aspects of analysis. We will re-examine some of these here, for a closer inspection focusing on the parts here italicized will help us to see this pattern of emphasis and de-emphasis, and thereby to understand the root cause of the illusion of unity.

First, Urmson. As we saw in Chapter 3, after noting in more general terms than Strawson the fact of diversity among analytic philosophers, Urmson nonetheless says that they were united at least in the *view* that analysis was at least one of the most important tasks of the philosopher; and by analysis, they meant something which, *whatever precise description of it they chose*, at least involved the attempt to *rewrite* in different and in some way more appropriate terms those *statements* which they found philosophically puzzling. (1956, vii, my emphasis)

These 'precise descriptions', of which Urmson is so dismissive, surely would have included the analysts' respective takes on the nature of philosophical analysanda, as well as Beaney's 'modes' of analysis (see p. 42), and the role Russell ascribed to synthesis in his overall method of 'analysis'. However, Urmson glosses over these substantive philosophical disagreements only to focus on the overtly linguistic aspects of analytic practice and expression: the *rewriting* of philosophically puzzling *statements*. Insofar as there was a common method of analysis, he implies, this was it; thus, like Strawson, Urmson arrives at a linguistic conception of philosophical analysanda, philosophical analysis, and AP itself by focusing on the empirical features of the practice rather than the ideas that informed it and constituted it a method.

Similarly, Warnock – who is otherwise very good at teasing out the differences among the analysts – makes a statement that fits this pattern of emphasis and de-emphasis. As we saw in Chapter 3, he claims that the analysts all held 'the *view* that the day-to-day labors of the philosopher consisted overwhelmingly in the *analysis of language*', specifically the analysis of '*statements* of fact' (1958: 57f, first and last italics added). Like Strawson and Urmson, Warnock illustrates 'the commonly accepted *notion* of "analysis"' (58f, my emphasis) by describing the empirical features of the expressions of particular analyses:

> The search for philosophical analyses always *took the form* of an attempt to formulate a sort of *linguistic equation*. On the *left* of the equation was to be the expression to be analyzed, and on the *right* another expression, usually *longer* and more explicit, designed to be synonymous with or equivalent to the first.... (59, my emphasis)

Here, the focus is on analysandum and analysans as linguistic entities with spatial extension and standing in spatial relations, hence most likely in the form of written language, visual symbols – just as with Strawson and Urmson.

Several times now I have said that the pattern under consideration is one of emphasizing the empirical and de-emphasizing the ideational. This is not entirely correct, however, for the authors cited as exemplifying it do allow *some* ideas to stand alongside the empirical features they highlight. Both Urmson and Warnock explicitly say that the analysts have a 'view' in common: respectively, that analysis was at least one of the most important tasks of the philosopher, and that the day-to-day labors of the philosopher consisted overwhelmingly in the analysis of language. Warnock also says that they had a common 'notion' of analysis. Thus, the aversion to views or ideas seems to be selective. In fact, the move away from the ideational and toward the empirical is made only when the ideas in question might be taken in a robustly metaphysical direction. They allow the linguistic thesis (a *view* or *notion*) to be articulated, but the kinds of views that might be expressed in response to questions about the nature of philosophical analysanda – ideas that might have to do with propositions construed as Ideal or mental entities – are assiduously avoided. When such questions arise, or if one is pressed to prove 'the linguistic nature of the enterprise', the pattern is called into play. Following the pattern, we avoid the realm of theory altogether and focus on the empirical, where we are limited to what Willard earlier described as words – and, by extension, propositions, analysis, and even (under the linguistic thesis) philosophy itself – in 'the only philosophically unmuddled sense ... [, namely,] that in which words [etc.] are simply one subset of physical objects and events'. In practice, this is how the pattern functioned. Thus, it is fundamentally a pattern of emphasizing the empirical over the *metaphysical* rather than just the ideational, and particularly of emphasizing the empirical aspects of language over its (potentially) robustly metaphysical aspects.[11]

This pattern, or rather the mentality behind it, is the root cause of the illusion of unity. There are several names that apply equally well or badly to it: three of them are 'empiricism', 'positivism' and 'naturalism'. These terms have been used in a variety of ways in the history of philosophy; but, in the modern period, their principal versions have been inspired by a common ideal: modern science. Thus, as Charles Taylor has noted, the focal sense of 'naturalism' nowadays has to do with the view that 'nature ... is to be understood according to the canons which emerged in the seventeenth-century revolution in natural science' (1985: 2). The same could be said for the focal meanings of positivism and empiricism: overwhelmingly, the variations on these themes in the modern era have been stimulated by the idealization of the emerging empirical/natural/ positive/physical sciences (as they are variously called) as setting the standard for knowledge. Consequently, they can all be seen as manifestations of a *scientistic drive* in modern thought. Thus, we will add 'scientism' to our list of terms for the mentality behind the illusion-generating pattern of emphasis and de-emphasis, and we will use it as an umbrella term capturing the empirical, positivistic and naturalistic aspects of the pattern.

The claim, then, is that this scientistic mentality is the root cause of the illusion of unity, and hence of the illusory TC. For the moment, we leave open the question of *how* the scientistic mentality played this role, and insist only that, regardless of *how* it played that causal role, *that* it did makes it part of the explanation for AP's pre-baptismal rise. Of course, a complete explanation of AP's peculiar career requires that we specify the *how* of its role, and also that we explain the illusion of promise. It will turn out that scientism explains this other illusion as well, and hence comes as close as anything to being the fundamental *explanans* of AP's peculiar career. In the next chapter, we will explore the shape of scientism in turn-of-the-twentieth-century Britain. This will give us insight into the connection between scientism and the illusion of promise, and into the manner (the *how*) of scientism's role in both it and the illusion of unity.

Chapter 6

The Root of the Illusion of Promise

The Scientistic Thesis

One of the most commonly made observations about AP is that it appears to have some deep and abiding connection to modern science.[1] This observation is usually inspired by the prevalence of scientistic tendencies within the analytic tradition, both on the individual and the corporate levels. The implicit suggestion, if not the explicit claim, is usually that *scientism* – the view that knowledge can be obtained best or only via the methods of modern science – is what has primarily animated the analytic tradition; that the best explanation for the prevalence of these tendencies is that scientism bears a systemic relation to AP, pervading the analytic tradition *as such* and hence as a whole. I will call this *the scientistic thesis*.

Scientism is *Not* a Defining Doctrine

In thinking about how a view like scientism could be systemically related to a philosophical school, it is most natural to think in terms of *defining doctrines*. These are views that, taken together, define a philosophical school, and that one *must* accept in order to belong to it – they are individually necessary and jointly sufficient conditions of membership. If scientism was a defining doctrine of AP, this would *ipso facto* make it a systemic feature of the school: because one could not be an analyst without accepting it, it would necessarily pervade the school.

Perhaps because this is the simplest and most obvious way for a view to be systemically related to a philosophical school, most claims stating or approximating the scientistic thesis are interpreted this way by those who seek to refute them. For instance, Brian Leiter attempts to refute Bruce Wilshire's characterization of AP as given to scientism with the sarcastic retort that the latter is 'apparently unaware of the dozens of major, self-described "analytic" philosophers who are critics ... of scientism in its various forms (Alvin Plantinga, George Bealer, John McDowell,

Hilary Putnam, Thomas Nagel, etc.)' (Leiter 2002).[2] Of course, it is *clearly* not the case that every analytic philosopher explicitly accepts or has accepted scientism. Even in the early to middle periods of AP, there are clear cases of analysts who rejected scientism, either explicitly or implicitly (in practice). Avrum Stroll and Hans-Johann Glock point to the philosophers of ordinary language and/or common sense – Moore, the later Wittgenstein and the 'Oxford school' – as counter-examples to the scientistic thesis (Stroll 2000: 1ff; Glock 2004: 430f). In fact, Glock argues that not even the early Wittgenstein can be read as endorsing a scientistic view of philosophy. And, as Glock observes, 'a definition of analytic philosophy that excludes not just Wittgenstein but also Moore and Oxford philosophy is a nonstarter' (431), thus the scientistic thesis must be wrong.

It is true that a definition which excludes core, canonical analysts is hopelessly flawed. Stroll and Leiter also must assume this in their refutations – otherwise their tactic of refutation by counter-example would not work. But they must also assume that they are refuting the claim that scientism was/is a *defining doctrine* for AP; and this assumption, unlike the first, is on shaky ground. As indicated above, the fact that many analysts did not and do not personally endorse scientism is so obvious that it would be foolish to propose it as a defining doctrine of AP; thus it is no surprise that most statements or approximations of the scientistic thesis stop short of doing this. What they do, rather, is to note features or patterns within AP that are highly suggestive of scientism. Except for the occasional incautious remark, they do not assert that all analysts endorse scientism or that it is a defining doctrine of the school.

Let's consider a few examples. First, in Wilshire's case, he clearly announces that 'rather than the old standby of attempting to define by adducing necessary and sufficient conditions ... I will try a kind of ostensive procedure' by pointing to 'actual instances of the "analytic" habit of mind' (2002: 2). And this is exactly what he does. By reflecting upon concrete cases that he (rightly or wrongly) takes to be illustrative of *characteristic* analytic views, attitudes and practices, Wilshire demonstrates that 'there is an analytic habit of mind that tends to pinch down the fullness of experiencing', and which 'diminishes fullness, weight, and sustaining presence of the world experienced by us and ... of our own experiencing selves' (17). This he reasonably takes to be a symptom of a scientistic orientation in AP itself.

Second, David Cooper has observed that 'analytical philosophy has generally proved ... friendly and sympathetic to science':

Where the traditional ambitions of philosophy have appeared to conflict with the claims of science, the response has typically been sanguine acceptance of a reduced role for philosophy – as conceptual analysis, the logic of scientific theory, or whatever. Beyond this, it has often been the explicit aim to provide analyses which will accommodate apparently recalcitrant phenomena to the scientific understanding. Tarski's 'scientific semantics' is scientific not only in the sense of 'exact', but in that of bringing semantics, through its elimination of intensional notions, into 'harmony with the postulates of the unity of science and of physicalism'. Behaviorism and materialism in the philosophy of mind, and the various breeds of 'anti-cognitivism' in ethics, have been motivated by a similar quest for harmony. (1993: 10)

Cooper makes an important observation which, although it is a digression from our main point, will be profitable to consider briefly since it will help to clarify what might count as a scientistic view of philosophy. His opening line notes that wherever science has advanced, philosophy has retreated. This is a manifestation of scientism that sometimes gets overlooked in the debate about scientism and AP. Glock's argument that the early Wittgenstein rejected scientism provides an example. The metaphilosophy of the *Tractatus*, Glock says, 'rejects ... scientism, the imperialist tendencies of scientific thinking which result from the idea that science is the measure of all things. Wittgenstein insists that *philosophy* cannot adopt the tasks and methods of science. There should be a *division of labor* between science and philosophy's second order reflection on our conceptual apparatus' (Glock 2004: 431). Glock argues as if making philosophy into a science is the only move allowed by scientism. But this cannot be right, since the refusal to make philosophy into a science is also perfectly consistent with scientism, so long as this disqualifies philosophy as a field of knowledge. One way to state the thesis of scientism is to say that x is a field of knowledge if and only if x is a science, where a science is a field that studies some region or aspect of the world, some range of phenomena, by means of a certain method called 'scientific'. Thus understood, scientism allows for two options *vis-à-vis* any academic discipline: either it is both a science and a field of knowledge or it is neither. To insist that 'philosophy cannot adopt the tasks and methods of science' is to take the latter option. And, indeed, the *Tractatus* view of philosophy is not only that it is not a science, but that it is not a field of knowledge: it tells us nothing about 'the world', does not contribute to or expand knowledge, but only clarifies knowledge we already possess. Thus it remains connected to and has a role in 'the knowledge business', but not as a field of knowledge – rather as 'a janitorial service for science' (Solomon 1999: 221). Altering the traditional scope and methods of philosophy to show that it is *not* a science is no less a manifestation of scientism than altering them to show that it *is* one.

Returning now to our main point, Cooper does not say that scientism was a *view* accepted by all analysts. His observation concerns the fact that *other* views, aims, methods and practices, adopted by a *significant number* of analysts – enough to make them *characteristic* of the movement – overwhelmingly exhibit a pattern of amenability to scientism. Like the pattern of emphasis and de-emphasis observable in some earlier analysts' characterizations of their school and its method, this suggests a scientistic bias, and perhaps even an underlying commitment to scientism; but Cooper stops short of claiming that scientism was a defining doctrine of AP.

All the most promising statements and approximations of the scientistic thesis are like this – they draw our attention to certain patterns and tendencies in AP that seem to suggest a significant background role for scientism; but they refrain from making it a defining doctrine since it so obviously is not. Thus, John McCumber approximates the scientistic thesis when he claims that AP originally and overwhelmingly 'excluded ... forms of inquiry that appeal to nonscientific criteria of validation, such as faith, tradition or aesthetic insight' (2001: 49).[3] Similarly, Pascal Engel observes that more recent AP 'mimics the scientific style of inquiry, which proposes hypotheses and theories, tests them in the light of data, and aims at widespread discussion and control by the peers' (1999: 222). Like Wilshire and Cooper, McCumber and Engel do not say that scientism was a *view* accepted by all analysts; in fact, they say nothing about views at all. Their observations are about analytic *practice*; and what they say, in essence, is that it is/was such as to offer no offense or challenge to scientism. Especially in McCumber's case, what he notes is that there is an observable pattern of acceptance and rejection or avoidance in the realm of analytic practice that suggests a scientistic bias. But, while it is natural to suppose that practice, especially philosophical practice, takes its cues from theory, he does *not* say that scientism was a defining doctrine for AP.

At this point, it should be clear that, frequently, when something like the scientistic thesis is proposed, it is not proposed as the claim that scientism was or is a defining doctrine for AP; thus, the second assumption behind it is quite false, and is best counted as an instance of the straw-man fallacy. At the same time, it *is* a challenge to see how scientism could be systemically related to AP without being a defining doctrine. Thus, the proponents of the scientistic thesis have an obligation to go beyond noting suggestive patterns, tendencies and habits by explaining exactly *how* scientism plays its systemic role in AP; and that is what I will now attempt to do.

The Cognitive and the Non-Cognitive in Science, Culture and Philosophy

The fact that scientism fails to be a defining doctrine for AP should come as no surprise, since, as indicated in Chapter 2, there seem to have been *no* defining doctrines for AP at any point in its history. This, combined with the fact that AP was initially presented by its practitioners as having a defining doctrine and was received as such by its adherents at large is the basis for the illusionist thesis. Under that thesis, the focus of historical research on AP shifts. Instead of looking for its 'real' defining doctrines, we will accept that there never were any, and hence that AP was never a philosophical school (or movement or tradition). Though AP was born in a revolution conducted by a movement that inspired a tradition all in the context of academic philosophy, AP is not a philosophical entity in the relevant sense. This fact liberates us from the need to explain it in philosophical terms. As a non-philosophical, more purely *social* entity, it may be explained in non-philosophical, more purely sociological terms. And this opens up new avenues for explaining the systemic role of scientism in AP.

Neil Levy (2003) takes a step in the right direction when he argues that AP functions and develops ('reproduces') much as Kuhnian 'normal science' does, and thus that a formal analogy exists between the two. 'Normal science' is a way of operating – in science or, by analogy, some other discipline – that depends on paradigms and exemplars rather than rational insight into first principles or foundational assumptions. Paradigms, according to Kuhn, are 'universally recognized scientific achievements that for a time provide model problems and solutions to a community of practitioners' (1970: viii). A solution to a problem becomes a paradigm when a sufficient number of practitioners in some community of inquiry agree that it is overwhelmingly successful, and when they see the success as mainly following from the views and methods that contributed directly to the solution rather than from luck or individual genius. As a result, the community seeks to abstract those views and methods and apply them to similarly structured problems, perhaps in different areas, to achieve similarly structured – and similarly successful – solutions.

Thus Levy observes that 'acceptance of a paradigm is simultaneously the acceptance of an ontology and a methodology' (2003: 292). But, then, to accept a paradigm is to adopt a dogmatic posture that is out of step with traditional philosophical ideals and aspirations. As Levy puts it, the adoption of a paradigm 'puts an end to debate about fundamentals' (292) thereby allowing practitioners to get on with the work of problem-solving *within* the paradigm.

Paradigms, then, provide clusters of background assumptions constraining such things as the selection of worthwhile problems or questions as well as acceptable solutions or answers to them. 'Good' problem-solution combinations are those judged to be sufficiently similar to the paradigm case. These similar 'concrete problem-solutions' (Kuhn 1970: 187) are 'exemplars'; they serve as models of work *within* the paradigm by exemplifying how the relevant features of the paradigm-case can be abstracted and applied to other problems. Because exemplars are logically posterior to paradigms, they 'need not be shared by the scientific [or other disciplinary] community as a whole' (Levy 2003: 294). By contrast, a paradigm must be, since, for all practical purposes, it is definitive of the discipline as a whole so long as it remains its paradigm. In fact, belonging to the discipline or the disciplinary community is determined in essentially the same way that 'good' problem-solutions are: by judging their similarity to the paradigm. If a practitioner's methods and aims are similar enough to those prescribed by the paradigm, then he is a member of the community, and his work is work of the discipline.

What Levy suggests, then, is that AP is the result of some community of philosophers having taken the work of Frege and Russell as a paradigm (2003: 293). Taking this 'paradigmatic turn' (295) altered the shape of philosophy not only in the obvious sense that the specific content of the paradigm began to shape philosophical practice as philosophers began to try to emulate it, but also in the sense that operating under a paradigm *at all* was a departure from traditional philosophical practice. One of the aspirations of traditional philosophy is to have no unexamined assumptions, to be 'presuppositionless'. Even if this goal is in the end unachievable, the mere attempt to achieve it requires that continual attention be paid to the theoretical foundations of one's practices not merely as a philosopher, but as a human being. This is implicit in the Socratic mandate to live an 'examined life', and it is part of what makes second-order reflection on the nature and methods of philosophy – i.e. metaphilosophy – part of philosophy itself. Since this is so, philosophy cannot take any paradigm for granted the way normal science does. As Levy puts it, 'philosophy cannot follow the normal sciences and leave its own foundations unexamined;

not, at least, without ceasing to be philosophy' (2003: 300). And yet, AP does seem to have taken an unphilosophical 'paradigmatic turn' insofar as it 'tends to channel its students away from' such reflection 'and in the direction of work on its puzzles' (300) – puzzles that fit within the Frege–Russell paradigm.

Now, it may be questioned whether Levy has identified the correct paradigm, since it is hard to see how the work of Frege and Russell could have served as a paradigm for the ordinary-language side of AP (though it must be admitted that all the problems currently taken to be at the 'core' of AP are problems that fit that paradigm). Still, Levy is on to something in his more general suggestion that AP is the result of some community of philosophers modeling philosophy on normal science by making it a thing of inquiry under paradigms and exemplars rather than a thing of reflection upon ultimate foundations. We will seek to develop this idea here.

First, we note that normal science, in the abstract, is not something that could easily be taken as a model. Rather, it would be by modeling itself on a particular instance of normal science, on science during one of its normal periods, that AP came to function as a normal science. Second, we note that to model a discipline on a particular instance of normal science *just is* for that discipline to adopt the paradigm definitive of that instance. Fundamentally, the dynamic of 'modeling' would be no different from what goes on within an instance of normal science as scientists attempt to apply the going paradigm to an ever expanding range of problems. Modeling philosophy on an instance of normal science would simply be an extension of this effort beyond the recognized disciplinary boundary of (a particular) science itself, into the realm of problems customarily associated with *another* discipline: philosophy. That is, this 'modeling' would have to take the form of an attempt to make philosophy 'scientific' according to the paradigm of a certain period of normal science. Thus, third, we note that this 'modeling' suggests a fundamental role for scientism as the primary ideational motivation for the paradigmatic turn that founded AP.

Fourth, we note that making scientism an explanation for the adoption of a *paradigm* explains how it could be systemically related to AP without its being a defining doctrine. One of the things true of paradigms but false of defining doctrines is that neither they nor the reasons for adopting them have to be explicitly recognized, understood and accepted in order to play their role. Although *instituting* a paradigm requires cognitive awareness and acceptance of some set of views by a community of inquiry, once a tradition of inquiry is established under a paradigm its *preservation* does not usually require a continued awareness of any of its founding ideas. As Levy says, 'once a paradigm is accepted, the scientist [or philosopher] can simply assume it: she does not have to rehearse previous findings, nor need she defend much of her methodology' (2003: 294). Instead, a community of inquiry need only conduct its work in accordance with the methodology their paradigm prescribes. Eventually, reinforced by habit, the practices involved will take on the character of a Wittgensteinian 'form of life' in which the practices themselves become relatively automatic and self-perpetuating. At this point, the ideational content of the paradigm can be ignored, even forgotten, and yet the paradigm itself will be sustained through its historical, causal connection to those living practices, which are themselves sustained largely by non-cognitive mechanisms.

Indeed, not even *initiation* into such a form of life will require a cognitive grasp of the ideational principles that originally informed the paradigm, much less the original reasons for adopting it. Instead, transmission of the paradigm to new members of the community takes place via a well-attested mechanism called 'norm conformism'. The *conformist transmission* model of social learning (introduced by Boyd and Richerson 1985) claims that, as a result of natural selection, human beings simply 'possess a propensity to preferentially adopt the cultural traits that are most frequent in the population' (Henrich and Boyd 1998: 219), where 'most frequent' means 'most common' in some specified, local population. This propensity is not, in the usual case, something of which humans are fully aware; rather, it guides human behavior without announcing itself. Conformist transmission operates via various mechanisms of direct social learning, together glossed as *infocopying* (Henrich and Gil-White 2001: 172ff). This includes not only the imitation of behaviors at the mechanical level, but also the ability to infer and emulate the goals toward which those behaviors are directed. In fact, the 'imitation' involved in infocopying need not take the form of the simple parroting of behavior, but can take more subtle forms of emulation, such as sliding one's political opinion along a continuum so that it is brought closer to that of an admired model.

Sociologists have identified at least two forms of conformist transmission. One of these, *norm conformism*, is a matter of adopting the most common *interactional* practices in a given population. This enables a person to maximize the probability of well-coordinated interactions with others, something that, on average, is necessary for various forms of social success. Norm conformism plays an important role in generating and maintaining social boundaries by facilitating the preservation and transmission of various sets of social norms that function as principles of inclusion and exclusion for various sorts of human groups or communities. The sorts of norms transferred by norm conformism essentially involve other people – they are *interactional* practices. Consequently, if an individual was to discover a way of interacting with others that was intrinsically superior to the existing interactional norms in his community (for instance, discovering that one can celebrate a young woman's coming of age by means of something like a *quinceanera* rather than by so-called 'female circumcision'), he would not be perfectly free to institute a change on his own. In changing his own interactional behavior, he would run the risk of being misunderstood, of offending people's social sensibilities, being perceived as a 'renegade', and thus of ending up a social outcast or worse. For this reason, the items transmitted by norm conformism tend to be quite resistant to change. This stability makes them suitable for grounding the unity of various human collectivities, and hence for serving as principles of inclusion and exclusion for them. And, once such a collectivity comes into existence, norm conformism is sufficient to preserve its unique culture by preventing deviations and socializing new members to the majority norms.

Taking the idea of Kuhnian paradigms and normal science together with that of norm conformism, we can explain how a view might bear a systemic relationship to a community of inquiry *without* all or even any of its members so much as grasping it, let alone endorsing it: (1) A variety of views and motives will be operative in the adoption-context of any paradigm, *within* the paradigmatic problem-solution, *behind* it, in the problem-solution progenitor's mind, and *behind* its adoption as a paradigm, in the minds of those who take it as a model. (2) Once established, a Kuhnian paradigm prescribes a method, and hence certain norms of practice within the community. Because inquiry in the sciences is cooperative and cumulative, the method of inquiry and its practices will be interactional in nature, and will be preserved and transmitted via norm conformism. Thus, (3) once those practices have been established as a 'form of life', the founding views in and behind the paradigm and its adoption may drop completely out of sight *without* hampering the preservation of those practices. But (4) those founding views will forever maintain a connection to the paradigm, not only historically, but also in the qualitative shape of the form of life itself. The views become, as it were, *fossilized* in the practices themselves, so that they and only they will be the *true* explanation for why the form of life is the way it is.

The fossilization of the cognitive in the non-cognitive, of views in practices, occurs not only at the level of the whole (the disciplinary community), but repeats itself microcosmically at the level of the parts (individual members). When its individual members acquire the community's practices, they thereby take the paradigm's fossilized founding-views into themselves. This connection will not remain limited to the form of habits of external practice. Rather, acquisition of the practices will naturally ramify into the development of attitudes and even explicit views *about* them, usually at least to the effect of 'this is how it is done'. Thus, at the individual level, the fossilization of the paradigm will be reinforced by what Van Fraassen calls a 'stance': 'a cluster of attitudes, including propositional attitudes (which may include some factual beliefs) as well as others, and especially certain intentions, commitments, and values' (2004: 128), inclining the individual toward the preservation of those practices.

In this way, at both the corporate and individual levels, the cognitive elements in and behind a paradigm and its adoption become fossilized in non-cognitive processes and states. But these non-cognitive phenomena are inherently fossils *of* those original cognitive phenomena. Thus a paradigm's founding views, those in and behind it and its adoption, remain logico-historically connected to the communal form of life and the individual stances and habits of practice the paradigm inspires, despite the latter's non-cognitive nature. Since this is so, and since, on this account, the correct explanation for the existence of a paradigm and its associated non-cognitive phenomena (form of life, habits, stances) terminates in its founding views (and motives), there is a sense in which we can speak of the latter, and particularly the *views*, as 'presuppositions' of the former. Here I am suggesting that we follow Collingwood who, anticipating Kuhn by more than two decades, spoke not of 'paradigms' but of 'absolute presuppositions' (1939: 65–67; 1940: ch. 4). For Collingwood, 'absolute presuppositions' are fundamental assumptions not only of sciences and other academic disciplines, but also of cultures or epochs in human history. Like the views in and behind a paradigm and its adoption after it is well-established, 'absolute presuppositions' are not, in the usual case, explicitly and consciously endorsed. However, they can be brought to light. In fact, according to Collingwood, this is the special business of metaphysics – to root out and describe the absolute presuppositions of some group or epoch.[4] The language of 'presuppositions' emphasizes the ideational character of these ultimate, explanatory entities, and also the logical or quasi-logical aspect of their relation to the paradigm/form of life/characteristic stance.

The proposal, then, is that AP came about through an attempt to model philosophy after science in one of its normal periods, and that scientism, as *a* if not *the* principal ideational factor behind this paradigmatic turn, is a founding assumption, an absolute presupposition, not only of work *within* the analytic tradition, but, more importantly, of the very *existence* of the tradition itself. In this way, scientism will be systemically connected to AP, understood not as a philosophical system, but as a social system founded *by* and hence in some sense *upon* scientism.

The Paradigmatic Turn: When and Why?

We cannot here trace the manifold ways in which work in AP exhibits scientistic tendencies. This has been admirably done elsewhere,[5] and in any case would not speak directly to the *systemic* relation of scientism to AP. Instead, it would reveal only another suggestive pattern. What we seek is the explanation for the existence of so many scientism-suggesting patterns within AP, and especially the pattern of emphasis and de-emphasis behind the illusion of unity. The ground covered in the section above gives the answer in the abstract. But now we must try to make it more concrete by locating the moment of the paradigmatic turn in actual history, by linking the emergence of AP to some specific period of normal science. Levy does not do this for us. Thus, he does not explain why or when the paradigmatic turn occurred. Consequently, as he himself admits, though his proposal 'has the virtue of accounting for a number of the characteristic features' of AP, it 'is not yet a fully satisfying explanation' since 'to achieve that, we need to go further, and explain why [AP] took the paradigmatic turn' (2003: 296). But this can only be explained by discovering *when* it took that turn, for the appeal of the normal-science paradigm for that period will give us the *why*.

Our task is made easy by the fact that the TC points us to the turn of the twentieth century, and easier still by the fact that Russell, in a short historical essay from 1928, specifically locates the origins of what became AP in the context of a wider and more general drive toward a scientific philosophy. There, he divides the philosophical world of the early twentieth century into three main factions: the adherents of classical German philosophy (Kantians and Hegelians), the pragmatists and Bergson, and a group he loosely calls the 'realists'. Although the origins of the realist movement date back to the last quarter of the nineteenth century, Russell chooses as a convenient inaugural event the revolt against Idealism which began around 1900. Against the Idealist background, he says, this realism stood out as a new and revolutionary philosophy.

Based on this description alone, a contemporary reader might suppose that Russell is using 'realism' as a name for what eventually became known as AP. After all, the revolt against Idealism is the very event in which Moore and Russell's move toward AP is generally supposed to have begun. This impression would be strengthened by Russell's description of the realists as being 'characterized by analysis as a method' (1928: 267). However, it is clear that he has in mind a much broader movement than the one ordinarily designated by the name 'analytic philosophy'. Among the realists, Russell counts James, Frege, Husserl, Meinong, Moore, himself, Couturat, and the American New Realists. The primary unifying characteristic of what Russell called 'the new philosophy' of the realists was that:

> it abandons the claim to a special philosophical method or a peculiar brand of knowledge to be obtained by its means. It regards philosophy as essentially one with science, differing from the special sciences merely by the generality of its problems, and by the fact that it is concerned with the formation of hypotheses where empirical evidence is still lacking. It conceives that all knowledge is scientific knowledge, to be ascertained and proved by the methods of science. (1928: 268)[6]

Russell here recounts as an event in actual history an occurrence of exactly the kind of 'modeling' that Levy hypothesized. And, as we predicted, scientism itself was operative in the modeling; for the view 'that all knowledge is scientific knowledge, to be ascertained and proved by the methods of science' is the heart of scientism.

Why was there such a widespread interest in making philosophy scientific? And according to what paradigm was the attempt proceeding? The second question is easy to answer. The paradigm of Newton's work, especially in his triumphant theory of universal gravitation, was the paradigm for science until the advent of Einsteinian relativity and quantum mechanics in the early twentieth century – and even then certain methodological features of the Newtonian paradigm were retained, and still are, though they have been weakened somewhat by later twentieth-century developments in the philosophy of science. A full answer to the first question would require its own book, so all I can hope to do here is to give it in outline. Fortunately, many very good books have been written on the subject, and the outline that I will give relies heavily upon them.[7] In general terms, the answer is to be found in the fact that, as Wilfred Sellars once remarked, 'the most difficult task of philosophy has always been to define itself in meaningful ways' (1974: 4). Difficult as self-definition always may have been, it had become even more difficult by the turn of the twentieth century, when, in addition to being philosophy's most difficult task, it became its most pressing task as well. As we shall see, the new exigency and increased difficulty attaching to self-definition were precipitated by the rise of the modern sciences in general and the emergence of experimental psychology in particular.

The Newtonian Paradigm and the Scientistic Drive of Modernity

A large part of the story of philosophy, especially Anglo philosophy, from the late medieval period on, is the story of the development and influence of the experimental method of knowledge which eventually became the distinguishing mark of modern science. By the close of the seventeenth century, the experimental method had achieved no small success in 'explaining' the phenomena of the natural world. At that time, the progression of scientific thought which began with the *via moderna* of the late medieval period and continued in the work of the natural philosophers of the early renaissance period and then of Copernicus, Galileo, Brahe and Kepler, came to a sort of culmination in the work of Newton (cf. Cohen 1960).

In Newton's work, we have for the first time in the history of science a breakthrough that is not only intellectual but cultural. The saga of modern science's struggle to gain legitimacy under the oppressive rule of tradition is well-known. Though there were many significant intellectual achievements prior to Newton, the activities of the modern scientists (or 'natural philosophers' as they were called until the late nineteenth century) were viewed with suspicion – or, at best, puzzled curiosity – by British and European culture at large. This all began to change with Newton, who, as E.A. Burtt has observed, 'enjoys the remarkable distinction of having become an authority paralleled only by Aristotle to an age characterized through and through by rebellion against authority' (1932: 201f). The extent to which he was held not merely in respect but in awe by his contemporaries, near-contemporaries, and later generations can only be fathomed by tracing the extent to which his work was taken as a paradigm not only in the developing sciences, but even in what we would now consider the humanities – indeed, our familiar disciplinary divisions did not exist at the time, and came about mainly through the attempt to model all putative fields of knowledge on Newtonian physics. According to Harry Prosch, 'the general attitude' among Newton's contemporaries and succeeding generations was that 'the great man had broken the ground, that he had in fact shown us where and how the foundations of heaven and earth were laid'. As a result:

> Those who were to come after him ... had now only to follow faithfully the method by which he had succeeded so well in uncovering these foundations. Their tasks were understood simply to consist in building upon these foundations, of filling out the picture, spinning out the consequences, and going on to the analysis of other natural forces than those of inertia and gravitation, as he had advised – and in the way that he had advised. (1964: 68)

Though he does not use the term, Prosch is describing the adoption of Newton's work as a paradigm. But, because our contemporary disciplinary divisions did not exist, to take Newton's work as a paradigm *for science* was *ipso facto* to take it as a paradigm for knowledge *as such*; and, in light of the subsequent division(s) between the sciences and the humanities, we can say this produced a drive toward *scientism* in all putative fields of knowledge. As Prosch goes on to say:

> as time went on more and more men everywhere came at length to suppose this 'scientific' or 'experimental' method to be the method of acquiring knowledge – so much so that the conviction became stronger and stronger that what could not be known by the use of this method was not a fit subject for knowledge at all. (1964: 77)

Consequently, to understand the Newtonian paradigm is to understand the constraints placed upon knowledge-in-general in post-Newtonian Britain.

Many interesting examples and anecdotes could be used to illustrate the contours of the Newtonian paradigm; however, considerations of space prohibit this approach. Instead, I will simply list its main features. The Newtonian paradigm mandated:

(1) That the *objects* of knowledge should be (a) sense perceptible, (b) quantifiable, and thus (c) analyzable into 'atoms' which would serve as correlates of mathematical units, and (d) calculationally determinable;
(2) That the method should (a) be grounded in careful, empirical observation, (b) exhibit mathematical precision and certainty, and thus (c) involve a calculational technique, and (d) be analytic, discovering the basic realities or atoms which will correspond to calculational units.

(3) That pieces of knowledge or 'scientific *truths*' should (a) involve *no* speculative 'hypotheses' but be grounded entirely in empirical observations, (b) be expressed in the form of a mathematical equation relating the quantifiable aspects of observable phenomena, involving *no* reference to the qualitative structures of things. (c) have some practical, preferably *predictive*, use, and (d) be of a kind that could be built upon by later thinkers, and thus form part of a cumulative body of knowledge.

Under the Newtonian paradigm, these features became not exactly *requirements* but *ideals* or *desiderata* for knowledge, so that any bit of purported knowledge, the method by which it was acquired, and the object(s) about which it claimed to be, had to at least approximate a great many, if not all, of these ideal features in order to be taken seriously.[8]

With the bulk of intellectual effort directed toward emulating this paradigm, not only in Britain but throughout the Western world,[9] the possibility of using *other* methods to acquire knowledge and the need for a philosophical grounding of the scientific method itself were increasingly ignored.[10] Notwithstanding attempts, like those of the Continental Rationalists, to suggest that the empirical sciences needed a firm philosophical grounding in a system of *a priori* metaphysics, and attempts, like Hume's, to show that there were disturbing epistemic problems latent in scientific method (especially with regard to its reliance upon sense-perception, causal relations and induction), Western culture at large was swept away in the direction of the Newtonian paradigm under a haze of naïve optimism; hence the drive toward scientism in modern thought.[11]

The Newtonian Paradigm and the *Method* of Philosophy

The first step toward AP was, of course, Moore's and Russell's revolt against British Idealism. In Moore's case, the revolt was motivated by his concern for common sense, but his main point of attack had to do with the distinction between thought and object in the act of consciousness (cf. Preston 2006a). For Russell, the main motive and focal issue is usually taken to be the logic of relations. Important as these issues are both in their own right and to the emergence of AP, neither one is the catalyst that caused the movement to crystallize. Not even Russell's later work in logic, from 'On Denoting' through *Principia Mathematica* played this role. But for the scientistic, and more specifically *positivistic*, pattern of emphasis and de-emphasis that enabled the illusion of unity to arise, these and other developments in early twentieth-century British philosophy never would have been seen as coalescing into a single approach to philosophy, hence there would have been no AP such as in fact emerged.

It is of no little significance, then, that positivism was an overwhelming presence in Britain at the turn of the twentieth century. Although Idealism was then the orthodoxy in British academic philosophy, Carré rightly describes its tenure as a 'brief interruption' in the otherwise steady emergence of 'a distinctive British method and doctrine' in philosophy (1949: ix f). Carré has in mind the British empirical tradition broadly construed – a tradition which, by the late nineteenth century,[12] had come to be seen as tracing a path from Bacon and Hobbes through Locke, Berkeley, Hume, Hartley, and on to the Mills.[13] Common to all these figures and forming the core of the tradition, at least as its late nineteenth-century representatives understood it, was an epistemological outlook that today is usually called 'empiricism', but which, in mid- to late-nineteenth-century Britain was just as likely to be called *positivism*.

The term 'positivism' was popularized by the Frenchman Auguste Comte, who used it as a name for his philosophical and religious system. However, it also names a general philosophical outlook centered on the view that human knowledge is limited to the objects of sense-experience and the relations among them. Comte's most famous view is perhaps his 'law of three stages', according to which human understanding passes through three successive stages of development: the theological, the metaphysical, and the positive. These stages are distinguished by the type of *explanans* characteristic of each: in the theological stage, supernatural agents; in the metaphysical stage, abstract essences or natures. In the positive or scientific stage, however, 'the mind has given over the vain search after absolute notions, the origin and destination of the universe, and the causes of phenomena, and applies itself to the study of their laws – that is, their invariable relations of succession and resemblance' (Comte 1969 [1830]: ch. 1). It is this view of knowledge that characterizes positivism in the general sense, and it is clearly implied in items (3a) and (3b) of the Newtonian paradigm.

Positivism in this general sense was present in British thought well before the Newtonian revolution, but during and after that revolution it became increasingly pervasive. It bears an obvious resemblance to the view of knowledge developed in the British empirical tradition, especially in its Humean form; but the explicit formulation of versions or approximations of the view by Bacon, Hobbes, Locke, Berkeley, Hume and the Mills was just the tip of a much larger cultural iceberg. The majority of British empiricists/positivists are forgotten to the history of philosophy because they were practitioners rather than theorists, working in the educated professions such as medicine, law, religion and politics. For instance, Locke's ideas about knowledge were strongly influenced by his co-worker in the employ of Lord Ashley, the physician Thomas Sydenham. Unlike other physicians of his day, Sydenham was content to correlate ailments with effective cures on the basis of experience and observation, without trying to understand why the cures worked – the very model of what would later come to be called 'empiricism' and 'positivism' (cf. Zimmer 2004: 243–46).

A moment ago I said that positivism became increasingly pervasive in post-Newtonian British thought. Although true on the whole, it is curiously false of English academic philosophy. In the early volumes of *Mind*, there appear a series of articles describing the recent and present states of philosophy in the major British universities and in a few select areas outside of Britain. Henry Sidgwick's contribution reveals that Cambridge was very much in the clutches of the *zeitgeist* during the post-Newtonian era. By the first quarter of the nineteenth century, 'the official recognition of [metaphysical and moral] studies had dwindled to the merest shadow of a shade … . Philosophy had, for all practical purposes, lost its old place in the Cambridge scheme of studies; and a new place had not yet been found for it' (Sidgwick 1876: 236). The things closest to philosophy that went on in that setting were discussions of methodology; but, Sidgwick notes, a training in mathematics and physics rather than in traditional philosophy was the standard preparation for taking part in such controversies. In fact, mathematics and physics came almost completely to take the place of philosophy at Cambridge. Sidgwick notes that a peculiarly English use of 'philosophy' as synonymous with 'physics' had been 'especially at home at Cambridge since the time of Newton' (237). From Newton's time until the first decade of the nineteenth century, the philosophical curriculum at Cambridge consisted only of Locke and Paley – both 'scientific' philosophers. After that, however, interest in philosophy proper seemed to disappear entirely, in favor of the continually growing interest in mathematics and philosophy-as-physics, on the one hand, and classics on the other.

Testing practices at Cambridge reflected the diminution of interest in philosophy proper. By around 1830, students in mathematics and the sciences were exempted from writing exams in philosophy: 'the traditional papers on "Locke and Paley" were, for the first time, avowedly constructed for the πολλοι [i.e. the common people] only: whose brains not being burdened with mathematics were supposed to have room for a modicum of moral reflection' (Sidgwick 1876: 241). By 1839, they were abolished entirely. That same year, Whewell began to lecture on moral philosophy, thereby maintaining at least a spark of more traditional philosophizing at Cambridge. However, moral philosophy at Cambridge was, for a long time, to wear what Sidgwick describes as a 'badge of inferiority' (242) as compared with mathematical and classical studies. On the whole, he says, the course of study at Cambridge generated interest in 'hypothetical extensions of physical explanations' and a preference for 'exactness of method and certainty of results in comparison with breadth and completeness of view' (245) – the same attitude that would later come to characterize AP.

It is clear from this portrait of Cambridge that philosophy as a unique field of knowledge was struggling for survival. This picture is reinforced in Mark Pattison's description of philosophy at Oxford as having 'no substantive existence of its own' but being only 'an appendage of our classical training' (1876: 90). W.R. Sorely was later to marvel at this negative assessment, since British Idealism was thriving at Oxford during this period:

> the first few years of *Mind* do not adequately reflect what was yet the fact that the type of thought inspired by Kant and Hegel was at the time among the most living forces in English philosophy. It had attracted a number of the most distinguished teachers and in some of the universities had captured the ablest students. It is astonishing that in the first number of *Mind*, in an article on Philosophy at Oxford, Mark Pattison could speak of 'the present stagnation of philosophical thought among us'. (1926: 413)

However, Pattison's neglect of the Idealists makes sense when one recognizes that he was judging the scene by the standards of the Newtonian paradigm. Although Idealism may have been thriving, the philosophical training it afforded was not, as he thought it ought to have been, 'intellectual discipline, not training in investigation, in research, in scientific procedure, but in the art of producing a clever answer to a question on a subject on which you have no real knowledge' (1876: 89). Pattison's lament, therefore, is not that philosophy had no presence at Oxford, but that such philosophy as they had did not proceed by the method prescribed by the Newtonian paradigm. This is not a biased judgment, for it was affirmed by Idealism's adherents as well. H.S. Holland wrote of Idealism's first appearance at Oxford in the person of his teacher, T.H. Green:

Oxford lay abjectly imprisoned within the rigid limitations of Mill's logic. Individualistic sensationalism held the field. Life was to be reduced to mechanical terms. Scientific Analysis held the key to the universe. Under this intellectual dominion we had lost all touch with the Ideals of life in Community. There was a dryness in the Oxford air, and there was singularly little inspiration to be felt abroad. We were frightened; we saw everything passing into the tyranny of rational abstract mechanism ... Then at last, the walls began to break. A world of novel influences began to open to us. Philosophically the change in Oxford thought and temper came about mainly through the influence of T.H. Green. He broke for us the sway of individualistic Sensationalism. He released us from the fear of agnostic mechanism. He gave us back the language of self-sacrifice, and taught us how we belonged to one another in the one life of high idealism. We took life from him at its spiritual value. (in Carpenter 1959: III, 483f)

Thus, both its proponents and its opponents agreed that Idealism was non-scientific and anti-scientistic; they disagreed only about whether this was a virtue. And it was because Pattison saw it as an unparalleled vice that he refused to acknowledge it as contributing one whit to the vitality of philosophy at Oxford.

Meanwhile, the British empirical tradition continued to develop outside the universities and other institutions of the cultural 'establishment'. In the nineteenth century, its leading figure was John Stuart Mill, and its positivistic bent is underscored by the readiness with which Mill and his fellows embraced Comte and his early system (before its religious aspects became apparent). Mill was the first of a British group of Comtist (as they were frequently called) sympathizers that came to include G.H. Lewes, the young Alexander Bain (founder of *Mind*), George Grote, George Holyoake, George Eliot and Harriet Martineau, who would become Comte's first English translator. Many of this group established personal contact with Comte in the 1840s through correspondence and reciprocal visits, and they even provided him with financial support when he fell on hard times in 1844. All along, Mill and Lewes used their connections with the press to make Comte known to the British populace. As a result, his views became well-known in Britain, and, despite the fact that none of these figures endorsed the religious side of Comte's philosophy, a small number of Positivist churches sprang up (though they met with little success).

It was over the religious aspects of his system that Comte's relationship with his British sympathizers began to turn sour. Toward the end of

his life, Comte became increasingly concerned with the religious side
of his system, insisting that his bizarre 'Religion of Humanity' was an
indispensable part of the only genuine system of scientific philosophy
– his own. As a result, he became more a cult-leader than a scientific (or
scientistic) philosopher. But, like the British populace at large, he found
his erstwhile sympathizers unwilling to accept his 'scientific' religion.
Thus it came to be that Martineau expressed the common sentiment of
the group when she insisted that she accepted the '"positive philosophy"
not as the "particular scheme propounded by any one author" but as the
"philosophy of fact", of empirical science in general' (Wright 1986: 67).
Thus it became clear that Comte's British sympathizers were positivists
but not Positivists, agreeing with Comte only on what Mill calls 'the
fundamental doctrine of a true philosophy':

> We have no knowledge of anything but Phaenomena; and our knowledge
> of phaenomena is relative, not absolute. We know not the essence,
> nor the real mode of production, of any fact, but only its relations to
> other facts in the way of succession or of similitude. These relations
> are constant; that is, always the same in the same circumstances. The
> constant resemblances which link phaenomena together, and the
> constant sequences which unite them as antecedent and consequent, are
> termed their laws. The laws of phaenomena are all we know respecting
> them. Their essential nature, and their ultimate causes, either efficient
> or final, are unknown and inscrutable to us. (1965 [1865]: 6)

This is precisely the positivism made requisite by the Newtonian
paradigm – a fact not lost on the science-minded in Comte's home
country of France. Comtean Positivism had done better on its native soil
than it had in Britain; but even there its totalizing character encountered
resistance, especially after Comte took his 'religious turn'. Thus, in his
1877 report on the state of philosophy in France, Théodule Ribot distinguished between 'Positivism, which is a rounded and finished doctrine
claiming to be unchangeable' and 'the positive spirit, which is only a
method of philosophizing' (374f). The former, he reported, was on its
way out (thanks in part to Comte's religious turn); but the positive spirit
was strong, thanks largely to 'the introduction into France of *a much wider
positivism*, often spoken of among us by the name of "*contemporary English
philosophy*" ... represented in different degrees by Stuart Mill, Herbert
Spencer, Bain, Lewes, [T.H.] Huxley, and Tyndall' (374f, my emphasis).
Taking Ribot's list together with the previous list of Comtist sympathizers,
we get a sense of just how pervasive the positive spirit was in Britain in the

late nineteenth century. Between the two we have represented not only philosophy, but also psychology, natural science, history and literature, as well as influential movements of social reform (utilitarianism, socialism, secularism) that were ultimately triumphant in shaping twentieth-century Western culture.

The Newtonian Paradigm and the *Matter* of Philosophy

Almost unanimously in the aforementioned *Mind* series, the state of philosophy is linked to the freedom it was given, in this or that institution, to keep pace with the scientistic drive of modern thought, yet *without* dissolving into science, as it seems nearly to have done at Cambridge. Another point of near unanimity is that the required reading of Locke seems to have been the mark of a modern curriculum. Locke provides at once an epitome of philosophy in the emerging British empirical tradition and a crucial modification of that tradition. The common core of this distinctive British approach was a broad empiricism whose orthodox form eventually became that of a Newtonian-paradigm-prescribed positivism. Beginning with Locke – the first of this tradition to operate under the Newtonian paradigm – this empirical bent had been coupled with the view that psychological phenomena are the proper subject matter of philosophy. In consequence, the proper philosophical method had been narrowed to *introspective* empirical observation combined with reductive analysis (of secondary qualities to primary, etc.). This combination of method and subject matter was to serve as the orthodox metaphilosophy of the British (but also French and German) positivistic tradition until the end of the nineteenth century.

Locke's metaphilosophical innovations were developed in direct response to the Newtonian paradigm. Since Newtonian physics told us all that was worth knowing about the external world, there was no longer any need for a speculative, philosophical worldview. Philosophy, therefore, was to leave the external world to the physicists – an early case of the same scientism-inspired retreat mentioned by Cooper (see pp. 126, above) – and to study atomic moments of experience, variously called perceptions, sensations, ideas, impressions, etc. by those in the emerging empirical tradition. These were understood to be introspectively percep- tible, and hence empirically given.

This characterization of its subject matter allowed the empirical philosophy to lay claim to using an analytic method (i.e., breaking the flow of experience into its 'atoms') that involved careful, empirical observation, just as the Newtonian paradigm prescribed. Perceptions were not, however, quantifiable in any obvious way, thus they could not serve well as correlates of mathematical units. As a result, they were not calculationally determinable, and neither the method nor the knowledge it produced could be mathematically precise. These were significant departures from the paradigm, but for a time it was not certain that they would put philosophy thus construed beyond the pale of science: initially, it was not clear how a closer approximation to the paradigm could be achieved in 'mental science', and it was possible that the relations between sensations might be regular enough to establish a set of non-mathematical 'laws' of correlation. Thus, there was hope that the empirical philosophy in its Lockean form might yield observationally verifiable truths that, though not mathematically expressible, would have a practical, possibly even a predictive, use. In this way, philosophy was to become a kind of 'mental science'.

It turned out, however, that the same subject matter could be approached in a way that approximated the Newtonian paradigm more closely – the way of experimental psychology. Experimental psychology dealt with mental phenomena not introspectively, but through the medium of correlated phenomena that were publicly observable and presumed to be quantifiable. In the British context, the first experimental psychologist was Hume's contemporary David Hartley, who in 1749 published a theory according to which psychological phenomena are correlated with physiological phenomena – vibrations in the brain and nerves. It was not immediately recognized that Hartley's approach was a competitor for the title 'mental science'. Like the other sciences, it took some time to recognize experimental psychology as a generically different endeavor from the philosophy of the day – in this case that of the empirical philosophers. Thus, for over a century the quasi-scientific, psychological philosophy of the British empiricists coexisted with the more fully scientific psychology of Hartley and his followers as two aspects of one and the same philosophical endeavor. This is why G.C. Robertson, in the second volume of *Mind*, places Hartley alongside Hume as a major figure in British *philosophical* thought, noting that 'psychology ... cannot be neglected in a history of philosophic thought in England, where it has been so steadily cultivated without being too carefully discriminated from philosophy proper' (1877: 358).

However, by the time of Robertson's writing, events had already been set in motion that would lead to the dissolution of the British alliance between philosophy and psychology. By 1860, the German researcher Gustav Fechner had laid the foundations for a quantitative approach to psychology and had formulated what was to become the first widely accepted psychophysical equation, purporting to reveal a logarithmic relation between the intensity of a sensation and the magnitude of its stimulus. This became the guiding 'exemplar' of the Newtonian paradigm in psychology from that point onward. Work in this vein was continued by Helmholtz and Wundt, whom Robertson explicitly mentions as exemplifying 'the best *philosophical* work' being done in that day (1876: 2, my emphasis).

Given his high opinion of Wundt, it is not surprising that Robertson chose him to author the *Mind* article on the state of philosophy in Germany. In it, Wundt emphasizes the emergence of a new realist movement in German academic philosophy (as opposed to the transcendental Idealism which had been dominant in the first half of the nineteenth century) that 'connects itself much less closely than the idealistic movement with Kant, joining on rather to Locke and Hume or Auguste Comte' (1877: 517). Their common feature, and the one that the 'realists' found so appealing, was their embodiment of 'the positive spirit'. In connection with this realistic movement, Wundt notes the prevailing positivistic opinion that 'for the present there can be no question of setting up comprehensive metaphysical systems which, like those that have just gone down, must seem to the next generation phantastic illusions rather than works of science' (518). 'The time is passed', Wundt says,

> when philosophy can hope to live apart from the other sciences. We see …, at the present time, all interest turned on those two depart-ments of philosophy that are of most account for the building up of a universal science, namely, Psychology and the Theory of Cognition. … The philosophical movement in Germany presents everywhere the spectacle of preparation for a step to be taken forward. (518)

But the step that was taken was not what Robertson and those in the British tradition would have expected or hoped for. Rather than the founding of either a universal science or a scientific philosophy, what occurred was the founding of a new 'special science' – psychology. As their quantitative methods became better defined, the experimental psychologists began to feel that the progress and scientific standing of their work suffered as a result of being conjoined to the qualitative, subjective approach of the philosophers. The problem was not unique to Britain, and is aptly illustrated by the events that led to the founding of the American Philosophical Association, which grew out of the American *Psychological* Association in 1901.

The American Psychological Association was founded in 1891, when the differences between experimental psychology and philosophy were still only vaguely recognized. Consequently, membership was initially available both to psychologists and to philosophers. Naturally, therefore, meetings of the Association often featured papers on topics more properly philosophical than psychological. Before long, both parties began to realize that their interests and endeavors were too different to manage under the head of a single professional association. In his report on 'The First Twenty-Five Years of the American Philosophical Association', H.N. Gardiner reminisced that:

> the state of affairs ... was satisfactory neither to the philosophers nor to the psychologists. The philosophers were fully aware of the anomalies of a situation in which their claims were allowed only on sufferance; the psychologists were disposed to regard these claims as an impertinence and to resent the intrusion of the philosophical camel into the psychological tent. (1926: 146)

Gardiner reports that in 1896 and again in 1898 motions were made to reorganize the Association so as to include a philosophical contingent separate from the psychological contingent. By 1898, no formal action had been taken, but an informal division was created by organizing the Association's annual-meeting program by subject matter. The result was, in effect, two separate programs, one psychological and the other philosophical. This was repeated in 1899 and 1900, thereby creating 'a situation that was becoming intolerable' (Gardiner 1926: 147). By 1901, the philosophers had had enough, so they started their own association.

Thus we see that, toward the end of the nineteenth century, the alliance between psychology and philosophy was beginning to dissolve, mainly because of the latter's subjective approach to mental phenomena and its consequent lack of mathematical precision. This stood in stark contrast to experimental psychology, which approximated the Newtonian paradigm much more closely. As a result, it became clear that philosophy was not a mental science.

The Crisis in Philosophy at the Turn of the Twentieth Century

By around 1900 it was becoming clear that the empirical philosophy's gambit to remain a field of knowledge under the Newtonian paradigm had failed, and it was again forced to face the challenge of 'defining itself in a meaningful way'. Idealism still held sway in the universities, but its approach to philosophy was increasingly meaning*less* to a culture that, in the last quarter of the nineteenth century, had embraced Newtonian-paradigm scientism even more fully.[14] Consequently, one might suppose that it would have soon died of natural causes if Moore and Russell hadn't done the job first. Gilbert Ryle describes this situation in an illuminating retrospective located, by no coincidence, in the Introduction to a 1963 collection on the history of AP. Ryle reports that, between the time of F.H. Bradley's undergraduate career and that of his own (c. 1865–1920), the academic world had shifted, both demographically and in terms of general interest, in the direction of the sciences. Whereas the universities had once been populated largely by clergy, both in the faculty and the student body, by Ryle's time theologians had become quite scarce. Instead, the universities were populated with students in a number of secular fields, especially the natural and applied sciences. In terms of general interest, the hot topics of the day came from the work of Cantor, Maxwell, Mendel, Marx, Frazer and Freud (Ryle 1963: 3). With the shifting intellectual tendencies of that roughly fifty-year period, Ryle observes that:

> the moment could not be long delayed when philosophers would challenge one another, and be challenged by their new academic colleagues, especially the natural scientists, to state unequivocally what sort of an enquiry philosophy was and what were the canons of its special methods. Already surrendering its historic linkage with 'mental science' or psychology, and no longer remembering its former claim to be the science of things transcendental, philosophy looked like losing its credentials as a science of anything at all. (4f)

With the advance of the special sciences under the Newtonian paradigm, philosophy had been deprived of every answer it had previously given to this question. It would require a new and very creative answer in order to preserve itself as a field of knowledge – as Russell put it in 1914: 'philosophy ... if it is to be a genuine study ... must have a province of its own, and aim at results which the other sciences can neither prove nor disprove' (1914b: 18). A new subject matter had to be found for philosophy, but one which would be unique among the sciences. And, of course, in order to qualify philosophy as a science, it had to be something that could be approached via a roughly scientific method. The situation was fertile ground for that revolution in philosophy that has come to be known as the linguistic turn, with its well-defined, if ill-conceived, metaphilosophical program.

The Linguistic Thesis as a Solution to the Crisis

Since the time of Locke, it had been established that the method of philosophy had to be analysis rather than construction. The only question was, *analysis of what?* In his great *Essay*, Locke had divided the sciences into three types: physics, or natural philosophy, was to study the nature of things; practics, which included ethics, was to study the right and how best to attain it; semiotics, which Locke also calls 'logic' and 'the doctrine of signs', was to study 'the Nature of Signs, the Mind makes use of for the understanding of Things, or conveying its Knowledge to others' (1975 [1690]: 720). Under the Newtonian paradigm, philosophy could not be a physical science. Of the two remaining possibilities, ethics was the least promising (as the history of scientistic theories of ethics attests). That left semiotics as the only remotely promising avenue for developing a scientific philosophy. According to Locke, there are two kinds of signs: ideas, which are signs for things external to the mind, and words, which are signs for ideas. Since the main business of the empirical philosophy was the study of ideas, it counted as a semiotic science on Locke's view. But, as we have seen, the rise of experimental psychology put an end to the notion that the direct study of ideas by introspection was a scientific endeavor. What remained was the study of words, the study of language as a symbol-system.

In the struggle to be scientific, language had certain advantages over ideas as a subject matter for philosophy. The main problem with ideas had been their unshakable subjectivity. By contrast, words – at least in their 'philosophically unmuddled sense' – are empirically given, and hence objective in the sense that matters for science. Benson Mates lauds the advantages of taking language as one's subject matter for this very reason:

> A sentence, at least in its written form, is an object having a shape accessible to sensory perception, or, at worst, it is a set of such objects. ... in general we find that as long as we are dealing with sentences, many of the properties in which the logician [or philosopher] is interested are ascertainable by simple inspection. Only reasonably good eyesight, as contrasted with metaphysical acuity, is required .... (1972: 10f)

The concreteness of linguistic symbolism also facilitated a closer approximation to the mathematical precision mandated by the Newtonian paradigm. The analysis of ideas had always involved a certain vagueness regarding just where one experience ended and another began, and hence just what the units of analysis were (e.g., just what counted as a *simple* idea). By contrast, language, especially in written form, presents us with empirical symbols whose boundaries are easy to demarcate at all levels of analysis – letters, words, sentences, etc. – so it is a great deal clearer what might count as a *unit* in language than in thought.

Moreover, the phenomenon of *synonymy*, so crucial to the notion of philosophical analysis from Moore onward, facilitated the satisfaction of another paradigmatic ideal: philosophical truths (analyses) could be given the form of (as we have seen Warnock describe them) 'linguistic equations'. Of course, synonymy itself was (and is) a mysterious phenomenon – if linguistic meaning *itself* was puzzling, two words or sentences having the same meaning could be no less so. However, this was one of the metaphysically threatening aspects of language that was suppressed by the positivistic pattern of emphasis and de-emphasis that led to the TC – a pattern that Ryle, too, engages in. Though Ryle was quite aware of the deep metaphysical disagreements over the nature of meaning, he merely alludes to this by characterizing the word 'meanings' as a 'trouble-making plural noun' (1963: 8) in the very act of emphasizing the analysts' *common* focus on meanings as the subject matter of philosophy. Thus, though Ryle insists that 'philosophers no more examine the private and momentary images and impressions that are the material of psychology, than they examine the English or Russian phrases or sentences that are the material of philology' (7f), he provides no positive characterization of 'meanings' in the sense relevant to the new philosophy. Absent such a characterization, it was natural in this overwhelmingly scientistic era to focus on the empirical features of philosophical practice and, within it, of language, as being the only features of any significance. As Russell had earlier observed, 'whatever presents itself as empiricism is sure of wide-spread acceptance, not on its merits, but because empiricism is the fashion' (1944b: 697).

In any case, as Ryle goes on to say, 'it is ... no freak of history that the example and the reputation of Moore's analytic method of philosophizing proved so influential; since here was a philosopher practising a specific method of investigation, with obviously high standards of strictness' (1963: 5). The emphasis here is on Moore's method, but method and matter are to a large extent complementary, and I submit that it was in no small measure due to the facts that (1) Moore was perceived as applying his method to language-empirically-construed, and that (2) the above-noted aspects of language lent themselves to a close approximation of the Newtonian paradigm in both matter and method that Moore's work was perceived as 'scientific' by some. For instance, upon reading *Principia Ethica*, Lytton Strachey wrote to Moore:

... it has not only laid the true foundations of Ethics, it has not only left all modern philosophy *bafouée* – these seem to me small achievements compared to the establishment of that Method which shines like a sword between the lines. It is the scientific method, deliberately applied, for the first time, to Reasoning. (in Levy 1979: 234)

And when Russell combined Moore's method of analysis with the mathematical logic of his *Principia*, the Newtonian paradigm was almost completely realized in philosophy, for now meanings could be translated into a notation and a 'language' that, like mathematics itself, represented only the formal/structural features of ordinary language and ordinary experience, retaining none of the latter's connotative or qualitative features or associations. Thus, it enabled 'linguistic' symbols to be manipulated with the mechanistic precision of a mathematical calculus. Indeed, when Ramsey declared Russell's theory of descriptions a 'paradigm of philosophy', what he was really noticing (whether or not he realized it) was that it was an exemplar, in philosophy, of the Newtonian paradigm.

Much more could and ideally would be said here about the nature, history and development of turn-of-the-twentieth-century scientism; but considerations of space prevent it. I am particularly conscious of having to skip any discussion of the development of mathematical logic in the late nineteenth century and its interesting and illustrative intersections with the British positivistic tradition. Be that as it may, the sketch given here is sufficient to ground our explanation for the illusion of promise: in the early twentieth century, anything approximating the Newtonian paradigm in any field would have seemed promising, but even more so in philosophy given its turn-of-the-century crisis. The conception of philosophy prescribed by the linguistic thesis did approximate the Newtonian paradigm, and in a way that averted the crisis precipitated by the rise of psychology as a separate science – hence its acceptance counts as a further case of the retreat of philosophy in response to the advance of Newtonian-paradigm science.

Of course, the Newtonian paradigm was soon forced to share its glory with those of Einsteinian relativity and of quantum physics, but paradigm-shift takes time, especially when centuries-old habits of thought and practice stand in the way; and, in any case, the introduction of these new paradigms did relatively little to change the general methodological features of the Newtonian paradigm, except to diminish somewhat the emphasis on empirical observation by making theoretical physics socially acceptable. Thus, the crisis precipitated by the advance of the sciences was still being felt by philosophers in the 1930s. In fact, again by no coincidence, it is discussed by Montague in the same essay in which he gives us one of our two earliest uses of 'analytic philosophy':

> Disillusionment and a mood of defeatism is making itself felt throughout our entire guild. How can we go on with speculative theories about the constitution of reality when the winds of scientific knowledge in physics, chemistry, biology, and psychology are sweeping around us and covering the once fertile fields of fancy with the arid sands of fact? ... now, perhaps, we shall find that Comte was right, and that metaphysical conceptions are quite as useless and far less exciting than the gods and ghosts of our fathers. (1933: 5)

Indeed, as one surveys the intellectual landscape of the late nineteenth and early twentieth centuries, there is no better, and arguably no other, explanation than scientism for the framing and adoption of the linguistic thesis, the illusion of promise, the illusion of unity, the TC, and thereby the advent and rise of AP.

Chapter 7

Conclusion

In the Introduction, I set out to explain AP's peculiar career. It involves, I said, two peculiarities: one philosophical, the other sociological. The philosophical peculiarity was that AP's original outlook initially was thought to be so promising that it generated a revolution in Anglo-American philosophy, but it came to be seen as so badly flawed that it was completely abandoned, all in the span of roughly half a century. The ground covered in Chapters 4–6 explains this peculiarity by casting the rise and fall of AP as the latest stage of what has been for several centuries now an ongoing cycle in philosophy – the cycle created by philosophers trying, failing, and trying again, to find a place for philosophy in a culture increasingly pervaded by a scientistic outlook or 'stance'. The cycle was sped up in AP's case because its rise depended heavily on illusions so obvious that they could not be maintained long even by those who wanted AP to succeed; consequently a quick fall was inevitable.

The sociological peculiarity, I said, consists in the fact that AP has maintained its dominant position in the academy even though the original reason for its dominance has long since been undermined. This is explained by the fact that AP has never been a philosophical school, movement or tradition, but rather a non-philosophical movement, that eventually became a tradition, within the social sphere of academic philosophy. As a thing of practices under an accepted paradigm, the ideational content of the linguistic thesis was really just window-dressing for the movement. Wittgenstein once observed that 'a wheel that can be turned though nothing else moves is not part of the mechanism' (1953: para 271); how much more a wheel that can be *lost* without causing the mechanism to falter even a little! Additionally, paradigms are much more flexible than defining doctrines as principles of group inclusion. On the defining-doctrine model, identity of belief is the criterion of group membership. By contrast, the paradigm model requires only similarity of problems, practices and results. It thereby allows for much more wiggle-room in determining what and who falls within the group-boundaries (see Chapter 6, note 8).

One might wonder how, if the linguistic thesis was necessary to prevent philosophy from falling into obsolescence after the rise of experimental psychology, AP managed to escape that fate once it abandoned the linguistic thesis. The answer in brief is that the period 1900–c. 1965 saw a great many developments in science, philosophy and culture that caused Newtonian-paradigm scientism to wane. The advent of Einsteinian relativity and quantum mechanics chastened those who saw Newton as 'showing us where and how the foundations of heaven and earth were laid', while developments in the philosophy of science and the closely related field of epistemology were quickly making it impossible to maintain the triumphal scientism of previous generations. Meanwhile, developments in the philosophy of language, metaphysics, and what we now call the philosophy of mind were beginning to suggest that, wherever their foundations might be laid, there were more things *in* heaven and earth than had been dreamt of under Newtonian-paradigm scientism. Thus, by the time the linguistic thesis was abandoned, it was no longer needed.

But, although the linguistic thesis was no longer needed, the name 'analytic philosophy' was – for two reasons. First, by that time, AP had carved out a valuable social space in the Anglo-American academy, and the preservation of that social space required the preservation of the name, which by that time was firmly established as the unique designator for the analysts as a group. Deprived of the illusory appearance of ideational unity in the linguistic thesis, falling under that name was the only *definite* phenomenon that made the analysts an 'us' that could be contrasted with a 'them', and it was certainly the only point of unity the analysts still had that bore even the slightest suggestion of their being a philosophical school. It was also the only public point of unity-suggesting contact between linguistic and post-linguistic AP. Thus, retaining the name was the only way for post-linguistic analysts to show the world that they were one with each other and with the earlier analysts in such a way that they and no one else rightfully belonged together in the social space carved out by the earlier analysts.

Second, the name had to be retained to save face. The history of AP resembles a peculiar combination of Tynianov's *Lieutenant Kije* and Andersen's *The Emperor's New Clothes*. In the former, some smudged letters on a military roster lead the Russian Czar to believe that a man named Kije is enlisted in his army. Rather than risk the Czar's displeasure by correcting him, his attendants quickly create a grandiose, fictional biography for Kije. When the Czar decides that he must meet Kije, his attendants complete the fiction by telling him that Kije has died a glorious death in battle – with the result that an empty coffin is given a state funeral and buried. In the case of AP, we have a fictional school of philosophy invented because of a kind of blurred philosophical vision that focused only on the empirical and the practical without penetrating to the ideational and theoretical, and this to avoid the ire of the then-ruling paradigm for knowledge.

Unlike *Kije*, however, when the ideational substance of the group (such as it was) underwent the kind of radical shift that should have resulted in recognition that 'analytic philosophy' was dead, this was not recognized, or at least not admitted. The preservation of a desirable social status hung in the balance; but also, to admit it would have been to admit that the progenitors and supporters of AP were either foolish or dishonest. Here Andersen's tale becomes the better analog. In it, a pair of charlatans come to town claiming to make clothes of a material that 'possessed the wonderful quality of being invisible to any man who was unfit for his office or unpardonably stupid'.[1] The emperor hires them to make an outfit for him, thinking that he will use it to test the worthiness of his court officials. However, when it turns out that no one, including the emperor himself, can see the material, everyone from the emperor to the peasants pretends that they *can* see it rather than risk being marked ignorant and unfit for office; everyone, that is, except a young child, who does not understand 'the rules' of the social system that make compliance with the charade advantageous. The child remarks, loud enough for others to hear, that the emperor has nothing on at all. Word of this pronouncement spreads though the crowd until they all exclaim: 'But he has nothing on at all!' At this point, everyone including the emperor sees the truth, and everyone *except* the emperor and his aids drops the charade. Thus the tale ends: 'he [the emperor] thought to himself, "Now I must bear up to the end." And the chamberlains walked with still greater dignity, as if they carried the train which did not exist.'

This is analogous to what happened when AP transitioned from its linguistic to its post-linguistic phase. AP had been emperor to the philosophical profession for several decades by then, during which time it had been 'dressed' in the insubstantial robes of linguistic philosophy. When the transition came about, to say that the demise of linguistic philosophy was the demise of AP would have been to admit that nothing else of a philosophical nature garbed the movement, and that it had been naked all along. Thus, the progenitors and supporters of AP would have been made fools, having been bamboozled by the illusions of the TC, or possibly villains, insofar as they had a hand in creating, promulgating and perpetuating the illusions. But making this admission was not socially necessary – at least not then. Given that AP was thoroughly entrenched in the academy and dominant in the profession, the analysts had only to *act* as if all was well, for any dissent could be construed as a sign of stupidity and unsuitability for the profession. Thus, like the emperor and his chamberlains, the analysts decided to 'bear up to the end' by retaining the name 'analytic philosophy' and the social space reserved under it.

Without either defining doctrines or a clear paradigm to follow, however, the practices that occupied the analytic space became increasingly disparate, and the analytic form of life increasingly incoherent – 'eclectic' – as individual practitioners began to move further away from earlier paradigms and exemplars. Of course, there are still traces of AP's founding scientism to be found within its social space, in the form of habits of thought and practice in individual practitioners who identify with AP. Depending on their prevalence, these may in some cases translate into tendencies that color the social space, and thereby AP, as a whole – hence the suggestive patterns of amenability to scientism so frequently observed in AP. And then there is that social space *itself*, whose very existence counts as a trace of AP's founding scientism, preserved within the social structure of the academy.

So it is that AP exists now mainly as a set of stances, habits and tendencies occupying a certain social space within the structure of the academy and of the philosophical profession – all of which appear increasingly baseless as they drift further from any explicit connection to the scientistic paradigm they were designed to serve, and as that paradigm itself continues to fade into obsolescence. And this brings us round to the worries about AP surveyed in Chapter 1: the puzzle, the crisis and the worries about hegemony, legitimacy and AP's effects on culture.

The ground we have covered reveals that there is good cause for concern in each of these areas. Though AP has no defining doctrines, and though it no longer has a clear paradigm to emulate, it does have at least one perennial feature: the failure or refusal to articulate its fundamental philosophical commitments. This is a failure of which analysts have been at least marginally aware ever since AP *as such* came into being in the early 1930s: Stebbing drew attention to it in 1932, Collingwood in 1933, and Nagel in 1936. The latter noted that leading analysts were then hard at work on the theory of meaning, hoping to solve the problem. However, none of their attempts succeeded in providing a definitive view for the school at large. Thus, in 1975, Gustav Bergmann could reflect:

The beginning of the [twentieth] century witnessed the rise of a movement sometimes referred to ... as the linguistic turn in philosophy.

By now, having reached maturity, it has jelled into two extremes. Both sides agree that, since, taken literally, all ontological discourse turns out to be about nothing, ontology is a futile enterprise. Or, to put the same thing differently, they agree that there is no such thing as ontology. [They] disagree on what they believe can be "saved" from it by "interpreting" it as they do. According to one side, the salvage operation results in a body of statements of the kind linguists and other scientists make about the language people speak. The other side replaces language and the scientist by the geometrical designs called calculi and the mathematical logician, respectively. ... *There are, scattered throughout the discourse, arguments and reflections in support of both beliefs. Yet they have so far not been supported by a connected line of reasoning both fully explicit and conclusive.* (1992: 318, my emphasis)[2]

It should not be missed that this characterization is thoroughly in line with the traditional conception. But more relevant to our present concern is the fact that, like Stebbing, Collingwood and Nagel, Bergmann charges AP with having failed to give an adequate account of its own methods and metaphilosophy. And, of course, things only got worse after the demise of linguistic philosophy, for AP then lacked not only a clear account of its fundamental commitments, but also the illusory *appearance* of unity that it had enjoyed previously.

In light of this, it is perhaps no surprise that contemporary historians have been unable to locate any substantive points of agreement unique to analytic philosophers, and hence definitive of AP. Moreover, it is perhaps no surprise that analysts now – or rather *still* – find themselves unable to give an account of their school's fundamental philosophical commitments. As noted in Chapter 2 (pp. 47ff.), both the current puzzle about AP's nature and the metaphilosophical crisis it signifies are longstanding features of the analytic movement that simply went unnoticed or ignored until recently. Indeed, in light of the current crisis in AP, the early warnings from Stebbing, Nagel and especially Collingwood appear prophetic. They were quite correct to note a strange lacuna in the AP of their day, consisting in the fact that, by the mid 1930s, no one had succeeded in working out the details of the linguistic thesis in a way that enjoyed either strong initial plausibility or unanimous support among the analysts – despite the fact that, as Wisdom's 1931 account shows, some analysts were already representing their school as possessed of a sufficiently well-developed, common method.

Similarly prophetic is Schlick's warning about the consequences of failing to make clear the ideational principles that define our philosophical groups. After noting both that philosophical groups are defined by their ideational principles and that it is natural for those principles to evolve through refinements and modifications (see pp. 62, 64f.), he says:

> If, alongside the evolved outlook, an 'orthodox' movement still continues to exist, which clings to the first principles in their original form and meaning, then sooner or later some terminological distinction of the old from the new will automatically come about. *But where this is not clearly so,* and where, to the contrary, the most diverse and perhaps contradictory formulations and interpretations of the principles are bandied about among the various adherents of a 'movement', then a hubbub arises, whose result is that supporters and opponents of the view are found talking at cross purposes; everyone seeks out from the principles what he can specifically use for the defence of his own view, and everything ends in hopeless misunderstandings and obscurities. (1932: 259, my emphasis)

This dynamic has occurred repeatedly in AP, both on the real and the illusory planes. On the plane of the real, the history of AP follows an evolution from the Platonic realism of Moore and Russell to logical atomism, to linguistic philosophy ideal and ordinary, and finally to post-linguistic eclecticism. Moore and Russell made their original principles clear enough, but the refinements and modifications that led to each of the other phases were not made clear at all. Each transition was simply a matter of its supporters 'seeking out from the original principles what they could specifically use for the construction of their own view', without making clear either the original principles themselves or the refined and modified principles that they themselves accepted. This inattention to ideational principles opened the door to an illusory plane upon which a school came to be, subsuming all of these transitions as its parts or phases. Rather than 'terminological distinctions of the old from the new automatically coming about', a single term – 'analytic philosophy' – was coined and maintained despite substantive and ever increasing ideational divergence on the real plane.

All along, AP has been characterized by the 'hopeless misunder-standings and obscurities' that Schlick says arise from failing to make a movement's ideational principles clear – witness the linguistic misinter-pretations of Frege, Moore and Russell, and the obscurity in which the analytic notion of 'meaning' has been perennially shrouded. Witness also the astonishing variety of answers now being given to the question 'What is AP?' Indeed, the current debate over the nature of AP, as it plays out in work on the past, present and future of AP, is just the sort of 'hubbub' that Schlick says arises when a movement's principles are not made sufficiently clear: 'supporters and opponents' of AP are 'found talking at cross purposes' because they are not talking about the same thing. Since AP has never clarified its own principles sufficiently, those who seek to clarify them now – either in defense or criticism of AP – frequently impose upon the movement as a whole whatever principles they can 'specifically use for the defense of their own views'.

To escape from this 'hubbub', we need only recognize that there is no good philosophical solution to the puzzle about AP's nature, and that it therefore cannot avert its metaphilosophical crisis. AP has a nature, of course, but it is that of a social group rather than a philosophical group. It abandoned philosophical status when it took its 'paradigmatic turn', and in doing so rejected the traditional philosophical imperative to examine one's presuppositions down to the foundations.

That AP involved the explicit rejection of this fundamental philosophical task is suggested in Collingwood's discussion of AP's 'skepticism' about traditional philosophy. After noting the duty to state one's metaphilosophical theory, Collingwood observes that 'analytic philosophy does indeed involve a constructive philosophical doctrine, but, true to its character as a form of skepticism, declines the task of stating it' (1933: 146). Collingwood saw that this was a problem only from the traditional philosopher's standpoint, while for those who accepted it 'a great part of the attraction of the analytic method lies in its claim to have done away with the old idea of constructive philosophy' (146). Thus, the analyst 'not only neglects this duty [to state his fundamental principles] but makes a merit of neglecting it and asserting that he has no constructive or systematic theory of his own' (145). Thus it is not so much that the analysts failed to fulfill this fundamental philosophical duty as it is that they *rejected* it *as* a duty. This rejection would be a natural result of a 'paradigmatic turn' to the *modus operandi* of normal science.

The great detriment of a paradigmatic turn, however, is that it neutralizes philosophy's most significant practical benefit: its ability to destroy prejudices by turning them into well-founded views or, if they cannot be made so, by showing them to be ill-founded and thereby dispensing with them. The overt attempt to liberate oneself from what Husserl calls 'persuasions begotten without insight, through psychological [or social!] mechanisms, and with no better justification than widespread prejudices' (Husserl 1900–01: I, 114f) comes as close as anything to counting as an essential part of a philosophical approach to life.[3] But to take a paradigmatic turn is to abandon oneself to such mechanisms, at least as concerns the content and presuppositions of the paradigm itself.

It is also to cut oneself off from frank and often fruitful dialogue about one's own fundamental assumptions. As Collingwood observes, given the analysts' unwillingness to articulate their principles, the traditional philosopher has no recourse but to insist that the analysts' 'professed skepticism is merely a veiled claim to exempt these principles from criticism ..., while assuming their truth and sufficiency' (1933: 147). And in fact the analysts have not infrequently been accused of exploiting this blank space in the theoretical substructure of their school in order to evade criticism. For instance, in his Foreword to the second edition of Mundle's *A Critique of Linguistic Philosophy*, P.L. Heath observes of ordinary-language philosophy specifically that:

> to assail the movement or its supposed doctrines as a whole was ... to be accused of tilting at windmills which existed ... only in the imagination of the critic; while to pitch directly into the statements of individual authors was not uncommonly to be told that the views in question were untypical, or outdated, or had been misconstrued, or at any rate were not shared by anybody else, so that very little overall damage could be done in this way. (in Mundle 1979 [1970]: 1f)

Similarly, Ian Jarvie notes in the Preface to a recent edition of Gellner's *Words and Things* that the analysts – and again specifically the later ordinary-language philosophers – engaged in a form of 'intellectual sleight-of-hand' by means of which 'key ideas are never stated, rather insinuated by attacking disapproved ideas, and ... there is a systematic denial of all attempts by outsiders to state these ideas' (in Gellner 2005 [1959]: xv). Against Gellner himself, 'the tactics were to deny that there was a movement or school; to admit there once was one, briefly, but that things have moved on, hence that Gellner was out of date ...' (xxii).

As a feature of ordinary-language philosophy, this evasiveness is usually seen as the result of Wittgensteinian 'quietism', his view that philosophy should not espouse any views. However, the pattern of avoiding mention of AP's fundamental commitments transcends Wittgensteinian ordinary-language philosophy, being a feature not only of 'Oxford philosophy' but also the earlier ideal-language philosophy, and hence of AP on the whole – a fact explained by the hypothesis that AP liberated itself from the duty of articulating its first principles by taking its 'paradigmatic turn'.

Given this history, it is difficult to see genus revisionism in the history of AP as anything other than the latest manifestation of this pattern of evasion; for it simultaneously perpetuates and justifies the pattern by insisting that '*of course* there are no defining doctrines; philosophical traditions aren't *that* sort of thing!' To adopt this view in the history of *philosophy*, however, is simply another manifestation of positivism, for it amounts to the insistence that certain figures and factions simply belong together (i.e., they are correlated in a certain way), and that no further explanation is either required or allowed. Thus the residual influence of Newtonian-paradigm scientism is still at work distorting our perceptions of AP. And though not overtly positivistic in this way, differentia revisionism also participates in the pattern of evasion, attempting to sweep AP's problem under the rug by directing us to the wrong defining doctrines.

In light of its historical pattern of evasion, there does seem to be some merit to the complaints about AP being what we described in Chapter 1 as a 'hegemony in the worst sense', wherein far-reaching professional and pedagogical decisions are guided by prejudice rather than principle. To disprove this charge, AP would have to articulate its fundamental philosophical commitments; however, whereas this may have been possible at an earlier stage, when the Newtonian paradigm was still in place and when analytic practice could be tied directly to it, it is quite hopeless now that AP has become so eclectic. All we can reasonably hope for now is that individual philosophers from every tradition, and especially those who identify with AP, will start to take seriously the project of articulating and scrutinizing their own fundamental commitments, so that they can discuss and defend them if the need arises. In this way, they will at least make some progress toward transforming prejudices into well-considered views, and will make possible the kind of dialogue among opposing parties that paradigm-dogmatism rules out. We may also hope that such dialogue might be made a priority in the philosophical profession, with representatives of different schools working to clarify the differing fundamental commitments that divide them. Paraphrasing Russell, the aim would be that philosophers 'learn to regard the philosophical enterprise as a unity, not as a collection of warring schools and traditions'. There is no reason that such a metaphilosophical dialogue couldn't be pursued with the same energy that, among analysts, is regularly directed to whatever narrower problems are currently in fashion; and there is every reason it should, for the issues involved have been the elephant in academic philosophy's parlor for most of the last century.

I would hope, of course, that this book might make a small contribution toward awakening contemporary analysts to this duty. But even if it has no appreciable effect on the future of philosophy, it has been worth writing purely for historical reasons. As A.C. Grayling has recently observed, 'history has to be got right before it distorts into legend and diminishes into over-simplification, which is always what happens when events slip into a too-distant past' (2006: 2). History has to be got right, in other words, to prevent historical illusions. This is the case even when the history in question is the history *of* an illusion.

Notes

Preface

1   On the connection between positivism and historical studies see Hughes 1960: 22–30.

Introduction

1   In some regions – notably Britain – '*analytical* philosophy' is more common than '*analytic* philosophy'. These are best understood as variants of the same term.

2   I will sometimes invoke the language of 'necessity', 'essence' and 'nature' in talking about analytic philosophy. Such talk is grounded in intuitions consistent with views in the ontology of groups and of social reality similar to those given in Pettit 1993 and Searle 1995, as well as with a Kripkean view of names. I will not be able to say much about these matters as space is limited and, though essential to the views presented here, they are too far from the center of the case I wish to make to allow for systematic treatment.

Chapter 1

1   URL = <http://www.philosophicalgourmet.com/analytic.htm>. In recent years, Brian Leiter's *The Philosophical Gourmet Report* (*PGR*) has become a highly regarded resource among analytic philosophers. The *PGR* is a ranking of graduate programs in philosophy. Though it is not a scholarly work, it is useful as an index of contemporary analytic culture. Principally, it serves as something of an axiological meter insofar as it reveals (extensionally) what counts as good work among analytic philosophers. Moreover, insofar as Leiter has his finger on the pulse of contemporary analytic culture, his observations about analytic philosophy are frequently indicative of the contemporary analytic self-understanding. Quotations from

the *PGR* are taken from the most recent edition; however, many of these statements appeared in earlier versions as well. In such cases, the date of the earliest version still available online will be noted in brackets. The URL for the *PGR*'s homepage is listed in the bibliography. URLs for the subsidiary pages from which quotations are taken are given in the notes.

2   URL = \<http://www.philosophicalgourmet.com/meaningof.htm\>.

3   There are important connotative differences among these terms. However, all are normally used to make distinctions between groups of philosophers along ideational lines. Since the ideational (or conceptual, or theoretical, or viewish) aspect of such groups is crucial to the present discussion, I will emphasize it to the exclusion of whatever connotative differences there may be among the terms (this will be further justified in Chapter 3). For brevity, I will frequently speak of 'schools' without listing 'movements' and 'traditions'. In such cases, and as context dictates, it should be understood that I intend 'school' to play surrogate for the whole genus of which these sorts of group are species (to my knowledge, this genus does not have a widely accepted name).

4   URL = \<http://www.philosophicalgourmet.com/analytic.htm\>.

5   Leiter himself notes that it is not possible to draw philosophically substantive distinctions between contemporary analytic philosophizing and the philosophizing of Kant, Hegel, Descartes or Aristotle (2004b: 12).

6   On the metaphysical aspect of this project, see Loux 1998: 4; Moore 1953: 1f, 24f; Whitehead 1941: 4; Willard 1967: 523; Naugle 2002.

7   See Thomas Aquinas, *Summa Theologiae*, IIa IIae, 45.1.

8   On issues of pluralism and hegemony in American academic philosophy, see also McCumber 2001 and Wilshire 2002. Lachs' piece, a letter to the editor of the American Philosophical Association's 'Proceedings and Addresses', is brief and brilliantly written. It makes an excellent introduction to many of the concerns addressed in this chapter. His target is not analytic philosophy as such, but contemporary academic philosophy in its professionalized state; however, because of its dominance in that arena, analytic philosophy receives the lion's share of his attention. In addition to its original published form, it is available online in two locations: \<http://www.politicaltheory.info/essays/lachs.htm\> and \<http://www.apa.udel.edu/apa/governance/edletters/#Lach\>.

9   Its pervasiveness in connection with professional issues combined with its current eclecticism recently led Bernard Williams to declare

'analytic philosophy' a purely professional, rather than a philosophical, designation (1996: 25).

10   URL = <http://www.philosophicalgourmet.com/analytic.htm>.

11   Leiter has taken pains to make the data representative of general opinion by recruiting a large pool of evaluators. He notes that, for the 2004 edition of the *PGR*, he sent surveys to 451 philosophy faculties, 266 of whom responded. While this is just a fraction of the total number of professional philosophers in the English-speaking world, it can hardly be said that the *PGR* relies on the idiosyncratic opinions of a very few.

12   URL = <http://www.philosophicalgourmet.com/reportdesc.htm>.

13   URL = <http://www.philosophicalgourmet.com/meaningof.htm>.

14   See also the extended discussion of analytic style in Ross 1998. Ross concludes that 'the style that now characterizes (post-)analytical writing is now so broad that it includes all other schools as well – provided only that they are writing for fellow professionals' (68).

15   I quote from Healy's weblog, in which he gives a survey of his preliminary results (URL = <http://www.kieranhealy.org/blog/archives/2005/01/27/specialization-and-status-in-philosophy/>). The full results are given in a paper that Healy is currently revising for publication. I refer to this unpublished work with the author's permission.

16   See, for example, the comments about analytic philosophy in Chapter 1 of Eleonore Stump's forthcoming Gifford Lectures on the problem of evil.

17   For discussion of analytic philosophy's ineffectual history with ethics, see Williams 1996. Some will be surprised to see the philosophy of religion included here, particularly on account of Alvin Plantinga's use of formal techniques to achieve a veritable resurrection of what was, at the mid twentieth century, looking to be a dead field. This sociological fact, however, should not be mistaken for a philosophical one. While the use of formal techniques by philosophers of religion has made it possible for the field to flourish in a socio-academic context already committed to technical philosophizing, it has not yielded a host of fresh insights directly applicable to the religious lives of non-philosophers. In the twentieth century, fresh ideas in the philosophy of religion – such as process theology and open theism – tended to be proposed by traditional, 'speculative' philosophers or by theologians.

18   At the same time, they are not indifferent to the way analytic philosophy has affected the philosophical experience of 'ordinary

people', for they advise that philosophers 'should learn how to present ideas clearly to all kinds of audiences, and not just to fellow aficionados of the fake barn'.

19   Until 2005, this was posted on the Centre's website, at <http://www. soton.ac.uk/~philosop/cpap1.htm>. In 2005, The Centre for Post-Analytical Philosophy was renamed 'The Centre for Philosophy and Value'. Shortly thereafter, the pre-2005 site and its content disappeared from the web. The current Centre's web page is located at <http://www.philosophy.soton.ac.uk/postgraduate-pages/centre. htm>.

Chapter 2

1   Thus A.P. Martinich and David Sosa note that 'Analytic philosophy would be easier to define if it had kept to its early form in Great Britain at the beginning of the [twentieth] century' (2001a: 1).

2   I do not mean to commit to a complete 'Millian' view of proper names, but only to the phenomenologically obvious fact that whatever descriptive content the terms constituting a proper name may normally have, it usually plays no essential role in their function *qua* name. Indeed, the descriptive content may drop completely out of sight. To borrow Kripke's example, 'Dartmouth' need not, and usually does not, bring to mind *a place at the mouth of the river Dart* in order to do its work as a name (Kripke 1980: 26).

3   While there are important differences between definitions and descriptions (or characterizations), both have in common that they can be good, bad, better, worse, more or less accurate, successful, etc. depending upon how well they capture that which they are definitions or descriptions *of*. I will frequently ignore the differences between definitions and descriptions in order to focus on *evaluating* them in these terms.

4   It is significant that, as we shall see in Chapter 3, the name 'analytic philosophy' was introduced only in the early 1930s, when, according to Weitz, there was consensus about this linguistic conception of philosophical analysis.

5   We will see in Chapter 3 that Warnock makes a similar observation.

6   URL = <http://www.philosophicalgourmet.com/analytic. htm#foot3>.

7   *Genealogy of Morals*, Second Essay, section 13.

Chapter 3

1 The only exception of which I am aware is Reck (ed.) 2002. Reck speaks of 'early analytic philosophy' as dating 1880–1930 (ix). The beginning date of 1880 is far enough from the turn of the twentieth century to count as a deviation from the TC. However, like several others we've seen, it is a deviation controlled by the TC itself, for the date is set at 1880 in order to accommodate Frege's role in AP. Frege has always been recognized as bearing some important relation to AP, but there has been debate about whether he should be considered a mere influence or a full-fledged founder. Shifting the starting date for AP in this way is consistent with the latter view. The other central figures of the early period are – according to Reck, Moore, Russell, Wittgenstein and Carnap – all perfectly consistent with the TC.

2 For many sociologists, a *social group* is no mere collection of human beings, but one characterized by a set of specific traits such as a fully saturated communication structure (one in which each member has a personal relationship with every other member), and a 'we' mentality grounded in shared activities and intentions (cf. Putnam and Stohl 1990; Frey (ed.) 1994).

3 Martin Kusch's (2000) work on the sociology of philosophical knowledge provides an excellent framework for understanding the interplay of ideational and social aspects in philosophizing without ignoring either or reducing one to the other.

4 Of course, when I say that these are the 'earliest known' uses, I primarily mean known *to me*. However, the extant historiographical literature on analytic philosophy does not suggest anything different. Earlier cases may exist, of course; but, if they do, they must be tucked away in works more obscure and forgotten than the ones to which I make reference here, for they seem to have eluded the majority of researchers working in the area. Moreover, a February 2004 discussion on Russell-l (an email discussion group managed by Andrew Bone of the Bertrand Russell Research Centre, McMaster University) supports the conclusion that there is no known use of 'analytic philosophy' prior to 1933. The discussion was specifically about early uses of the term, and the prize for the earliest use went to Michael Beaney, who pointed us to its occurrence in Collingwood's 1933 monograph (discussed below). I have since found the occurrences in Wisdom and Montague.

5 Collingwood 1933. The term appears in the table of contents; the corresponding text occupies pp. 137–50.

6 Stebbing voices reservations about lumping the British proponents of analysis together with the non-British proponents, for, as she clear-sightedly observes: 'there are important differences between their conceptions of metaphysics and those of [the British proponents]; consequently, there are corresponding differences in the method used' (1933: 74 n). One wonders how the history of twentieth-century philosophy would have been different if the scruples of Stebbing, Nagel and Collingwood had been the norm.

7 It should be noted that this would have been an international linguistic and academic community, as Collingwood was located at Oxford and Wisdom at Cambridge, while Montague and Nagel were in the US. Montague spent his career at several American institutions – in 1933, he was on the faculty of both Barnard College and Columbia University. Nagel was at Columbia for most of his career, but spent 1934–35 traveling Europe on a Guggenheim fellowship – whence his 1936 report.

Chapter 4

1 URL = <http://www.umass.edu/philosophy/PDF/Aune/feigl.pdf>.

2 'Collective intention' is Searle's term (Searle 1990, 1995). Although there is some disagreement over the details, it is widely accepted by those working on the ontology of social reality that the existence of a social object requires that a group of people have a set of common views and beliefs that circumscribe the object and its role in their social world.

3 I don't mean to suggest that I base my view of the development of AP on any particular theory in social ontology or the philosophy of language. My references to Kripkean baptism and collective intentionality are meant as heuristic devices, to help illustrate the kinds of considerations and intuitions that lie behind my account. (See Introduction, note 2)

4 The elided material mentions some pragmatists and American New Realists as secondary influences. As in other cases we have surveyed, these departures from the TC seem to to count as uncharacteristic extensions of certain aspects of it and hence to presuppose it.

5 Cf. Peter Hylton: 'the idea of analysis itself gets us nowhere until we put constraints on the process. ... Both the vindication of the

process, and the constraints to be put on it, must be the result of philosophical thought. They are presuppositions of the process of philosophical analysis, and cannot themselves be justified by appeal to it. Whatever else philosophical analysis may be, it cannot be a *starting point* for philosophy' (1996: 213).

6   For a more complete reconstruction of Collingwood's critique of AP, see Beaney 2001.

7   Cf. Smith 1994: 27. It is a popular half-truth that the logical positivists purged themselves of the verification principle by dint of their own intellectual power and integrity (cf. Soames 2003: I, xiii). In fact, the core of the refutation that eventually led them to abandon the principle was being articulated from outside the analytic movement in the early 1930s. The same half-truth in a more general form is frequently applied to AP as such (cf. Searle 1996: 2).

8   Aune (1998: 8 n) notes that Carnap was the last to finally give up on the principle, and has him doing so after David Kaplan found a counter-example to the formulation Carnap gave it in his 1956 article.

Chapter 5

1   I have already mentioned the disagreements between Dummett and Sluga (in Chapter 2). Nicholas Griffin has also challenged Dummett's interpretation of Frege (Griffin 1998), as have Gordon Baker and Peter Hacker (Hacker 1997: 52f; Baker and Hacker 1983, 1984, 1987, 1989). See also Resnik 1981.

2   Cf. Dummett 1993, index entries under 'third realm' and 'thoughts not contents of the mind'.

3   Though published in 1953, *Some Main Problems of Philosophy* consists in the texts of lectures given in 1910–11. The lecture from which these lines were taken was given in 1910.

4   Only in the last decade or so has it finally begun to lose its grip on the minds of analytic philosophers, thanks mainly to historians of analytic philosophy such as Tom Baldwin (1990, 1991).

5   Russell had already objected to the logical positivists' 'linguistic bias' in his 1940 volume.

6   Russell's relationship to the logical positivists makes an interesting study *vis-à-vis* the illusionist thesis. Despite their obvious disagreement over the linguistic thesis, Russell nonetheless had a

high regard for their work and does not vituperate them as he does the later Wittgenstein. Though Russell did address some of their differences (see note 5, above), their mutual respect seems to have led Russell and the positivists to treat each other with kid gloves, or perhaps even to fail to notice the extent of their differences. In his contribution to the forthcoming *Cambridge Companion to Carnap*, Chris Pincock provides a detailed study of this dynamic in the Russell–Carnap relationship. His essay begins with the observation that 'Russell and Carnap were constantly at odds on a number of fundamental philosophical issues. What is striking about their relationship is that these deep divisions were apparently overlooked in their early exchanges in the 1920s. By the 1930s and 1940s it must have been clear to both that their views were incompatible. Still, there is little outward sign of these conflicts and, especially in their autobiographical writings, the tendency is towards flattery over philosophical engagement.' The failure of these two to directly engage one another over their differences would have helped to facilitate the illusion of unity.

7   Cf. Russell 1944a: 19; 1959: 211f; 1968: 57. Wittgenstein's influence on Russell during the period 1912–14 is of tremendous importance both for understanding the later development of Russell's thought and his relationship to analytic philosophy as traditionally conceived. The scope of that influence exceeds the matter of Russell's linguistic turn in logic and math, but this was certainly one manifestation of it, and it is the aspect most relevant to our current study. It is also an aspect that affected Russell very deeply, since, as he was to recount in several of his autobiographical writings, this doomed the hopes he had had that philosophy could satisfy his religious longings by demonstrating the existence of something transcendent. For more on Wittgenstein's influence see Blackwell 1999; Stevens 2005; and Carey, forthcoming.

8   He may not have. We must recall that, in 1912–14, even Wittgenstein had not worked out his thoughts to the point where he felt he could write them out in a complete treatise, and it was not until 1919 that he did. Russell, who knew Wittgenstein's views only through discussion and letters, did not have even so 'systematic' a presentation as the *Tractatus* to lean on in trying to make sense of them. Such a situation inevitably lends itself to eisegesis; and, as the case of the logical positivists shows, not even their complete written presentation in the *Tractatus* was enough to prevent this.

9   On the non-linguistic interpretation of Russell, see the essays in Monk and Palmer 1996.

10   Klement 2005 has Russell resorting to a linguistic view of propositions during his logical atomist phase. This may be correct – there are clear cases where he uses the term in that sense. Even so, it is clear during this period that he held a view of *meaning* as picturing, and the material covered above indicates that his view of 'picturing' was at no time linguistic.

11   Insofar as these descriptions begin by noting a view/theory and then attempt to explain the view in terms of behaviors/practices, the pattern might also be interpreted as an attempt to *reduce* the ideational/theoretical to the sensible/practical. Ultimately, this would bespeak the same scientistic mentality.

Chapter 6

1   In addition to the cases discussed below, see Putnam 1992: ix f; Sorell 1991; Clarke 1997; Willard 1998: 28; Capaldi 2000; Margolis 2003.

2   URL = <http://www.utexas.edu/law/faculty/bleiter/hoekemawilshire.html>. This is part of an exchange that began with David Hoekema's review of Wilshire 2002 in Notre Dame Philosophical Reviews (URL = <http://ndpr.nd.edu/>).

3   McCumber sees this as a result of the academic-philosophical profession making concessions to McCarthyism – an attempt to avoid anything that might get it into trouble. Even if this is true, it cannot be the whole story, for analytic philosophy's scientistic tendencies transcend the McCarthy situation, having their root, along with analytic philosophy itself, in Britain around the turn of the twentieth century.

4   Even when brought to consciousness, however, Collingwood denies that absolute presuppositions can be argued for as other presuppositions can. Instead, like the adoption of a paradigm, they are justified only by what they make possible, be it grand scientific discoveries or a humble but satisfying form of social organization. This results in the same kind of radical incommensurability between cultures and epochs that Kuhn says exists between periods of normal science under their different paradigms. Though I cannot develop this theme here, I reject this radical incommensurability (see Margolis 2003 for a good discussion of this issue). All I want to take from

Collingwood is the notion that practices, paradigms, forms of life, and stances involve ideational presuppositions that explain them and that can in principle be rooted out and brought to consciousness through appropriate modes of inquiry, historical, philosophical, and so on.

5   Cf. Taylor 1985; Capaldi 2000; Wilshire 2002; Margolis 2003. *Caveat lector:* some of these authors have understandings of *scientism* different from each other and from my own.

6   See also Collingwood's descriptions of the realists in his 1939 volume.

7   See Burtt 1932; Carré 1949; Husserl 1954; Cohen 1960; Copleston 1963; Prosch 1964; Gregory 1977; Wright 1986; Cashdollar 1989; Sorell 1991; Yeo 1993; Reuben 1996; Reed 1997; Michell 1999.

8   This is characteristic of the way disciplines function when they have taken a 'paradigmatic turn' – as indicated in 'The Cognitive and the Non-Cognitive in Science, Culture and Philosophy', belonging to the discipline is a matter of *emulating* the paradigm rather than *accepting* a view under a particular verbal formulation, and such emulation is expected to involve departures from it as well as substantial similarities. There is no clear line limiting just how great the differences may become before an attempt at work within the discipline is ruled beyond the pale. Though not entirely arbitrary, the bases for judgments of 'sufficient similarity' to a paradigm are much more nebulous than the bases for judgments of whether someone 'accepts the same view' as others. This leaves the matter open to substantial influence from intellectual fashion and the relatively arbitrary consensus it generates.

9   This eventually led the West to 'sensate culture', as documented in Sorokin 1941.

10   On this matter, the case of Whewell is most instructive. See Yeo 1993.

11   And, insofar as the paradigm seemed to require it, an ever-increasing range of phenomena was treated as empirical, quantifiable and mathematically determinable. The methodological strictures of the paradigm were sometimes taken to have ontological consequences, in which case they were taken to prescribe a mechanistic materialism. This seems to have been the tendency in France and Germany. In Britain, however, the tendency was to see these as methodological strictures only. See Gregory 1977; Yeo 1993.

12   See Yeo 1993: ch. 7 on the development of this late nineteenth-century 'orthodox' view.

13 In his 'Prefatory Words' to the first volume of *Mind* (which was to become the leading journal in the analytic world for many years), George Croom Robertson groups these figures together as representative of a line of British thought that had not hitherto received sufficient institutional support, with the consequence that British philosophy remained unscientific. The journal itself was supposed to aid in remedying that situation.

14 The shift has much to do with the rise of Darwinism. See Yeo 1993: 25f.

Chapter 7

1 Available in many editions. These quotations are from the version at URL = <http://hca.gilead.org.il/emperor.html>.

2 This was published posthumously in 1992, but was written in 1974–75.

3 This is not to say that there are no philosophers who have taken the opposite view. Hume stands out as one who seemed perfectly satisfied with making natural propensities the source of human behavior. For him, even reasoning itself was ultimately the product of blind instinct. However, for a philosopher to take such a position is to endorse what Kai Neilsen has called *anti-philosophy philosophy* (Couture and Nielsen 1993: 3–4 n).

Bibliography

Addis, L. (1989), *Natural Signs*. Philadelphia: Temple University Press.

Allen, D. (1976), *The Naturalist in Britain*. Princeton: Princeton University Press.

Ammerman, R. (ed.) (1965), *Classics of Analytic Philosophy*. Indianapolis: Hackett.

Aune, B. (1998), 'Feigl and the Development of Analytic Philosophy at the University of Minnesota'. URL = <http://www.umass.edu/philosophy/PDF/Aune/feigl.pdf>.

Ayer, A.J. (1982), *Philosophy in the Twentieth Century*. London: Weidenfield and Nicolson.

Ayer, A.J., *et al.* (1963), *The Revolution in Philosophy*. London: Macmillan.

Baillie, J. (ed.) (1996), *Contemporary Analytic Philosophy: Core Readings*. New Jersey: Prentice Hall.

Baker, G. and Hacker, P. (1983), 'Dummett's Frege or Through a Looking-Glass Darkly'. *Mind* 92: 239–46.

(1984), *Frege: Logical Excavations*. Oxford: Blackwell.

(1987), 'Dummett's Dig: Looking-Glass Archaeology'. *Philosophical Quarterly* 37: 86–99.

(1989), 'The Last Ditch'. *Philosophical Quarterly* 39: 471–77.

Baldwin, T. (1990), *G. E. Moore*. London: Routledge.

(1991), 'The Identity Theory of Truth'. *Mind*, New Series, 100.1: 35–52.

Beaney, M. (1998), 'What is Analytic Philosophy? Recent Work on the History of Analytic Philosophy'. *British Journal of the History of Philosophy* 6.3: 463–72.

(2001), 'Collingwood's Critique of Analytic Philosophy'. *Collingwood and British Idealism Studies* 8: 99–122.

(2002), 'Decompositions and Transformations: Conceptions of Analysis in the Early Analytic and Phenomenological Traditions'. *Southern Journal of Philosophy* 40: 53–99.

(2003), 'Analysis'. *Stanford Encyclopedia of Philosophy*. Ed. E. Zalta. URL = <http://plato.stanford.edu/archives/sum2003/entries/analysis/>.

Bell, D. (1999), 'The Revolution of Moore and Russell: A Very British Coup?', in O'Hear (ed.) 1999: 193–208.

Bergmann, G. (1992), *New Foundations of Ontology*. Madison: University of Wisconsin Press.

Biletzki, A. and Matar, A. (1998), 'Preface', in Biletzki and Matar (eds) 1998: xi–xiv.

Biletzki, A. and Matar, A. (eds) (1998), *The Story of Analytic Philosophy: Plot and Heroes*. London and New York: Routledge.

Blackwell, K. (1999), 'The Early Wittgenstein and the Middle Russell', in A. Irvine (ed.), *Bertrand Russell: Critical Assessments of Leading Philosophers*. New York: Routledge.

Blanshard, B. (1962), *Reason and Analysis*. London: George Allen & Unwin.

Boyd, R. and Richerson, P.J. (1985), *Culture and the Evolutionary Process*. Chicago: University of Chicago Press.

Burge, T. (1999), 'A Century of Deflation and a Moment about Self-Knowledge'. *Proceedings and Addresses of the American Philosophical Association* 73.2: 25–46.

Burtt, E.A. (1932), *The Metaphysical Foundations of Modern Physical Science*. London: Routledge and Kegan Paul.

Capaldi, N. (2000), *The Enlightenment Project in the Analytic Conversation*. Dordrecht: Kluwer.

Carey, R. (forthcoming), *Russell and Wittgenstein on the Nature of Judgement*. Bristol: Thoemmes Continuum.

Carnap, R. (1934), 'On the Character of Philosophical Problems', in Rorty (ed.) 1967: 54–62.

— (1956), 'The Methodological Character of Theoretical Concepts'. *Minnesota Studies in the Philosophy of Science* 1: 38–76.

Carpenter, S.C. (1959), *Church and People 1789–1889*. 3 vols. London: SPCK.

Carré, M.H. (1949), *Phases of Thought in England*. Oxford: Clarendon.

Cashdollar, C.D. (1989), *The Transformation of Theology, 1830–1890: Positivism and Protestant Thought in Britain and America*. Princeton: Princeton University Press.

Charlton, W. (1991), *The Analytic Ambition*. Oxford and Cambridge, MA: Blackwell.

Clarke, D.S. (1997), *Philosophy's Second Revolution*. La Salle: Open Court.

Coffa, J.A. (1991), *The Semantic Tradition from Kant to Carnap*. Cambridge: Cambridge University Press.

Cohen, I.B. (1960), *The Birth of A New Physics*. New York and London: W.W. Norton.

Cohen, L.J. (1986), *The Dialogue of Reason: An Analysis of Analytical Philosophy*. Oxford: Clarendon.

Collingwood, R.G. (1933), *An Essay on Philosophical Method*. Oxford: Clarendon.

(1939), *An Autobiography*. Oxford: Clarendon.

(1940), *An Essay on Metaphysics*. Oxford: Clarendon.

Comte, A. (1969 [1830]), *Cours de Philosophie Positive*, published in English (1853) as *The Positive Philosophy of Auguste Comte*, trans. H. Martineau, excerpted in P. Gardiner (ed.), *Nineteenth Century Philosophy*. New York: The Free Press, 133–43.

Cooper, D. (1993), 'Analytical and Continental Philosophy'. *Proceedings of the Aristotelian Society* 94 (1993–94): 1–18.

Copleston, F. (1963), *A History of Philosophy*. Vol. 7. New York and London: Doubleday.

Corrado, M. (1975), *The Analytic Tradition in Philosophy*. Chicago: American Library Association.

Cottingham, J. (1988), *The Rationalists*. Oxford: Oxford University Press.

Couture, J. and Nielsen, K. (1993), *Metaphilosophie*. Calgary: University of Calgary Press.

Dennon, L. and Egner, R. (eds) (1961), *The Basic Writings of Bertrand Russell*. London: George Allen & Unwin.

Dummett, M. (1978), *Truth and Other Enigmas*. London: Duckworth.

(1993), *Origins of Analytical Philosophy*. Cambridge: Harvard University Press.

Einstein, A. (1944), 'Remarks on Bertrand Russell's Theory of Knowledge', in Schilpp (ed.) 1944: 278–91.

Engel, P. (1999), 'Analytic Philosophy and Cognitive Norms'. *The Monist* 82.2: 218–35.

Feigl, H. (1943), 'Logical Empiricism', in D.D. Runes (ed.), *Twentieth Century Philosophy*. New York: Philosophical Library. Reprinted in Feigl and Sellars (eds) 1949: 3–26.

Feigl, H. and Sellars, W. (eds) (1949), *Readings in Philosophical Analysis*. New York: Appleton-Century-Crofts.

Follesdal, D. (1997), 'Analytic Philosophy: What is It and Why Should One Engage in It?', in Glock (ed.) 1997: 1–16.

Forguson, L. (2001), 'Oxford and the "Epidemic" of Ordinary Language Philosophy'. *The Monist* 84.3: 325–46.

Frey, L. (ed.) (1994), *Group Communication in Context: Studies of Natural Groups*. Hillsdale: Lawrence Erlbaum.

Gabriel, G. (2002), 'Frege, Lotze, and the Continental Roots of Early Analytic Philosophy', in Reck (ed.) 2002.

Gardiner, H.N. (1926), 'The First Twenty-Five Years of the American Philosophical Association'. *The Philosophical Review* 35.2: 145–58.

Gellner, E. (2005 [1959]), *Words and Things*. London: Gollancz; Boston: Beacon.

Glock, H. (ed.) (1997), *The Rise of Analytic Philosophy*. Oxford: Blackwell.

(1999), '*Vorsprung durch Logik*: The German Analytic Tradition', in O'Hear (ed.) 1999: 137–66.

(2004), 'Was Wittgenstein an Analytic Philosopher?' *Metaphilosophy* 35.4: 419–44.

Grayling, A.C. (2006), *Among the Dead Cities*. New York: Walker and Co.

Gregory, F. (1977), *Scientific Materialism in Nineteenth Century Germany*. Dordrecht and Boston: Reidel.

Griffin, N. (1991), *Russell's Idealist Apprenticeship*. Oxford: Clarendon.

(1998), 'Dummett and the Origins of Analytic Philosophy'. *Philosophy and Progress* 24–25: 1–22.

(2003), 'Introduction', in Griffin (ed.) 2003: 1–50.

Griffin, N. (ed.) (2003), *The Cambridge Companion to Bertrand Russell*. Cambridge: Cambridge University Press.

Gross, B. (ed.) (1970), *Analytic Philosophy: An Historical Introduction*. New York: Pegasus.

Hacker, P. (1986), *Insight and Illusion: Themes in the Philosophy of Wittgenstein*. Oxford: Clarendon.

(1996), *Wittgenstein's Place in Twentieth-Century Analytic Philosophy*. Oxford: Blackwell.

(1997), 'The Rise of Twentieth Century Analytic Philosophy', in Glock (ed.) 1997: 51–76.

(1998), 'Analytic Philosophy: What, Whence, and Whither?', in Biletzki and Matar (eds) 1998: 3–34.

Hager, P. (2003), 'Russell's Method of Analysis', in Griffin (ed.) 2003: 310–31.

Hales, S. (ed.) (2002), *Analytic Philosophy: Classic Readings*. Belmont, CA: Wadsworth.

Hanna, R. (2001), *Kant and the Foundations of Analytic Philosophy*. Oxford: Oxford University Press.

Henrich, J. and Boyd, R. (1998), 'The Evolution of Conformist Transmission and the Emergence of Between-Group Differences'. *Evolution and Human Behavior* 19: 215–41.

Henrich, J. and Gil-White, F.J. (2001), 'The Evolution of Prestige: Freely Conferred Deference as a Mechanism for Enhancing the Benefits of Cultural Transmission'. *Evolution and Human Behavior* 22: 165–96.

Hintikka, J. (1998), 'Who is About to Kill Analytic Philosophy?', in Biletzki and Matar (eds) 1998: 253–69.

Hodgson, S. (1876a–c), 'Philosophy and Science'. *Mind* 1.1:67–81e; 1.2: 223–35; 1.3:351–62.

Hospers, J. (1953), *An Introduction to Philosophical Analysis.* Englewood Cliffs: Prentice-Hall.

Hughes, H.S. (1960), 'The Historian and the Social Scientist'. *The American Historical Review* 66.1: 20–46.

Husserl, E. (1900–01), *Logical Investigations.* 2 vols. Amherst: Humanity Books, 2000.

(1954), *The Crisis of European Sciences and Transcendental Phenomenology.* Evanston: Northwestern University Press, 1970.

Hylton, P. (1990), *Russell, Idealism, and the Emergence of Analytic Philosophy.* Oxford: Clarendon.

(1996), 'Beginning with Analysis', in Monk and Palmer (eds) 1996: 183–216.

(1998), 'Analysis in Analytic Philosophy', in Biletzki and Matar (eds) 1998: 37–55.

Jacquette, D. (2002), 'Philosophy of Language', in Hales (ed.) 2002: 11–20.

Klement, K. (2005), 'Russell's Logical Atomism', in E. Zalta (ed.), *The Stanford Encyclopedia of Philosophy.* URL = <http://plato.stanford.edu/ archives/win2005/ entries/logical-atomism/>.

Kripke, S. (1980), *Naming and Necessity.* Cambridge: Harvard University Press.

Kuhn, T. (1970 [1962]), *The Structure of Scientific Revolutions.* Chicago: University of Chicago Press.

Künne, W., Siebel, M. and Textor, M. (eds) (1997), *Bolzano and Analytic Philosophy.* Amsterdam: Rodopi.

Kusch, M. (2000), 'The Sociology of Philosophical Knowledge: A Case Study and a Defense', in M. Kusch (ed.), *The Sociology of Philosophical Knowledge.* Dordrecht: Kluwer.

Lachs, J. (2004), 'The Future of Philosophy'. *Proceedings and Addresses of the American Philosophical Association* 78.2: 5–14.

Leiter, B. (2002), 'Second Reply to Hoekema'. URL = <http://www. utexas.edu/law/faculty/bleiter/hoekemawilshire.html>.

(2004a), *The Philosophical Gourmet Report*, Blackwell. URL = <http:// www.philosophicalgourmet.com/>.

(2004b), 'Introduction', in B. Leiter (ed.), *The Future for Philosophy.* Oxford: Oxford University Press.

Leiter, B. (ed.) (2004), *The Future for Philosophy.* Oxford: Oxford University Press.

Levy, N. (2003), 'Analytic and Continental Philosophy: Explaining the Differences'. *Metaphilosophy* 34.3: 284–304.

Levy, P. (1979), *Moore: G.E. Moore and the Cambridge Apostles*. Oxford and New York: Oxford University Press.

Locke, J. (1975 [1690]), *An Essay Concerning Human Understanding*. Oxford: Clarendon Press.

Loux, M. (1998), *Metaphysics: A Contemporary Introduction*. London and New York: Routledge.

Magee, B. (1997), *Confessions of a Philosopher*. London: Weidenfeld and Nicholson.

Malcolm, N. (1942), 'Moore and Ordinary Language', in Schilpp (ed.) 1942: 343–68.

Margolis, J. (2003), *The Unraveling of Scientism*. Ithaca: Cornell University Press.

Marsh, R.C. (ed.) (1956), *Logic and Knowledge*. London: Allen & Unwin.

Martinich, A.P. and Sosa, D. (eds) (2001a), *Analytic Philosophy: An Anthology*. Oxford: Blackwell.

    (2001b), *A Companion to Analytic Philosophy*. Oxford: Blackwell.

Mates, B. (1972), *Elementary Logic*. New York: Oxford University Press.

McCumber, J. (2001), *Time in the Ditch: American Philosophy and the McCarthy Era*. Evanston: Northwestern University Press.

McGill V.J. (1942), 'Some Queries Concerning Moore's Method', in Schilpp (ed.) 1942: 481–514.

Mehta, V. (1963), *Fly and the Fly Bottle: Encounters with British Intellectuals*. Boston: Atlantic-Little, Brown.

Michell, J. (1999), *Measurement in Psychology*. Cambridge: Cambridge University Press.

Milkov, N. (2004), 'G.E. Moore and the Greifswald Objectivists on the Given and the Beginning of Analytic Philosophy'. *Axiomathes* 14.4: 361–79.

Mill, J.S. (1965 [1865]), *Auguste Comte and Positivism*. Ann Arbor: University of Michigan Press.

Monk, R. (1996a), 'What Is Analytical Philosophy?', in Monk and Palmer (eds) 1996: 1–22.

    (1996b), *Bertrand Russell: The Spirit of Solitude*. New York: The Free Press.

    (1997), 'Was Russell an Analytical Philosopher?', in Glock (ed.) 1997: 35–50.

Monk, R. and Palmer, A. (eds) (1996), *Bertrand Russell and the Origins of Analytical Philosophy*. Southampton: Thoemmes.

Montague, W.P. (1933), 'Philosophy as Vision'. *International Journal of Ethics* 44.1: 1–22.

Moore, G.E. (1899), 'The Nature of Judgment'. *Mind*, New Series, 8.30: 176–93.

(1942a), 'An Autobiography', in Schilpp (ed.) 1942: 3–39.

(1942b), 'A Reply to My Critics', in Schilpp (ed.) 1942: 535–677.

(1953), *Some Main Problems of Philosophy*. New York: Macmillan.

Mulligan, K., Simons P. and Smith B. (2006), 'What's Wrong with Contemporary Philosophy?' *Topoi* 25.1–2: 63–67.

Mundle, C.W.K. (1979 [1970]), *A Critique of Linguistic Philosophy*. Oxford: Clarendon.

Munitz, M.K. (1981), *Contemporary Analytic Philosophy*. New York: Macmillan.

Nagel, E. (1936a-b), 'Impressions and Appraisals of Analytic Philosophy in Europe'. *The Journal of Philosophy* 33.1: 5–24; 33.2: 29–53.

Naugle, D. (2002), *Worldview: The History of a Concept*. Grand Rapids: Eerdmans.

Nehamas, A. (1998), *The Art of Living: Socratic Reflections From Plato to Foucault*. Berkeley: University of California Press.

O'Hear. A. (ed.) (1999), *German Philosophy Since Kant*. Cambridge: Cambridge University Press.

Ongley, J. (2005), 'In This Issue'. *The Bertrand Russell Society Quarterly* 127: 3–4.

Pap, A. (1949), *Elements of Analytic Philosophy*. New York: Macmillan.

Pattison, M. (1876), 'Philosophy at Oxford'. *Mind* 1.1: 82–97.

Peirce, C.S. (1905), 'What Pragmatism Is', in H.S. Thayer (ed.) *Pragmatism: The Classic Writings*. Indianapolis: Hackett, 1982.

Pettit, P. (1993), *The Common Mind*. New York: Oxford University Press.

(2003), 'Groups with Minds of Their Own', in F. Schmitt (ed.), *Socializing Metaphysics: The Nature of Social Reality*. Lanham: Rowman & Littlefield.

Pincock, C. (forthcoming), 'Carnap, Russell and the External World', in *The Cambridge Companion to Carnap*. Cambridge: Cambridge University Press.

Pojman, L. (2001), 'Introduction: Philosophy in the Twentieth Century', in *Classics of Philosophy*. Vol. 3. Oxford and New York: Oxford University Press.

Preston, A. (2004), 'Prolegomena to Any Future History of Analytic Philosophy'. *Metaphilosophy* 35.4: 445–65.

(2005a), 'Conformism in Analytic Philosophy: On Shaping Philosophical Boundaries and Prejudices'. *The Monist* 88.2: 292–319.

(2005b), 'The Implications of Recent Work on the History of Analytic Philosophy'. *Bertrand Russell Society Quarterly* 127 (August): 11–30.

(2006a), 'G.E. Moore', in J. Fieser and B. Dowden (eds), *The Internet*

Encyclopedia of Philosophy. URL = <http://www.iep.utm.edu/m/moore. htm>.

(2006b), 'Analytic Philosophy', in J. Fieser and B. Dowden (eds), *The Internet Encyclopedia of Philosophy*. URL = <http://www.iep.utm.edu/a/ analytic.htm>.

Prosch, H. (1964), *The Genesis of Twentieth Century Philosophy*. Garden City: Doubleday.

Putnam, H. (1992), *Renewing Philosophy*. Cambridge and London: Harvard University Press.

(1998), 'Kripkean Realism and Wittgenstein's Realism', in Biletzki and Matar (eds) 1998: 241–52.

Putnam, L. and Stohl, C. (1990), 'Bona Fide Groups: A Reconceptualization of Groups in Context'. *Communication Studies* 41: 248–65.

Reck, E. (ed.) (2002), *From Frege to Wittgenstein: Perspectives on Early Analytic Philosophy*. Oxford: Oxford University Press.

Reed, E.S. (1997), *From Soul to Mind: The Emergence of Psychology, from Erasmus Darwin to William James*. New Haven and London: Yale University Press.

Reinach, A. (1914), 'Concerning Phenomenology'. *The Personalist* 50.2: (1969): 194–221.

Resnik, M. (1981), 'Frege and Analytic Philosophy: Facts and Speculations'. *Midwest Studies in Philosophy*, 83–103.

Reuben, J. (1996), *The Making of the Modern University: Intellectual Transformation and the Marginalization of Morality*. Chicago: University of Chicago Press.

Ribot, T. (1877), 'Philosophy in France'. *Mind* 2.7: 366–86.

Robertson, G.C. (1876), 'Prefatory Words'. *Mind* 1.1: 1–6.

(1877), 'English Thought in the Eighteenth Century'. *Mind* 2.7: 352–66.

Rorty, R. (ed.) (1967), *The Linguistic Turn: Essays in Philosophical Method*. Chicago and London: University of Chicago Press. (Second edn 1992.)

Rorty, R. (1992), 'Twenty-Five Years After', in Rorty (ed.) 1967, 2e: 371–74.

Ross, J. (1998), 'Analytic Philosophy as a Matter of Style', in Biletzki and Matar (eds) 1998: 56–70.

Russell, B. (1894), 'On the Distinction Between the Psychological and Metaphysical Points of View', in K. Blackwell *et al.* (eds), *The Collected Papers of Bertrand Russell*, Vol. 1. London: George Allen and Unwin, 1983: 195–98.

(1900), *A Critical Exposition of the Philosophy of Leibniz*. London: George Allen & Unwin.

(1903), *Principles of Mathematics* (2e). London: George Allen & Unwin, 1963.

(1905), 'On Denoting', in Russell 1973: 103–119.

(1914a), 'On Scientific Method in Philosophy', in Russell 1918b: 97–124.

(1914b), *Our Knowledge of the External World*. London: George Allen & Unwin.

(1918a), 'The Philosophy of Logical Atomism', in Marsh (ed.) 1956: 177–281.

(1918b), *Mysticism and Logic*. New York: Longmans, Green and Co.

(1919a), *Introduction to Mathematical Philosophy*. London: George Allen & Unwin.

(1919b) 'On Propositions: What They Are and How They Mean'. *Proceedings of the Aristotelian Society*, Supp. Vol. 2: 1–43. Reprinted in Marsh (ed) 1956: 285–320; references are to the latter source.

(1920) 'The Meaning of "Meaning"'. *Mind*, New Series, 29.116: 398–404.

(1924), 'Logical Atomism', in Slater (ed.) 1997: 160–79.

(1928), 'Philosophy in the Twentieth Century', in *Skeptical Essays*. London: Allen & Unwin. Reprinted in Dennon and Egner (eds) 1961: 259–74.

(1940), *An Inquiry into Meaning and Truth*. London: George Allen & Unwin.

(1944a), 'My Mental Development', in Schilpp (ed.) 1944: 3–20.

(1944b), 'Reply to Criticisms', in Schilpp (ed.) 1944: 681–741.

(1945a–b), 'Papers on Philosophy', in Slater (ed.) 1997: 220–23, 223–33.

(1946), 'My Own Philosophy', in Slater (ed.) 1997: 67–82.

(1953), 'The Cult of "Common Usage"', in Slater (ed.) 1997: 610–14.

(1956), 'Philosophical Analysis', in Slater (ed.) 1997: 614–25.

(1959), *My Philosophical Development*. London: Unwin.

(1964), 'The Duty of a Philosopher in This Age', in Slater (ed.) 1997: 455–63.

(1968) *The Autobiography of Bertrand Russell*. Vol. 2. London: Allen & Unwin.

(1973), *Essays in Analysis*. Ed. D. Lackey. London: George Allen & Unwin.

Russell, B. and Whitehead, A.N. (1910–13), *Principia Mathematica*. 3 vols. Cambridge: Cambridge University Press.

Ryle, G. (1963), 'Introduction', in Ayer *et al.* 1963: 1–11.

Schilpp, P.A. (ed.) (1942), *The Philosophy of G.E. Moore*. La Salle: Open Court.

(1944), *The Philosophy of Bertrand Russell*. La Salle: Open Court.

Schlick, M. (1932), 'Positivism and Realism', in Mulder and Van De Velde-Schlick (eds), *Moritz Schlick: Philosophical Papers*, Vol. 2. Dordrecht and Boston: Reidel, 1979: 259–84.

Searle, J. (1990), 'Collective Intentions and Actions', in *Intentions in Communication*, eds P. Cohen, J. Morgan and M.E. Pollack. Cambridge, MA: MIT Press.

(1995), *The Construction of Social Reality*. New York: The Free Press.

(1996), 'Contemporary Philosophy in the United States', in *The Blackwell Companion to Philosophy*. Oxford: Blackwell.

Sellars, W. (1948), 'Realism and the New Way of Words', reprinted in Feigl and Sellars (eds) 1949: 424–56.

(1974), *Essays in Philosophy and Its History*. Boston: Reidel.

Sidgwick, H. (1876), 'Philosophy at Cambridge'. *Mind* 1.2: 235–46.

Simons, P. (2001), 'Whose Fault? The Origins and Evitability of the Analytic-Continental Rift'. *International Journal of Philosophical Studies* 9: 295–311.

Slater, J. (ed.) (1997), *The Collected Papers of Bertrand Russell*. Vol. 11. London and New York: Routledge.

Sluga, H. (1980), *Gottlob Frege*. London: Routledge and Kegan Paul.

(1997), 'Frege on Meaning', in Glock (ed.) 1997: 17–34.

(1998), 'What Has History to Do with Me? Wittgenstein and Analytic Philosophy'. *Inquiry* 41: 99–121.

Smith, B. (1994), *Austrian Philosophy: The Legacy of Franz Brentano*. La Salle: Open Court.

Soames, S. (2003), *Philosophical Analysis in the Twentieth Century*. 2 vols. Princeton and Oxford: Princeton University Press.

(2006), 'What Is History For? Reply to Critics of *The Dawn of Analysis*'. *Philosophical Studies* 129: 645–65.

Solomon, R. (1999), *The Joy of Philosophy*. New York and Oxford: Oxford University Press.

Sorell, T. (1991), *Scientism: Philosophy and the Infatuation with Science*. New York and London: Routledge.

Sorely, W.R. (1926), '50 Years of "Mind"'. *Mind*, New Series, 35: 140, 409–18.

Sorokin, P. (1941), *The Crisis of Our Age*. New York: EP Dutton & Co.

Stebbing, L.S. (1933), 'The Method of Analysis in Metaphysics'. *Proceedings of the Aristotelian Society* 33 (1932–33): 65–94.

Stevens, G. (2005), *The Russellian Origins of Analytic Philosophy*. London and New York: Routledge.

Strawson, P.F. (1963), 'Construction and Analysis', in Ayer *et al.* 1963: 97–110.

Stroll, A. (2000), *Twentieth Century Analytic Philosophy*. New York: Columbia University Press.

Stump, E. (forthcoming), *Wandering in Darkness: Narrative and the Problem of Suffering*. Oxford: Oxford University Press.

Taylor, C. (1985), *Philosophy and the Human Sciences*. Cambridge: Cambridge University Press.

Urmson, J.O. (1956), *Philosophical Analysis: Its Development Between the Two World Wars*. Oxford and New York: Oxford University Press.

Van Fraassen, B. (2004), 'Précis of *The Empirical Stance*'. *Philosophical Studies* 121: 127–32.

von Wright, G.H. (1993), 'Analytical Philosophy: A Historico-Critical Survey', in *The Tree of Knowledge and Other Essays*. Leiden: E.J. Brill, 25–52.

Warnock, G.J. (1958), *English Philosophy Since 1900*. London: Oxford University Press.

Weitz, M. (ed.) (1966), *Twentieth-Century Philosophy: The Analytic Tradition*. New York: The Free Press.

Whitehead, A.N. (1941), *Process and Reality: An Essay in Cosmology*. New York: The Humanities Press.

Willard, D. (1967), 'A Crucial Error in Epistemology'. *Mind* 76: 513–23.
(1983), 'Why Semantic Ascent Fails'. *Metaphilosophy* 14.3–4: 276–90.
(1984), *Logic and the Objectivity of Knowledge: A Study in Husserl's Early Philosophy*. Athens, OH: Ohio University Press.
(1998), 'Who Needs Brentano? The Wasteland of Philosophy Without its Past', in R. Poli (ed.), *The Brentano Puzzle*. Aldershot: Ashgate.

Williams, B. (1996), 'Contemporary Philosophy: A Second Look', in *The Blackwell Companion to Philosophy*. Oxford: Blackwell: 25–37.

Williamson, T. (2004), 'Past the Linguistic Turn?', in Leiter (ed.) 2004.
(forthcoming), 'Must Do Better', in Greenough and M. Lynch (eds), *Proceedings of the 2004 St Andrews Conference on Realism and Truth*. Oxford: Oxford University Press.

Wilshire, B. (2002), *Fashionable Nihilism: A Critique of Analytic Philosophy*. Albany: State University of New York Press.

Wisdom, J. (1931), *Interpretation and Analysis in Relation to Bentham's Theory of Definition*. London: Kegan Paul.
(1934), *Problems of Mind and Matter*. Cambridge: Cambridge University Press.

Wittgenstein, L. (1921), *Tractatus Logico-Philosophicus.* London and New York: Routledge, 1974.

(1953), *Philosophical Investigations* (3e). Englewood Cliffs: Prentice-Hall, 1958.

Wright, T.R. (1986), *The Religion of Humanity: The Impact of Comtean Positivism on Victorian Britain.* Cambridge and New York: Cambridge University Press.

Wundt, W. (1877), 'Philosophy in Germany'. *Mind* 2.8: 493–518.

Yeo, R. (1993), *Defining Science.* Cambridge: Cambridge University Press.

Zeller, E. (1881), *A History of Greek Philosophy.* Vol. 1. London: Longmans, Green and Co.

Zimmer, C. (2004), *Soul Made Flesh: The Discovery of the Brain and How it Changed the World.* New York: The Free Press.

Index

Breinigsville, PA USA
21 November 2010
249776BV00002B/5/P